ECOCRITICISM
& THE FUTURE
OF SOUTHERN
STUDIES

Southern Literary Studies

SCOTT ROMINE, SERIES EDITOR

ECOCRITICISM
& THE FUTURE
OF SOUTHERN
STUDIES

EDITED BY

Zackary Vernon

AFTERWORD BY

Jay Watson

Louisiana State University Press | Baton Rouge

Published by Louisiana State University Press
Copyright © 2019 by Louisiana State University Press
All rights reserved
Manufactured in the United States of America
First printing

DESIGNER: Michelle A. Neustrom
TYPEFACE: Chaparral Pro
PRINTER AND BINDER: Sheridan Books, Inc.

LIBRARY OF CONGRESS CATALOGING-IN-PUBLICATION DATA

Names: Vernon, Zackary, editor.
Title: Ecocriticism and the future of southern studies / edited by Zackary Vernon ;
    afterword by Jay Watson.
Other titles: Southern literary studies.
Description: Baton Rouge : Louisiana State University Press, [2019] | Series: Southern
    literary studies | Includes bibliographical references and index.
Identifiers: LCCN 2019010079| ISBN 978-0-8071-7113-4 (cloth : alk. paper) |
    ISBN 978-0-8071-7209-4 (pdf) | ISBN 978-0-8071-7210-0 (epub)
Subjects: LCSH: Ecocriticism—Southern States. | American literature—Southern States—
    History and criticism. | Southern States—In literature. | Ecology in literature. |
    Environmental degradation in literature.
Classification: LCC PS169.E25 E24 2019 | DDC 810.9/975—dc23

CONTENTS

ECOCRITICISM
& THE FUTURE
OF SOUTHERN
STUDIES

Introduction

Southern Studies in the Age of the Anthropocene

ZACKARY VERNON

Whether we want to admit it or not, the US South, like the rest of the world, has entered the Anthropocene—a new geological epoch in the earth's history marked by human-induced changes to the environment.[1] After nearly 12,000 years of the Holocene—a relatively warm and stable period that fostered the explosive growth of human populations—a majority of scientists now agree that the Anthropocene has arrived, and with it, unprecedented disruptions to global ecosystems, including climate change, carbon and chemical emissions, depletion of the ozone layer, atmospheric aerosol loading, the loss of biodiversity, rising sea levels, ocean acidification, air toxification, and worsening floods and droughts.[2] In such a world, it has become increasingly difficult, if not impossible, to distinguish between what is natural and artificial, and thus the perception of nature as a wild and pristine space is a thing of the past.[3] The idea of the Anthropocene is and will continue having far-ranging cultural, political, and artistic ramifications, as we consider our place in and our responsibilities to this post-natural world.

Although people have been aware of environmental degradation and the need for widespread conservation efforts since at least the dawn of the Industrial Revolution, our generation is unique in that we know just how dire the consequences of the Anthropocene can and likely will be. Therefore, we bear the brunt of responsibility more than any other humans in the history of our species. Scientists and policy makers should not have to contend with this responsibility alone. All people and certainly all academics should be contributing to possible solutions. In her introduction to the groundbreaking 1996 collection *The Ecocriticism Reader: Landmarks in Literary Ecology,* Cheryll Glotfelty states that ecocriticism enables scholars to examine "the reciprocal relationships between humans and land, considering nature not just as a stage upon which the human story is acted out, but as an actor in the drama" (xxi). Given the consistent emphasis on land and place in southern literatures and cultures, ecocriticism proves to be an invaluable tool in analyzing texts that deal with the connections not only among individual subjects and culture but also sub-jects and the environment, and culture and the entire biosphere. While most literary critics pursue various cultural contexts, Timothy Clark argues that it is important to remember that "culture itself has a context—the biosphere, air, water, plant and animal life—and more radical ecocritical work tends to be, so to speak, *meta-contextual,* opening on issues that may involve perspectives or questions for which given cultural conceptions seem limited" (4). Jedediah Purdy, in his Pulitzer-nominated book *After Nature: A Politics for the Anthro-pocene* (2015), notes that from the period of colonization onward "there has been a link between how Americans have acted toward the natural world and how they have imagined it" (22). Undoubtedly, the arts and various cultural ex-pressions have played a major role in shaping, to use Lawrence Buell's famous phrase, the American environmental imagination, and therefore scholarship in ecocriticism and the environmental humanities is particularly crucial at pres-ent. As southernists, then, it is our responsibility to consider the intersections among southern environments and the literature, film, visual arts, philosophy, and politics of the region as well as to determine how southern cultures will respond to the impending pressures of the Anthropocene.

In 1996, Cheryll Glotfelty argued that in order for literary studies to re-main relevant, the field must address contemporary environmental issues: "In view of the discrepancy between current events and the preoccupations of the literary profession, the claim that literary scholarship has responded to contemporary pressures becomes difficult to defend" (xvi). In the interven-ing two decades since Glotfelty's assertion, we have witnessed ever-worsening disruptions to global ecosystems, and it is now more important than ever for scholars across academia to examine the cultural effects of this increas-ingly post-natural world. Since 1996, many subfields of literary studies have explored environmental issues through the publication of books and articles as well as through conferences and activist organizations. Southern studies, however, remains largely behind the curve. A survey of recent scholarship in the field reveals just how few publications have directly discussed environmen-tal issues; while some preliminary work of this sort has been accomplished in journal articles, in general the southern studies community has not incor-porated ecocriticism as much as other fields, including, more broadly, liter-ary studies and American studies. In recent issues of journals in the field—including *Mississippi Quarterly, south, Southern Cultures, Southern Literary Journal, Southern Spaces,* and *Southern Quarterly*—only a small percentage of articles addresses either past or present ecological concerns, and most are not firmly grounded in ecocriticism or environmental studies, but rather explore issues like landscape, geography, foodways, or agriculture.

The field's response in the form of environmentally oriented monographs and collections has also not been as robust as in other fields. Some examples of books that do engage specifically with southern and environmental studies are Lewis P. Simpson's *The Dispossessed Garden: Pastoral and History in Southern Literature* (1975), Martyn Bone's *The Postsouthern Sense of Place in Contemporary Fiction* (2005), Anthony Wilson's *Shadow and Shelter: The Swamp in Southern Culture* (2006), and Christopher Rieger's *Clear-Cutting Eden: Ecology and the Pastoral in Southern Literature* (2009). Some author-specific monographs and collections also bring together southern and environmental studies, such as Casey Howard Clabough's *Elements: The Novels of James Dickey* (2002), Donald M. Kartiganer and Ann J. Abadie's collection *Faulkner and the Natural World* (1999), Joseph R. Urgo and Abadie's collection *Faulkner and the Ecology of the South* (2005), and my collection, coedited with Randall Wilhelm, *Summoning the Dead: Essays on Ron Rash* (2018). Other recent southern studies collections have accomplished important work in this area. For example, Eric Gary Anderson, Taylor Hagood, and Daniel Cross Turner's collection *Undead Souths: The Gothic and Beyond in Southern Literature and Culture* (2015) contains a strong ecocritical perspective in some of its essays. Anderson, Hagood, Kirstin Squint, and Anthony Wilson's forthcoming collection *Swamp Souths: Literary and Cultural Ecologies* will also include chapters that utilize environmental studies. Additionally, the field of history has offered several books devoted to environmental issues in the region, including Albert E. Cowdrey's *This Land, This South: An Environmental History* (1983), Thomas D. Clark's *The Greening of the South: The Recovery of Land and Forest* (1984), Jack Temple Kirby's *Mockingbird Song: Ecological Landscapes of the South* (2006), and Paul S. Sutter and Christopher J. Manganiello's *Environmental History and the American South: A Reader* (2009). Ecocritical collections that adopt nationalist or transationalist foci regarding literature and culture—such as Glotfelty and Harold Fromm's *The Ecocriticism Reader: Landmarks in Literary Ecology* (1996), Tom Lynch, Glotfelty, and Karla Armbruster's *The Bioregional Imagination: Literature, Ecology, and Place* (2012), Joni Adamson and Kimberly N. Ruffin's *American Studies, Ecocriticism, and Citizenship: Thinking and Acting in the Local and Global Commons* (2013), and Scott Slovic, Swarnalatha Rangarajan, and Vidya Sarveswaran's *Ecocriticism of the Global South* (2015)—serve as significant models for how *Eco-*

criticism and the Future of Southern Studies approaches the field of ecocriticism and informs how I have sought to accomplish the work of greening southern studies. At present, *Ecocriticism and the Future of Southern Studies* stands alone in offering broad, foundational coverage of ecocriticism and a range of topics in southern studies, including race, class, gender, sexuality, literature, film, history, music, politics, media, foodways, and anthropology.

This collection is in part an answer to Jay Watson's call for more ecocritical southern studies research, which he articulated in his 2014 plenary address at the Society for the Study of Southern Literature Conference and again in his article "The Other Matter of the South" in *PMLA* in January of 2016. Watson argues that the fields of southern and environmental studies have much to contribute to one another. Specifically, southern studies can provide for environmental studies a disruption of the "dominant paradigm for environmental thought" of "solitary reflection in pristine natural settings" (159).[4] In addition, Watson maintains that the recent transnational turn in southern studies can "help scholars practicing environmental studies in the United States look away from the national frameworks and nationalist ideologies in which the field arose (Nixon 236) and toward alternative models and strategies more responsive to global geographies and ecologies" (159). In contrast, environmental studies can benefit southern studies in that "current efforts to rehabilitate nostalgia, utopia, apocalypticism, and other discourses of temporal alterity as bases for environmental activism and critique (e.g., Buell 280–309; Nixon) can guide southern studies scholars to a deeper consideration of which pasts to claim and which forms of change to interrogate or contest in the field's ongoing work of negotiating tradition" (159). Building upon and responding to Watson's ideas, the contributors to this collection are attentive to the valuable contributions southern and environmental studies can make to one another, while also helping to build bridges between these two fields.

In the introduction to their recent collection *Keywords for Southern Studies* (2016), Scott Romine and Jennifer Rae Greeson ask, "What is southern studies *studying?*" (1). To answer this question is, of course, difficult because "the U.S. South is neither solid nor exceptional. It lacks (and therefore cannot be known in essentialist terms), a polity, and clearly defined boundaries" (2). A corresponding question could be asked of this collection: What is ecocritical or environmental southern studies *studying?* Daniel Spoth asks in this collection whether it is even possible to determine a distinctly southern environmental philosophy. Spoth's answer, and mine as well, is that one can no more determine a monolithic environmental philosophy for the region than one can a monolithic cultural identity. Instead, as Steven E. Knepper argues, "To study the southern states ecologically is to challenge the myth of a unified, organic South. While their climes are generally warm and wet, the southern states are ecologically diverse . . ." (264). Knepper continues, "To study the southern United States ecologically, then, is to study its amazing biodiversity. To study the environmental history of the southern states is to study a problematic past" (266). While we must remain careful not to reinscribe outdated notions of southern exceptionalism based on the region's environmental histories, I believe it is permissible to note that the South has been and continues to be a place of quantifiable environmental degradation and loss, such as vast carbon and chemical emissions from industrialized agriculture, mountaintop removal in southern Appalachia, and increasingly destructive rising sea levels and floods on the Gulf and Atlantic Coasts. Therefore, the US South is a site of environmental precariousness, in the same way that, as Lisa Hinrichsen observes in this collection, the Global South, more broadly, is today.

Therefore, throughout this collection, the US South is treated both as an imaginary space and at times a real place.[5] Joseph M. Thompson's idea, articulated in this collection, of the rhizomatic South provides a useful way of considering how southern cultures, both imagined communities and actual identifiable ecologies, circulate throughout the nation and beyond. In this regard, I follow Romine's assertion in *The Real South: Southern Narrative in the Age of Cultural Reproduction* (2008), when he states, "I am less interested in whether cultures and traditions are 'really' authentic than in what *counts* as authentic within stories of culture and tradition" (13). In this way, I am not interested in determining what states or landscapes count as southern, but rather for what purposes southern environments and southern environmentalisms may be evoked. Unlike so many times that the South is used to support problematic, regressive ideologies based on, among other things, race, class, or gender, southern environments can sometimes serve positive, progressive purposes. Local-, state-, and region-specific environmentalist groups—for instance, the Blue Ridge Conservancy, the North Carolina Sierra Club, Appalachians Against Pipelines, or the Southern Environmental Law Center—often utilize place, whether real or imagined, to categorize, control, and rally support for their causes.

This collection is not interested in reasserting outdated notions of southern "sense of place" or romanticizing folk cultures that supposedly remain closer to the land or more authentically engaged with agrarian cultures.[6]

Rather, the chapters of the collection seek to complicate traditional conceptions of "nature" and "sense of place," instead emphasizing the often dirty, polluted, compromised, natural/cultural spaces that we find in the US South. Taken as a whole, the contributors cultivate arguments similar to those of Bart H. Welling, who says, "we can find grounds for optimism that southern ecocriticism will participate actively in the important scholarly task of making sense of the non-sublime and ecologically degraded—but also culturally vibrant, profoundly interconnected, and potentially restorable—places where most of the Earth's inhabitants, human or not, actually live" (132). Similarly, in a 2013 review of the film *Beasts of the Southern Wild,* Patricia Yaeger argues that "We must dirty ecology . . ." if we are ever to understand the irrevocably compromised, post-natural state of life in the region and the world in the age of the Anthropocene.

On one hand, the South is an ideal fit for environmental research because it has long fascinated travelers and locals alike with its varied landscapes and exotic indigenous flora and fauna;[7] the region has also possessed a range of agricultural traditions (a plantation system fueled by slavery, sharecropping, tenant farming, yeomanry, back-to-the-land experimental farming, industrial factory farming, and, most recently, organic, biodynamic, and sustainable farming); and, finally, the South still hosts vast swathes of green spaces, both those that are protected and those in need of protection, both publicly and privately owned.[8] On the other hand, though, southern studies as a field is not uniquely burdened with the need to address the interconnections between local and global environmental issues. *All* lives, regardless of location, are inextricably bound to the environment—to the physical world that provides us with the sustenance and shelter and pleasure needed for our species to survive and flourish. Understanding this is important, because the future health of humanity and the planet will largely be determined by human choices that are made within the coming years and decades.

Many recent scholars, such as Ursula K. Heise, have sought to usher in a planetary turn in environmental scholarship, which attempts to balance global ecological considerations with emphases on local initiatives. Heise argues that this position is necessary but challenging, as it asks us "to envision how ecologically based advocacy on behalf of the nonhuman world as well as on behalf of greater socioenvironmental justice might be formulated in terms that are premised no longer primarily on ties to local places but on ties to territories and systems that are understood to encompass the planet as a whole" (10). As

Delia Byrnes highlights in her chapter of this collection, we must also remain attentive to the places between the local and the planetary; citing Terrell Scott Herring, Byrnes notes that the local/global binary "occludes the 'forgotten spaces' of region and microregion that remain crucial to disrupting the 'loopy binary' of the local/planetary circuit, which can too easily obscure the multiple scales (the sublocal and the bioregional, for example) that overlap within the 'planetary' (628)." Focusing our scholarly attention and activist endeavors on regional environmental concerns might, then, provide a way out of the limitations of thinking too locally or too globally.

This collection's timeliness is evident whenever one reads the daily headlines in the news, and as data comes in about the earth's rising temperatures and, correspondingly, its rising sea levels. Furthermore, the controversy over the Dakota Access Pipeline through the sacred lands of the Standing Rock Sioux tribe has drawn national attention to the connections between social and environmental justice. This can also be seen in water-related fights throughout the South—for example, when Virginia Tech professor and Appalachian studies scholar Emily Satterwhite was recently arrested while protesting the Mountain Valley Pipeline in Montgomery County, Virginia. Moreover, the inhabitants of Isle de Jean Charles in southern Louisiana, many of them members of the Biloxi-Chitimacha-Choctaw tribe, have been called the first climate refugees in the United States; they were slated for government-funded relocation in 2016, after their ancestral lands in Terrebonne Parish were lost to coastal erosion, sea-level rise, saltwater intrusion, and subsidence. Because of global warming, such floods in the South are no longer anomalies; rather, they are the new norm of the Anthropocene.

To address these environmental concerns, this collection, while grounded foremost in literary studies, also utilizes current interdisciplinary trends in environmental and southern studies. As a result, *Ecocriticism and the Future of Southern Studies* targets diverse audiences and makes vital connections across disciplines and between fields. While several of the contributors are established scholars in southern studies, many of them are emerging scholars, including graduate students and early-career professors. As I solicited chapters from top academics in the field, I often got the same response: scholars would express enthusiasm for the collection's topic, before saying that their own research is not ecocritical; yet in the same breath, many of them remarked that they had current or recent graduate students doing significant work in environmental studies. I believe this is evidence of the fact that ecocriticism is still relatively new and that it is a, if not *the,* burgeoning subfield for future generations of southern studies scholars.

Ecocriticism and the Future of Southern Studies is the first book-length collection of scholarship that applies interdisciplinary environmental studies research to analyses of the US South. In charting new directions for ecocritical approaches to southern studies, I have assembled rigorous, theoretically engaged essays that speak to a broad range of topics related to the South and both its built and natural environments. The sixteen chapters contained in this collection are divided into five sections, arranged thematically rather than chronologically. These sections include: 1) "Coal, Oil, and Southern Hazardscapes," 2) "Routes, Roads, and the Rhizomatic South," 3) "Farming and Foodways," 4) "Floods and Southern Water Studies," and 5) "Eco-dystopias." Each section provides original research that contributes to a range of fields, and, taken together, the collection's contributors create a chorus of voices emphasizing and demonstrating the fruitful connections between southern and environmental studies.

The first section of the collection explores several texts, films, and media that portray sacrifice zones in the United States—those internal resource colonies, many of which are found in the South and Appalachia. In these locations, environments tend to be treated as extractable and exploitable commodities, generally offering the rewards to more economically and politically powerful people outside these bioregions. This section begins with a chapter by Lisa Hinrichsen, in which she brings together an array of sources from the fields of ecocriticism and affect theory to examine Ann Pancake's novel *Strange as This Weather Has Been* (2007). According to Hinrichsen, Pancake interrogates the idea of southern "sense of place" by rendering place-sense remarkably strange. Rather than relying on outdated concepts of place and region, Pancake's novel urges readers to develop more realistic and ultimately more sustainable notions of community based on what Hinrichsen calls "bioregional affinity and an ecocosmopolitan vision of space and place." Pancake's Appalachia is both material and virtual, tangible and imaginary, and instead of merely celebrating or defending Appalachia and Appalachian identity, Pancake confronts the unsettling and often destructive cultural and environmental realities of a place that has been ravaged by mountaintop removal.

Delia Byrnes's chapter seeks to enliven productive conversations between southern studies and environmental humanities by arguing for an energy regionalism, which analyzes region, rather than nation or world, in conjunction with energy policy. Byrnes's research focuses on Gulf Coast texts—from literature and film to photography and digital media—and her chapter specifically examines *Petrochemical America* (2012), a hybrid work knitting together narrative photography and geography. Created by landscape architect Kate Orff and photographer Richard Misrach, *Petrochemical America* investigates a 150-mile stretch of the Mississippi River, from roughly Baton Rouge to New Orleans, known as "Cancer Alley" due to the unusually high rates of diseases and cancers that occur in communities, predominantly African American communities, in and near this area of intense oil refinement and petrochemical production. Through their writing and photography, Orff and Misrach suggest that the local inhabitants here, like those in coal communities in Appalachia, must contend with the many negative externalities of the energy industry without reaping any of the potential rewards. Furthermore, *Petrochemical America* often highlights the transition in these parts of Louisiana from antebellum plantations to oil refineries in order to demonstrate a legacy of ecological and racial exploitation that undergirds both systems.

The third chapter in this section, by Ila Tyagi, analyzes early Cold War era films that depict oil drilling in the Gulf of Mexico; these films, which Tyagi calls petrocinema, often portray oil extraction in a positive light, and perhaps not surprisingly, many of these films were sponsored by the oil industry itself. Surveying the oil-obsessed films of the midcentury, Tyagi finds that they collectively assert that the oil industry possesses superior scientific technologies, especially those that enhance sight, such as microscopes and polarizing filters; the industry then uses its sensory acuity to arrive at specialized forms of knowledge that seemingly benefit local communities but are really engineered solely to enrich those in the industry. Similar to the texts studied by Hinrichsen and Byrnes, the petrocinema of the postwar era was used strategically to help explain and justify in the national imaginary the corporate and industrial colonization of parts of the US South as well as the exploitation of those areas' resources. In her conclusion, Tyagi argues that in the same way that these films emerged in response to a period when offshore oil drilling in the Gulf was ramping up, there has been another spike in petrocinema since 2010 following the Deepwater Horizon oil spill, which was the largest US spill in history. However, unlike midcentury films that were sympathetic to the oil industry, new films level harsh critiques against the industry and seek to investigate the ways in which it negatively impacts both human and nonhuman communities on the Gulf Coast.

The collection's second section considers the environmental history of the South relative to the creation of routes and roads, both literal and metaphorical, throughout the region. This section begins with Scott Obernesser's examination of John Muir's posthumously published *A Thousand-Mile Walk to the Gulf* (1916), which chronicles Muir's experience in 1867 traveling from Indianapolis, Indiana, to Cedar Keys, Florida. While much recent scholarship has questioned southern cultural and environmental exceptionalism, many early naturalists were drawn to the region for the supposed extreme otherness of its native flora and fauna. Obernesser places Muir in this tradition, but he argues that Muir complicates simplistic notions of southern otherness by undermining strict North/South binaries based on his focused ecological study of the region. Obernesser also explores why Muir struggled to consider how issues of race and class are intertwined in the region's environmental history. Thus, the irony at the center of Muir's text is that although it enables him to progressively conceive his conservationist and preservationist environmental praxis, it ultimately precludes him, because of his utopic preference for pristine wilderness spaces, from analyzing how messy cultural conflicts surrounding race and class are inextricably bound to the environmental history of the United States.

Jimmy Dean Smith's chapter considers several texts by Harriette Simpson Arnow, John Ehle, and Cormac McCarthy, all of which prominently feature roads in southern Appalachia. According to Smith, one of the most obvious ways that humanity has attempted to dominate the natural world is through the creation of roads, which he claims is part of the larger rationalist master narrative in Western culture focused on control through both cultural and technological means. This is a particularly important subject to study in southern Appalachia, as it is a subregion that has been subjected to intense resource extraction alongside the extreme denigration of its peoples. Smith concludes his chapter by powerfully asserting the need to create an environmental praxis that will lead to a more sustainable, rather than apocalyptic, phase of the Anthropocene. He writes, "Building the right kind of roads, ones that recognize that human beings' place is *in* nature and not above it, is a start."

The final chapter in this section, by Joseph M. Thompson, focuses on the 1970s music of African American poet and songwriter Gil Scott-Heron. Thompson highlights several of Scott-Heron's most political songs—such as "The Revolution Will Not Be Televised," "Whitey on the Moon," and "South Carolina (Barnwell)"—to show how black individuals and communities have often suffered as a direct result of projects funded by the federal government and centered in the national military-industrial complex. Furthermore, Scott-Heron's songs assert that US defense spending tends to reentrench the oppression of African Americans; having spent much of his childhood in Jackson, Tennessee, and continuing to have a lifelong obsession with that place, Scott-Heron's critique of environmental racism is often anchored specifically in the US South. Thompson points out that the region's environmental racism is not exceptional. Rather, he argues that Scott-Heron's music encourages listeners to observe the South's place within much broader networks of racism and environmental degradation. Building upon the work of philosophers Gilles Deleuze and Félix Guattari, Thompson argues that the South is rhizomatic, in that, as he states, "the rhizome model could deal more accurately with the issue of historical causality by recognizing the multiplicity of roots and outcomes." This theory helps to further deconstruct lingering notions that there is a monolithic "South" with an identifiable origin; instead, the rhizomatic South is an ever-changing idea that has been and continues to be mobilized at certain times with certain ideological projects in mind. For Scott-Heron, the South of the mid-twentieth century was one in which several political and economic networks overlapped—Cold War military defense, the space race, and nuclear power production—to create toxic cultural and environmental threats to vulnerable communities of color.

The third section of *Ecocriticism and the Future of Southern Studies* examines how farming and foodways have been variously conceived and represented throughout the history of the region. Sam Horrocks tackles the perennially difficult topic of the Nashville Agrarians and the legacy of their 1930 manifesto *I'll Take My Stand*. Horrocks argues that it is important to realize that agrarian thinking existed long before the Nashville Agrarians, as well as after, in forms entirely independent of the problematic platform advanced in *I'll Take My Stand*. In other words, Horrocks suggests that southern studies must contend with the idea that agrarianism, even within the US South, is not always the southern-inflected version of the concept that necessitates immediate critique. After analyzing the many implicitly and explicitly racist and classist elements of *I'll Take My Stand*, Horrocks seeks to advance a new theory of agrarian ecologies. While Horrocks acknowledges that the Nashville Agrarians provided a fitting critique of how industrialization negatively impacts rural communities, he goes on say that the kind of agrarianism touted by the group was not agrarianism at all in the way that he defines it. Rather, the Nashville

Agrarians ironically supported an agrarianism that Horrocks maintains was based on the logic of industrialism. They built this platform on a nostalgic view of southern antebellum plantations, which featured characteristics more commonly associated with industrialism, especially the exploitation of both people and environments.[9] In addition, Horrocks evaluates several novels by William Faulkner, a contemporary of the Nashville Agrarians whose environmental vision diverged sharply from that of *I'll Take My Stand*. Horrocks asserts that because Faulkner accurately and unflinchingly highlights the exploitative practices of southern plantations, he promotes a truer agrarian ecology that is based on the mutually beneficial, but also inevitably messy, interconnectedness of human and nonhuman communities, rather than the destruction of both solely for the sake of profit.

In the second chapter of this section, Daniel Spoth highlights the intersections between environmentalism and foodways in the US South. Following recent scholars such as Jon Smith and Scott Romine, who have coedited an entire collection forthcoming on this matter, *Against Cornbread Nationalism: How Foodways Partisans Misrepresent the South*, Spoth is skeptical of much of the food writing and foodways scholarship that has focused on the region in recent years. In particular, Spoth questions the generally positive portrayal of foodways in the South and the tendency in both popular and scholarly writing to depict food in the region as ameliorating long-standing cultural tensions and involving a healthy and sustainable connection between people and the land. Furthermore, Spoth discusses what he calls visceral environmentalism, which is a "concern with the natural world stemming from affect rather than intellect, the guts rather than the brain." Spoth is careful to point out that with this theory he does not mean to reinscribe stereotypical notions of southerners being somehow closer to the soil than people in other parts of the United States. Instead, he suggests that the visceral obsession in environmental and food-related rhetoric is often used as a way to elide or circumvent thorny issues, such as race, class, and gender. Refusing to romanticize, fethishize, or commodify southern foodways, Spoth hopes to demystify them by highlighting positive traditions while never falling prey to the nostalgic and historically inaccurate depictions of the region as ever having been environmentally and culturally harmonious. Ultimately, for Spoth, visceral environmentalism enables us to acknowledge not the historically accurate interactions between humans and the environment, but rather the ways that humans have desired to see and thus depict their relationships with the environment. Visceral environmentalism, therefore, can lead us to a messy and synthetic but ultimately truer and more honest conception of the ecological history of the South.

The fourth section of the collection is devoted to floods and southern water studies and is comprised of chapters assessing literature, cinema, and cultures that are preoccupied with the region's complicated legacy of water management efforts and water-related environmental disasters. This section begins with Lucas J. Sheaffer's eco-rhetorical analysis of the speeches and writings of David E. Lilienthal, the leader of the Tennessee Valley Authority (TVA), a New Deal project created under Franklin Delano Roosevelt's administration to control floods, improve riverine navigation, bolster the economy, revolutionize the agricultural sector, and create electricity plants, many using hydropower. The TVA targeted the bioregion of the Tennessee River and its tributaries, a vast area that covers most of Tennessee as well as parts of Alabama, Georgia, Kentucky, Mississippi, North Carolina, and Virginia. Sheaffer focuses on three tropes that recur throughout Lilienthal's rhetoric: refrigerators, mosquitoes, and phosphates, each of which represents an environmental issue that Lilienthal proposes to fix by utilizing both technological and mechanical means, thus ensuring the economic, social, and physical health of the US South, or so Lilienthal claims. Sheaffer concludes that while the TVA accomplished many beneficial things for the area, Lilienthal's rhetoric must be interrogated to understand how the agency required southern communities to "acquiesce to the supremacy of their own anthropocentric needs and forsake the complex ecological implications of these decisions, actions, and words."

The next chapter, by Christopher Lloyd, analyzes the southern imaginary in relation to the floods that have continually devastated the South. Lloyd contends that literature has consistently and creatively responded to this waterlogged and water-obsessed region. After providing a useful inventory of this literary tradition, Lloyd focuses on the Mississippi River and how contemporary fiction utilizes the river's flooding as a representation of memory. Two such texts are Bernice L. McFadden's *Gathering of Waters* (2012) and Tom Franklin and Beth Ann Fennelly's *The Tilted World* (2013), both of which depict, among other floods, the Great Mississippi Flood of 1927. In addition to productively recalling previously forgotten or neglected elements of history, Lloyd asserts that we must also remain suspicious of how the watery past in these works is presented and for what ideological purposes.

Evangelia Kindinger's chapter continues the exploration of hydropolitics, or the intersection between water-related environmental issues and US politics. Kindinger provides an extensive summary and analysis of scholarship on global diasporas. The field of diaspora studies tends to focus on individuals or groups of people who are forced to leave their homes for religious, political, economic, cultural, or environmental reasons and seek a new life elsewhere. Most groups of people who are studied in this field leave their homes physically and then settle in an entirely new location, usually a different country. Kindinger expands diaspora studies by analyzing characters in the HBO series *Treme* (2010–2013), which follows the lives of New Orleanians after Hurricane Katrina. These characters do not adhere to traditional definitions of diaspora in that their movements are intranational, settling in other states within the United States or remaining in New Orleans. In both of these cases, however, the people have experiences like those in more conventionally understood diaspora scenarios—in particular, the sense of geographical, cultural, and personal alienation and consequent attempts to recover and re-create, if possible, a sense of self and community that existed prior to the diaspora. Kindinger suggests that the most successful characters in *Treme* are those who are able to retain elements of their prediaspora identities and incorporate them into healthy new ones informed by their diaspora experiences.

The final chapter in this section, by Sarah E. McFarland, also investigates Hurricane Katrina by examining Behn Zeitlin's 2012 film *Beasts of the Southern Wild*. Against the backdrop of Louisiana—a state that has often been overly accommodating to environmentally destructive industries that pollute the air and water without protecting its citizens—*Beasts* is a film that not only studies the ways human behaviors led to and exacerbated the destruction caused by Hurricane Katrina, but also provides a much broader analysis of the ways humans interact with the environment in the Anthropocene. McFarland contends that this is a particularly relevant film for this new geological epoch in that it celebrates storytelling that is attentive to the fragility of contemporary ecosystems and the ways in which we must recognize and respond appropriately to the interconnections between human and nonhuman communities at the local and global levels. McFarland powerfully argues that "ecologically-embodied storytelling"—as we see in *Beasts,* particularly in the young female African American protagonist Hushpuppy—is imperative to teach the people living in and through the Anthropocene how to adapt to life in this inevitable and globalized environmental crisis.

The final section of *Ecocriticism and the Future of Southern Studies* is devoted to eco-dystopias—i.e., narratives that marshal environmental imagery that is dystopic, if not downright apocalyptic; narratives that center on environmental catastrophes; and/or narratives that focus on the environmental ramifications of any kind of doomsday scenario. Joshua Myers's chapter scrutinizes graves and graveyards of the antebellum South; whereas people tend to associate graveyards with peace, tranquility, and natural splendor, Myers argues that funerary practices, both past and present, tend to mask environmental degradation and social oppression. Myers surveys the antebellum, proslavery novels of Caroline Lee Hentz to show that in them plantation owners use gravesites and the funerals of slaves to create a seemingly natural and pastoral space on the plantation. In turn, slaveholders deploy this space to conceal the various dystopic qualities of the southern plantation. Thus, Hentz's novels "present slavery as utopic by conflating the gravesites of slaves with idyllic nature."

Jonathan Villalobos's contribution to this section examines the ecological crises that came to the fore of American consciousness in the 1960s and 1970s, especially following the publication of Rachel Carson's watershed book *Silent Spring* in 1962. Villalobos contends that southern texts register broader American anxieties about environmental destruction and seek to highlight these issues in the region to counter notions that the South still existed as an isolated wilderness or a pastoral idyll. Specifically, Villalobos provides close ecofeminist readings of the scenes of sexual assault in James Dickey's *Deliverance* (1970) and Cormac McCarthy's *Child of God* (1973), both of which portray parallels between the violation of human bodies and the destruction of the natural world.

In the third chapter of this final section, John Moran observes that Florida is often depicted in various media as being the weirdest, wildest, and most criminal state not only in the South, but in the entire nation. As the quintessence of this way of depicting the state, Florida Man has become an internet meme with hundreds of thousands of fans. Florida Man (and occasionally Florida Woman) is depicted as engaging in strange, inexplicable, and often violent acts and, in most cases, being arrested for them. Moran demonstrates that such portrayals of Floridians can best be understood within a long tradition of climatological racism—i.e., the belief that different groups of people living in different places possess varying abilities and capacities, which are directly related to and dependent upon climate. An infamous example of climatological racism is the justification of slavery based on the idea that Africans were biologically predisposed to labor in the typical climate of Deep South plantations. Using whiteness studies and queer theory, Moran asserts that the stigmatization of Florida Man reveals the temperatist gaze of the supposedly more "civilized" peoples of the North (and Global North) who tend to value "metronormative and homonational whiteness, or a properly civilized and socially inclusive urban whiteness." Moran concludes that given the environmental consequences we are seeing and will continue to see due to climate change, the temperatist tendency to other those peoples associated with tropicality, animality, primitivity, and extreme environmental phenomena may be even more prevalent in the future.

In the final chapter of the collection, Robert Azzarello explores texts about the environmental past, present, and future of the city of New Orleans. In order to assess the significance of eco-apocalyptic narratives about New Orleans, Azzarello provides a useful review of scholarship regarding why the apocalypse has been a popular preoccupation across time periods, locations, and genres, and he uses this broader context to speak specifically about how the apocalypse functions in the environmental imagination. Examining texts by Valerie Martin, Katie Ford, and Moira Crone, Azzarello suggests that literature about New Orleans is inevitably obsessed with environmental catastrophes because the city itself is and will increasingly be threatened by disasters caused by climate change, especially ever-worsening hurricanes, floods, and sea-level rise. In a bleak but realistic and necessary conclusion both to the chapter and the collection, Azzarello asserts that the authors he has assembled, especially Moira Crone, have written "the history of the future," a harrowing peek into the planet's coming years which will be marked by environmental catastrophes and consequent social, political, and economic turmoil. The lingering question, then, of the Anthropocene is whether it is too late, or whether we may still stave off disaster, particularly in the coastal landscapes of the US South.

All of the essays in this collection demonstrate how effectively environmental studies can contribute to southern studies, and vice versa. Together these two fields form a new academic community engaged in groundbreaking conversations. The greening of southern studies and the southernization of environmental studies can catalyze alternative ways of seeing the region and its places and spaces, ultimately inspiring regional and environmental sensitivities that open new intellectual terrain, while also generating additional directions for activists who understand the overlaps between environmental and social justice in the region. About their collection *Keywords for Southern Studies*, Romine and Greeson say, "This geopolitical frame brings us a final critical consonance among the essays in this volume. Many of them share a note of urgency, an urgency directed not toward the loss of the object of study or the ambiguous state of the field but rather toward the present moment" (4). A similar sense of urgency is clear in the field of American ecocriticism, but it is particularly acute in southern ecocriticism, because environmental problems have been at certain times in the past and in many ways in the present particularly dire throughout the region. Communities of color, in particular, tend to experience far more detrimental impacts from contaminated air and water (e.g., the predominantly African American areas of Warren Country, North Carolina, which became the infamous site of a PCB landfill),[10] as well as the impacts of human-induced or, at the very least, human-exacerbated climatological events, such as hurricanes and floods (e.g., the loss of ancestral lands in Isle de Jean Charles and the severe devastation faced by Gulf Coast communities of color during Hurricanes Katrina and Rita).[11] For contemporary ecocritics, our urgent scholarly endeavors connect with the past and present but also look to the future. As Aaron Sachs observes, "Environmentalists, of necessity, are future-oriented: the whole point is to cultivate modes of interaction with nature that can be sustained over time" (348). The title of this collection, *Ecocriticism and the Future of Southern Studies,* may at first sound hyperbolic. However, given the immense risk of environmental catastrophes that we face in the US South in the age of the Anthropocene, I believe this title is fitting. Southern studies, if it is to remain relevant to future generations, must take seriously these environmental threats and explore how they were and are and will be addressed by the cultural expressions of the region.

NOTES

1. I began to cultivate some of these ideas in my brief article "The Anthropocene and the Future of Southern Studies," published in *Mississippi Quarterly,* vol. 68, nos. 1–2, 2015, pp. 32–34.

2. There remains some debate about who first coined the word "Anthropocene." However, in its current meaning, the word was both theorized and popularized in the early 2000s by scientists such as Eugene F. Stoermer and Paul J. Crutzen. In more recent years, scholars in the environmental humanities have adopted the term, utilizing it in a range of academic contexts.

3. For more information on why the term *nature* has fallen out of favor amongst environmental critics, see McKibben's *The End of Nature* and Morton's *Ecology without Nature.*

4. Steven E. Knepper makes a similar argument in his chapter of *Keywords for Southern Studies:* "Because of the South's environmental history and its current environmental challenges, southern studies can contribute to the move beyond wilderness and nature writing to a wider reckoning with the problems of humans' interaction with nonhuman nature" (268).

5. Applying the word *real* to any aspect of the South inevitably raises hackles and puts certain scholars—probably the majority these days—on edge, and rightfully so. For example, Romine states, "By real South, I refer to something more like the 'real'/'South': a set of anxious, transient, even artificial intersections, sutures, or common surfaces between two concepts that are themselves remarkably fluid . . ." (2–3).

6. For more information on "sense of place" in the southern context, see Vernon's "The Problematic History and Recent Cultural Reappropriation of Southern Agrarianism." For more on the importance of considering the global, as well as the local, in discussions about "sense of place," see Ursula K. Heise's *Sense of Place and Sense of Planet*.

7. See Fishman's *Journeys Through Paradise*.

8. While these relatively undeveloped areas are vast compared to much of the Northeast, I should note that they appear diminutive when compared to much of the Southwest.

9. See also Knepper 266–67.

10. See Bullard's *Dumping in Dixie*.

11. For more information on how ecological crises disproportionately impact marginalized people, especially the impoverished and communities of color, see Park and Miller, Nixon, and Reed. I briefly address the connections between social and environmental justice in my recent article "Environmental Pedagogy, Activism, and Literature in the U.S. South," published in *South: A Scholarly Journal*, vol. 50, no. 2, 2018, pp. 225–235.

WORKS CITED

Adamson, Joni, and Kimberly N. Ruffin, editors. *American Studies, Ecocriticism, and Citizenship: Thinking and Acting in the Local and Global Commons*. Routledge, 2013.

Anderson, Eric, Taylor Hagood, and Daniel Cross Turner, editors. *Undead Souths: The Gothic and Beyond in Southern Literature and Culture*. Louisiana State UP, 2015.

Bone, Martyn. *The Postsouthern Sense of Place in Contemporary Fiction*. Louisiana State UP, 2005.

Buell, Lawrence. *The Environmental Imagination: Thoreau, Nature Writing, and the Formation of American Culture*. Harvard UP, 1995.

Bullard, Robert D. *Dumping in Dixie: Race, Class, and Environmental Quality*. Westview Press, 1990.

Clabough, Casey Howard. *Elements: The Novels of James Dickey*. Mercer UP, 2002.

Clark, Thomas D. *The Greening of the South: The Recovery of Land and Forest*. UP of Kentucky, 1984.

Clark, Timothy. *The Cambridge Introduction to Literature and the Environment*. Cambridge UP, 2011.

Cowdrey, Albert E. *This Land, This South: An Environmental History*. UP of Kentucky, 1983.

Fishman, Gail. *Journeys Through Paradise: Pioneering Naturalists in the Southeast*. UP of Florida. 2017.

Glotfelty, Cheryll. "Introduction: Literary Studies in the Age of Environmental Crisis." *The*

Ecocriticism Reader: Landmarks in Literary Ecology, edited by Cheryll Glotfelty and Harold Fromm, U of Georgia P, 1996, pp. xv–xxxvii.

Glotfelty, Cheryll, and Harold Fromm, editors. *The Ecocriticism Reader: Landmarks in Literary Ecology.* U of Georgia P, 1996.

Heise, Ursula K. *Sense of Place and Sense of Planet: The Environmental Imagination of the Global.* Oxford UP, 2008.

Herring, Terrell Scott. "Review: Micro: Region, History, Literature." *American Literary History,* vol. 22, no. 3, 2010, pp. 626–34.

Kartiganer, Donald M., and Ann J. Abadie, editors. *Faulkner and the Natural World.* UP of Mississippi, 1999.

Kirby, Jack Temple. *Mockingbird Song: Ecological Landscapes of the South.* U of North Carolina P, 2006.

Knepper, Steven E. "Ecology/Environment." *Keywords for Southern Studies,* edited by Scott Romine and Jennifer Rae Greeson, U of Georgia P, 2016, pp. 264–75.

Lynch, Tom, Cheryll Glotfelty, and Karla Armbruster, editors. *The Bioregional Imagination: Literature, Ecology, and Place.* U of Georgia P, 2012.

McKibben, Bill. *The End of Nature: Humanity, Climate Change and the Natural World.* Bloomsbury, 2003.

Morton, Timothy. *Ecology without Nature: Rethinking Environmental Aesthetics.* Harvard UP, 2007.

Nixon, Rob. *Slow Violence and the Environmentalism of the Poor.* Harvard UP, 2011.

Park, Yoosun, and Joshua Miller. "The Social Ecology of Hurricane Katrina: Re-Writing the Discourse of 'Natural' Disasters." *Smith College Studies in Social Work,* vol. 76, no. 3, 2006, pp. 9–24.

Purdy, Jedediah. *After Nature: A Politics for the Anthropocene.* Harvard UP, 2015.

Reed, T. V. "Toward an Environmental Justice Ecocriticism." *Environmental Justice Reader: Politics, Poetics, and Pedagogy,* edited by Joni Adamson, Mei Mei Evans, and Rachel Stein, U of Arizona P, 2002, pp. 145–62.

Rieger, Christopher. *Clear-Cutting Eden: Ecology and the Pastoral in Southern Literature.* U of Alabama P, 2009.

Romine, Scott. *The Real South: Southern Narrative in the Age of Cultural Reproduction.* Louisiana State UP, 2008.

Romine, Scott, and Jennifer Rae Greeson. "Introduction." *Keywords for Southern Studies,* edited by Scott Romine and Jennifer Rae Greeson, U of Georgia P, 2016, pp. 1–5.

Sachs, Aaron. *Arcadian America: The Death and Life of an Environmental Tradition.* Yale UP, 2013.

Simpson, Lewis P. *The Dispossessed Garden: Pastoral and History in Southern Literature.* U of Georgia P, 1975.

Slovic, Scott, Swarnalatha Rangarajan, and Vidya Sarveswaran, editors. *Ecocriticism of the Global South.* Rowman & Littlefield, 2015.

Sutter, Paul S., and Christopher J. Manganiello, editors. *Environmental History and the American South: A Reader.* U of Georgia P, 2009.

Urgo, Joseph R., and Ann J. Abadie, editors. *Faulkner and the Ecology of the South*. UP of Mississippi, 2005.

Vernon, Zackary. "The Problematic History and Recent Cultural Reappropriation of Southern Agrarianism." *ISLE,* vol. 21, no. 2, 2014, pp. 337–52.

———. "Environmental Pedagogy, Activism, and Literature in the U.S. South." *South: A Scholarly Journal,* vol. 50, no. 2, 2018, pp. 225–235.

Watson, Jay. "The Other Matter of the South." *PMLA,* vol. 131, no. 1, 2016, pp. 157–61.

Welling, Bart. "Grounding Southern Ecocriticism." *Southern Literary Journal,* vol. 45, no. 1, 2012, pp. 129–33.

Wilhelm, Randall, and Zackary Vernon, editors. *Summoning the Dead: Essays on Ron Rash*. U of South Carolina P, 2018.

Wilson, Anthony. *Shadow and Shelter: The Swamp in Southern Culture*. UP of Mississippi, 2006.

Yaeger, Patricia. "*Beasts of the Southern Wild* and Dirty Ecology." *Southern Spaces,* 13 Feb. 2013. https://southernspaces.org/2013/beasts-southern-wild-and-dirty-ecology. Accessed 27 Aug. 2018.

I

COAL, OIL, & SOUTHERN HAZARDSCAPES

Stuck in Place

Affect, Atmosphere, and the Appalachian World of Ann Pancake

LISA HINRICHSEN

Was it worse to lose the mountain or the feelings that you had for it?
—ANN PANCAKE, *Strange as This Weather Has Been*

The South has always existed, as Edward Ayers writes, "on the edge of extinction," for "as long as people have believed there was a South they have also believed it was disappearing" (69). Though Ayers speaks primarily about the linguistic and imaginative construction of the region—"What We Talk About When We Talk About the South," as he puts it in his title—and the performance of a "sense of place" hinged on the loss of an always-mythical imagined community, the US South is and has been a site of real loss.[1] Against constructed, fantasized notions of the region—as an abundant paradise; a pastoral haven of order and simplicity; a feudal, aristocratic anachronism; a place cursed and ruined by its legacy of chattel slavery—there has been a parallel natural history of ecological dislocation and environmental degeneration, collapse, and commodification. Marked (but not exceptionally so) by the transition to modern ecological regimes characterized by the draining of the land by monoculture agriculture, asset-stripping, the exploitation of biocapital, heightened privatization, and shifts from production to consumption, the US South, like the broader Global South, is an increasingly precarious ecosystem.

In drawing on recent work in ecocriticism and affect theory, this essay focuses on West Virginian author Ann Pancake's 2007 debut novel, *Strange as This Weather Has Been,* and its story of a coal-mining family in Appalachia witnessing mountaintop removal. From its opening depiction of a young girl, Lace See, running down the road away from home, guilt-burdened but wanting to escape, *Strange as This Weather Has Been* explores the ambivalence of home as Pancake depicts Lace leaving on a scholarship to West Virginia University and then returning home after an unexpected pregnancy. Moving forward and backward in time and switching between different voices, Pancake traces the family's turbulent life raising four children in a trailer in a valley surrounded by mountaintop-removal mines, unfolding the types of feelings and memories rooted in this precarious place. In its attention to the imaginary ideals and intangible objects that ground Appalachia's material spaces and places, Pancake raises intriguing questions about the future of a southern "sense of place" through its illumination of the growing ecological sacrifice and segregation of people along economic and geographic lines. In tracing the intersection of regionalism, poverty, and multinational industry, *Strange as This Weather Has Been* makes, I argue, a southern "sense of place" strange, parsing the relevance of local identities in our globalized age, and articulating what it means to move from a traditional concept of region—one drawn from an anachronistic ideal at odds with contemporary ecological and economic reality—to a more sustainable understanding of community organized around bioregional affinity and an ecocosmopolitan vision of space and place.[2] In examining what the value of affect is to the ecological, Pancake's work speaks to Cheryll Glotfelty's call to "become place-based global thinkers" who "pay attention to the local and build a sustainable local culture without becoming narrowly provincial or exclusionary" (43), and challenges dominant modes of ecocriticism that, as Janet Fiskio notes, have largely focused on "the reinhabitation of the local community as a means of simultaneously regenerating ecological sensibility and participatory democracy" while neglecting the transnational and the global (301).

Like earlier literary and documentary work on coal mining in Appalachia—for example, James Still's *River of Earth* (1940) and Silas House and Jason Howard's collection of oral histories, *Something's Rising: Appalachians Fighting Mountaintop Removal* (2011)—Pancake's novel richly evokes Appalachia as a complex culture, a place enlivened by the embodied knowledge experienced by the people who live there. A native of Romney and Summersville, West Virginia, Pancake has spoken openly of her pride in the state and her anguish at the way her homeland has been ecologically ravaged by mountaintop-removal coal mining. Primarily occurring in West Virginia, Kentucky, Virginia, and Tennessee, mountaintop removal began in the 1970s as an extension of conventional strip-mining techniques. Often hidden away from major highways, mountaintop removal is a form of surface mining that involves the dramatic blasting apart of mountain summits to extract exposed coal seams. Dismantled and mined, the land is then reclaimed as flattops with rolling grasslands and shrublands, introducing a new ecosystem to replace what once was a mixed hardwood forest. Involving a multistep process of clearing, blasting, digging, and dumping waste, mountaintop removal has eliminated the need for miners by relying on increased mechanization responsible for introducing a wide range of toxic materials into the air, streams, and soil of the region. Despite impacting biological diversity, drinking water, and local communities, which have often organized in resistance, the practice continues, altering the landscape permanently due to the limitations of legislated reclamation.[3]

Citing Jack Turner's claims in *The Abstract Wild* (1996) that "only genuine love of our environment will incite us to save it," Pancake declares in a personal essay (2013) in *The Georgia Review* that, inspired by her sister Catherine Pancake's experience in making a documentary film about mountaintop removal, she composed *Strange as This Weather Has Been* "with the conscious aim of just trying to show the truth about the devastation of a place I loved with the hope of generating compassion for the living beings suffering because of this devastation. If people understood better, I thought, they would help make change" ("Creative Responses").[4] Yet in examining the dirty dimensions of mountaintop-removal mining, and in illustrating the living conditions of persons displaced by land expropriation and exploitation more broadly, Pancake's novel comes to parse, and even critique, this "love" in its unpacking of the social-ecological relations that modulate Appalachia as both concrete place and affective community.

As Patricia Clough suggests, affect does not merely indicate emotion, but our "bodily capacities to affect and be affected" (2), offering us enabling or disabling forms of activity and life. Understood as not merely (sentimental) feeling but as a model of relation, affect is, as *Strange as This Weather Has Been* reveals, pivotal to political and collective life, including current concerns about climate change, species extinction, pervasive toxicity, population growth, and industrial expansion. Wanda Vrasti asserts, "the hegemony of late capitalism is being fought on territories . . . such as the personal, the affective, and the aesthetic" (qtd. in Jensen), making understanding the "love" felt to accompany a southern "sense of place" crucial. While critiquing nostalgic narratives of place and community, displacing a traditional southern sense of place, Pancake underscores how community can potentially offer a value that is not properly accounted for under neoliberal logic. Her novel's focus on the "feel" of neoliberal deterritorialization, the psychological turmoil of environmental trauma, and the fragmentations of self underlying postmodernity more broadly, ultimately posits an economy of affect that transcends a sense of place as mere capital, pointing toward affective dimensions of ecology that are resistant to economic codification and that offer an alternative to the unfeeling neoliberal circulation of capital—"We exist," as her characters declare at one key moment, articulating their existence against national forgetting (314).

Yet Pancake's text consistently reminds us that place attachment can become a "resource in the articulation of environmental unconscious" (Buell 28) only if it allows us to imagine relational, rather than exclusionary or autonomous, forms of personhood, and to make connections between specific forms of local destruction and widespread instances of "strange weather" increasingly part of our interconnected global ecology. Noting the value of a politics of communal feeling that can potentially work against the "rationality" of neoliberal enterprise and atomized individualism, Pancake ultimately advocates what Floya Anthias (2008) has called "translocational positionality," a form of thinking beyond static locations, borders, nations, and identities toward an amalgamation of locations and belongings in ways that are sensitive to spatial *and* affective politics. "Was it worse to lose the mountain or the feelings that you had for it?" a character asks, before realizing that "to not care wasn't to save yourself at all. It was only another loss" (356). While cautioning against the fantasy of community taking precedence over the destruction of the mountain itself, leaving us with *only feeling,* Pancake acknowledges the central role affect plays in understanding the ecological.

In tracing the "temperature, weather," Pancake ties social habitation back to the ecological and material, revealing how both can remain invisible but influential. In reflecting on his upbringing in Appalachia, one character recalls how his fellow classmates "learned not to ask questions, to do as they were told, expect little, they were raised to expect disappointment," framing his immersion in this worldview in ecological terms: "this they absorbed from the air around them, a pessimism so pervasive . . . that Avery never recognized it— it was temperature, weather—until he left out [of his hometown in Appalachia] and realized how much the other people, at least the other white people, in this country perceived, expected, desired" (235). Seeing the once-invisible "temperature, weather" of working-class resignation, Pancake argues, means consciously confronting the depression and exploitation, the lack and scarcity, that is the underside of capitalism; and, from this vantage point, *Strange as This Weather Has Been* advances a vision of environmental justice intertwined with critiques of economic injustice. To make the atmosphere of Appalachia visible is to see how feelings such as the love of place and habits like the expectation of disappointment are generated in and through flows of financialization that transform place into capital, and environment into exploitable commodity.

As numerous critics have noted, public and private vulnerability to disasters is highly differentiated; risk and costs are displaced and transferred onto communities with the least political power, while rewards are expropriated by those who do not bear the danger. Recently, Rebecca Scott has delineated how conventional popular representations of Appalachia work ceaselessly to connect poverty and environmental destruction with fundamental difference, in the process reaffirming the imagined immunity of the mainstream from this type of suffering and asserting the logic of differential worthiness. Neoliberal cultures that allow the rich to prosper in a deregulated economy, as Henry Giroux and Lisa Duggan argue, are buttressed by images of the abject poor: images, like the ones that Pancake has a character recite, of "American poverty Appalachian-style: the shanties and decaying trailers, the retarded and the crazy, those without plumbing reeking on school buses, the ringworm and scabies and lice, your daily meal the free one at school, your clothes somebody else's first and everyone can tell" (235). In exposing holes in the protection of belonging promised by US citizenship, and drawing attention to the gap between an everyday experiential reality of American inequality and the mythic narration of an idealistic, innocent, and equal democracy, Pancake, through her description of environmental and social damage, spotlights the "kill spaces" of capitalism, and addresses what political economist Samir Amin calls the "lumpen development" model of social disintegration, pauperization, and super-exploitation that has affected those in economically and historically marginalized communities and produced environmental injustice.[5] As one character in *Strange as This Weather Has Been* wryly notes, "Seems like there are two laws. One for the rich people, and one for the poor" (117).

Underscoring the history of weak labor and environmental protections endemic to the South, and particularly to Appalachia, Pancake relentlessly details the landscape that forms the ground for this exploitation, situating the region's present-day destruction by mountaintop-removal mining within a larger history of exploitation for national gain. In delineating the logic of who can, in her words, "get away with what—where, when, and on whom," and in revealing that "the whole region had been killed at least once" (238), she gestures toward the deep history of the land, described as "regularly slaughtered for well over a hundred years" (238), subject to a state of disaster that must be ation only.

n only.

y.

thought of as "cumulative" and "governed by a different scale of time" defined by the "chronic, pressing, insistent, insidious" (239). The landscape is, as she renders it, a palimpsest of trauma: "Its gradual being taken away for the past hundred years, by timber, by coal, and now, outright killed, and the little you have left, mind thinking, heart knowing, a constant reminder of what you've lost and are about to lose. So you never get a chance to heal" (271).

Brimming with descriptions of a slaughtered landscape, *Strange as This Weather Has Been* depicts a world made up of sediment ponds, blast damage, blackwater impoundments, and fill, as "clawed-up," "cratered-out," and "amputated" (165)—land transformed, in short, into what Pancake calls "an amphitheater of kill" (213) distant from the highway, but felt via a kind of affective residue: "You had your quiet places, Grandma places, your places where peace would settle in your chest—then you had these places, places with a sharpness, a hardness, so utterly opposite all the rumpled deep green, you'd have to slow down and refocus your eyes" (157). Here the "sharpness" of the industrial mining contrasts with the comfort of "Grandma places," or environments associated with the lived knowledge gained from multigenerational inhabitation. In contrast, the "kill" places of industrial capitalism, the "used-up left-behind places," hardened by the wasting of nature, demand a different kind of perception and affect (157).

Importantly, Pancake does more in this passage than merely say we have to "refocus" and "slow down" to see environmental destruction properly: her novel also asks us, as part of what I am arguing is a broader project of articulating the role of affect to the ecological, what blindness is integral to the "Grandma places," and what forms of structural inequality and violence might be intertwined with ideas of comfort and the feeling of home. For, thick with memory, rich with fantasy, the South is, as Pancake evinces in her description of "Grandma places," a space both real and imaginary, both material and full of intangible affect: in her words, a "place sticky with history, history sticky in it" (236). In unfolding what Pancake means by calling Appalachia a "sticky" place, I draw upon Sara Ahmed's phenomenological work on the transference of emotions, in particular her argument in *The Promise of Happiness* (2009) that "[a]ffect is what sticks, or what sustains or preserves the connection between ideas, values, and objects" (230), Teresa Brenna's scholarship on the multisensorial dimensions of what it means to soak up "an atmosphere" in *The Transmission of Affect* (2014), and studies by geographers and political economists on "sticky places" and "slippery spaces" (Markusen 1999; see also Castree et al.

2004). Broadly, "sticky places" are frequented spaces that are significant in how we see ourselves and our relationships with others, rooted in an attachment to locality; "slippery spaces," conversely, reflect the way that globalization has made space seem more mobile and more ephemeral.

In *Strange as This Weather Has Been,* rural West Virginia is slippery, a hub for the global export of coal and chemicals, yet it is also sticky in the sense that it is a particular ecological space—one with natural resources for coal extraction, embedded in networks of corporate strategies, industrial structures, state priorities, and local and national politics that together create an experience of space and place not easily transported elsewhere. Coal functions as both artifact and organizing principle for a constellation of social relationships, creating a vision of home that is both comforting and carceral, sustaining if not sustainable, because it is tied to illness, death, and destruction: "We eat off it, dig in it, doctor from it, work under it. Us, we grow up swaddled in it, ground around our shoulders, over top our heads, we work both the top and the underside of the earth, we are surrounded" (151). It "swaddle[s]" but can also suffocate.

A product of this world, Lace See, Pancake's central protagonist, first articulates the stickiness of her rural home, or what she terms simply "the feel," when she "left out [of her hometown] and knew it by its absence" (4). In Morgantown, West Virginia, where she attends college, she feels overwhelmed by a "great swallowing lonesomeness . . . for known place" (98), and she experiences a slippery, discombobulating sensation "like I was all the time feeling like I wasn't touching nothing, and wasn't nothing touching me back" (4). Later, she spends a brief period in North Carolina, during which she feels similarly rootless, unreal, and ungrounded: "You walk only in the skin of the world, nothing in you reaching any deeper. So that you know how you're blowing away, feel always the airy empty insides of you" (136). Displaced from the mountains of West Virginia, Lace experiences spatial and psychic disorientation, a loss of depth that makes her feel ephemeral and "unstuck" from space and time, unhinged by a sense of placelessness. Weightless and shallow, with her sense of space and place eroded, she recognizes her dependence on a particular ecology to ground her. "West Virginia," she thinks, filled with homesickness, "I want to stay, I want to have, I want to be, without leaving" (136). "What is it about this place?" she asks herself, "What?" (10). She returns to the same question later, transforming a longing for home into a sentimental, even nativistic, articulation of place:

What is it? What makes us feel for our hills like we do? I waited. The chunging of cicadas around me, the under-burr of the other insects. Something small twisting through the always dead leaves. And although I didn't get an answer, I did know you'd have to come up in these hills to understand what I meant. Grow up shouldered in them, them forever around your ribs, your hips, how they hold you, sit astraddle, giving you always, for good or for bad, the sense of being held. It had something to do with that hold. (99)

"Home," as it is figured here, is more than a relationship to a mere physical landscape: transcending space, "home" encompasses the sticky temporality of shared experiences and memories, fusing the landscape with psychic life.

Yet if stickiness, as Ahmed delineates it, comes about through the binding of associations and affects that interpellate subjects, Pancake's novel plays with the tension between the need for "sticky places" to ground us and what it means to be "stuck in place," bound to an often mythic and limited version of locality. As Lace states, "for a long time I'd known the tightness of these hills, the way they penned. But now, I also felt their comfort, and worse, I'd learned the smallness of me in the away. I understood how when I left, I lost part of myself, but when I stayed, I couldn't stretch myself full" (10). The ethos of Appalachian belonging that ties identity to the materiality of homeplace decrees, as one character in *Strange as This Weather Has Been* states, that "[t]o leave home is not just to leave a piece of land and family and friends, it is to leave your reputation, the respect you've earned from others, your dignity, your place" (215). The paradox of staying, however, while seemingly resisting the loss tied to leaving, means, for Pancake's characters, the feeling of a diminishment of possibility: "I couldn't stretch myself full" (10). The exclusionary politics of community that this version of place offers—"you'd have to come up in these hills to understand what I meant"—form a type of comfort that is ultimately binding and inhibiting, offering an ethos of place, Pancake indicates, that resists the type of transpatial and relational understandings of community demanded by our current environmental crisis.

Pancake's vivid rendering in *Strange as This Weather Has Been* of the imaginary ideals, places, and intangible objects that ground Appalachia's material spaces and places thus offers a vision of ecology as relational, made up of material and virtual geographies crisscrossed by flows of nostalgia, desire, and hope. Yet in probing the difference between "sticky" and merely stuck, *Strange as This Weather Has Been* offers a poetics of place that complicates mainstream and celebratory forms of Appalachian self-conceptualization, positioning them as potentially unsustainable, particularly in the face of the "strange weather" of massive ecological destruction. Bryan T. McNeil notes how "natives of the region often describe an attachment to the land in romantic but vague terms," commenting on "the visceral experience of living in the coalfields" in ways that cement the identification of Appalachian people with a landscape—one rooted in the labor of mining (2). Mining, however, is not infinitely sustainable: as Robert J. Higgs writes in *Appalachia Inside Out: Conflict and Change* (1995), "the simple desire to earn a living is—and always has been—at odds with nostalgia and environmental concerns" (183). To put McNeil's observation more boldly, romantic fantasies about space and place can screen destructive realities, offering a feeling of rootedness that can prove toxic when bound to a polluted place.

In struggling to envision an environmental disaster that must be thought of as cumulative and chronic, and in processing the ethically fraught relationship between material place and imagined "sense of place," Pancake's protagonists run up against a set of imaginative and conceptual limits that make it hard to respond to environmental destruction. Faced with spills, valley fills, piles of overburden, and ongoing blasting, they feel unable to process the wreckage they see and feel: "it was even harder to take it all as real. It was like my mind didn't want to make a place for this here" (21). Seeing the scope of destruction from deforestation, flooding, mudslides, and the fouling of headwater streams takes on the gloss of obscenity: as one character relates, "it was like dirty pictures I was seeing . . . like looking at pictures of naked people. Like looking at pictures of dead bodies" (58). In tying together a perverted, "dirty" eroticism with death, this scene evokes an extinction fantasy that is potentially seductive and horrifying all at once.

Both made by coal and destroyed by it, needing the income it brings while aware also of the damage it creates, Pancake's characters, like all of us intimately indebted to an inherently ecologically destructive capitalism, can only disavow what they see and feel as "obscene," trying to preserve identity in the face of a deeply traumatic reality that they can neither ignore nor fully admit. As one character states, "It's like you can't get your eyes to adjust, the thing won't come into focus, but, no, not like the focus of your eyes, but your mind, your mind can't focus it" (29). If our current ecological crisis is a radical condition that not only constitutes a real and present danger but, as Slavoj Žižek suggests, also "questions our most unquestionable presuppositions, the very horizon of our meaning, our everyday understanding of 'nature' as a regular, rhythmic process" (34), then disavowal becomes necessary when one wants to continue to live without making radical changes. Living in this conditional state means operating in the "as if" of denial: "I know very well . . . but . . . I continue to act as if ecology is of no lasting consequence for my everyday life" (35).

In functioning as if place can remain a static ideal, rather than a lived reality inherently dynamic and fragile, the coal-producing communities of West Virginia are thus marked by a "relation of attachment to compromised conditions of possibility," which Lauren Berlant (2011) has termed "cruel optimism" (24). A relational dynamic whereby individuals remain attached to "clusters of promises" embedded in desired object-ideas ("the good life") even when they inhibit the conditions for flourishing and fulfilling such promises (24, 23), cruel optimism maintains attachments that ultimately prove injurious. In specifically addressing the end of the postwar good life fantasy and the rise of neoliberalism, Berlant positions cruel optimism as an affective condition that we live collectively, in that we are invested in the very institutions that ensure our precarity. Unable to give up forms of work, consumerism, love, and intimacy, we become reliant upon their toxic norms. Cruel optimism sustains us without being sustainable, because it ultimately makes us sick.

In *Strange as This Weather Has Been,* the fantasy that mountains can be continually mined without consequence proves cruel. Nodding to the costs of bodily affiliation with fossil fuels, and the many diseases and illnesses that can be traced back to sedimentation and dissolved minerals that drain from mine sites into nearby streams, Pancake's novel is littered with cancers, coughs, and pains that the characters envision will get better: "The disaster was carved into his body like grooves in a phonograph record, and the page about the prices, they played his skin back" (237). Economically dependent on a substance that proves toxic to human life, resistant to mobility but not desire ("I want to have"), the autochthonous identities that Pancake points to mean a vision of community dependent on (disavowed) ecological destruction to attain the "good" life.

In countering the colonization of West Virginia as a "national sacrifice zone," a resource colony written off for environmental destruction in the name of national interest, Pancake thus works to make "strange" the stickiness of Appalachian space and place, challenging modes of feeling that are toxic, and denaturalizing nativisitic modes of conceiving of community and environment. In looking for a solution to the cruel optimism of coal and in drawing our attention to how new forms of regionalism may prove useful in our globalized age, Pancake's characters come to discover forms of affiliation—parallel histories, political alliances, emotional solidarities—through "tunneling in" to the land. Researching the Buffalo Creek disaster, for example, one character "learned the February 26, 1972, dam bust was not Pittston's first, wasn't even the first one they'd had. . . . He tunneled into the history of slaghead disasters: Letcher County, Kentucky, 1923; Crane Creek, West Virginia, 1924; Buchanan, Virginia, 1942; Aberfan, Wales, 1966" (236). In digging down into the ground of West Virginia, Pancake's characters trace place-based affinities that offer the possibility of a new politics of solidarity that can exist across geopolitical borders, whereby they can understand themselves relationally with other lands and peoples across space and back through time, even potentially coming into relationships with the deep time of ecology, which involves complex, multi-causal states of affairs that have taken form through nonlinear histories.

As such, *Strange as This Weather Has Been* reveals how, as George Handley has written in another context, "going south can also mean going down under to bioregional spaces affected by history's violence" (91). "Going south," in this context, offers the possibility of "imagin[ing] transgressively across . . . a geography carved up by political and economic interests" (91). "Imagining transgressively," as Pancake delineates it in the form of her novel, means moving beyond the mere recording of machinations of economic and political inequalities—beyond literature as merely didactic—to think toward an Elsewhere that comes to eclipse the monolithic, static South, through tracing a new strange geography that puts bioregionally similar spaces and places into an integral conversation. In this form, *region,* as a term that describes the relationship of multiple places, has the potential to rhetorically link spaces into complex configurations, providing a lens or scale that can help identify, scrutinize, and respond to complex intersections of labor, environment, politics, and economics in particular sites on the landscape—intersections that point toward interconnections with other places, peoples, and cultures in ecocosmopolitan relation.

If, as Jon Smith has argued, white southerners' love of place is "largely just self-love dis-placed onto natural objects" (80), ecocosmopolitanism functions as a fetish-negating strategy that may help pry "white southern identity from its long, narcissistic gaze at its own ancestral navel" (95), reworking a form of love that misrecognizes the environment as a mere mirror for human life. Making the atmosphere of southern feeling "strange" means embracing an ethic of "out-of-jointness" that is productive for new collectivities not bound by the frameworks of traditional community. Against the mythologization of land as territory in ways that obscure ecocide, maintain oppression, obstruct solidarities, and determine "who counted for how much where," Pancake's novel thus offers us a model of "going south" that seeks to move us beyond a narcissistic fixation on individual, atomistic identity, destabilizing the boundaries between object and subject to introduce new ways of feeling about place and space. By moving beyond a subject-centered approach, by striving to make possible the analytical description of the "atmosphere" of a place, Pancake urges us to view human interiority and the exterior world as an intertwined assemblage, and to consider the affective potentialities of nonliving entities as well as nonhuman living entities: "What's a body. What's a woman, a man, a girl a boy a stream a tree a hill" (238).

Thus, in seeking to "create literature that imagines a way forward which is not based in idealism or fantasy, which does not offer dystopia or utopia, but still turns current paradigms on their heads," Pancake works to make strange the "stickiness" of southern place and space, denaturing the familiar parameters of what it means to belong and to inhabit its space, so as to turn from the past to the present, from the social to the geomaterial, from static nostalgia to activist activity, and from old notions of region to new recognitions of interconnected ecologies ("Creative Responses") and a vision of environmental activism in which "strangeness itself [must be] the locus of new forms of neighborliness and community" (Santner 6). In conclusion, as *Strange as This Weather Has Been* aptly shows, an economic model based on perpetual growth on a finite planet will inevitably fail, but not without first ravaging the ecologies of our land and psyches. Against this, Pancake offers a poetics of place that does not reassert myths linked to exceptional notions of land, but rather puts that land back into a larger map of interconnected bioregional communities able to respond to what she describes as a "kind of runaway loss," "an accelerated unraveling," that "is happening everywhere right now, on the level of the environment, of economics, and of human rights" ("Creative Responses").

NOTES

1. A "sense of place" references Eudora Welty's discussion in "Place in Fiction," wherein location is the "ground conductor of all the currents of emotions and belief and moral conviction that charge out from the story in its course" (128). Place has been a long-standing

trope seen to define southern literature, and writers and critics as different as Welty, William Faulkner, the Vanderbilt Agrarians, James Dickey, Louis D. Rubin Jr., James C. Cobb, and V. S. Naipaul have drawn on this concept to declare southern distinctiveness. More recent writing and criticism, however, points to the conceptual instability of place (see, for example, Jones and Monteith) and, as I've argued elsewhere, its foundation in fantasy (see Hinrichsen 2015).

2. As led by thinkers such as Peter Berg, Raymond Dasmann, Gary Snyder, and Stephanie Mills, bioregionalism is a school of thought that addresses environmental politics through a notion of the local that emerges from a biotically determined framework rather than traditional (but arbitrary) political boundaries such as nations, states, counties, etc. As such, it draws upon distinctly localized notions of scale and space in envisioning possibilities of sustainability and environmental justice. *The Bioregional Imagination: Literature, Ecology, and Place* (2012) provides a good overview. For more on ecocosmopolitanism, see Ursula Heise's *Sense of Place and Sense of Planet* (2008). Heise critiques both early and contemporary ecocriticism for its nostalgic sense of place, instead calling for an ecocosmopolitanism that focuses more on the relationship between the local and global.

3. The Surface Mining Control and Reclamation Act of 1977, which was partially a response to the 1972 Buffalo Creek disaster, in which a coal slurry impoundment ruptured and killed over 120 people, initiated legislated reclamation efforts by requiring that "all surface coal mining operations back-fill, compact [...] and grade in order to restore the approximate original contour of the land with all high-walls, spoil piles, and depressions eliminated." This legislation, which has been heavily revised since its inception, is not without problems: exceptions are regularly granted, and under SMCRA the economic value of the land supersedes its cultural (nonmonetary) value. Furthermore, reclamation does not replace the natural habitats of many local species, nor does it help with the destruction that radiates from the dig site: airborne debris, noise pollution, and downstream water supplies that are buried or impacted by leached toxins. See more about SMCRA at https://www.osmre.gov/lrg.shtm.

4. Catherine Pancake's film, *Black Diamonds: Mountaintop Removal and the Fight for Coalfield Justice* (Bull Frog Films, 2006) received a number of awards. Ann Hornaday in the *Washington Post* called it "a riveting and ultimately energizing documentary" that "provides a thumbnail economic and political history of coal mining in the state, a textured portrait of Appalachian life and a convincing case for ending the environmental scourge of decapitating mountains to get to the coal buried inside them."

5. See Amin's *The Implosion of Contemporary Capitalism* (2013) for more on "lumpen development." Amin builds upon the work of Marx, Lenin, and Mao Zedong to critique the worldwide dominance of large oligopolistic global corporations. Corporate monopolies, he argues, have become sufficiently powerful to control the productive system not only of Western developed countries but also of the Global South. No longer effectively regulated by national states, which have lost the political autonomy they once possessed, these companies have altered political economy to such a degree that electoral democracy no longer has the power to provide protection or progress for the increasingly generalized proletariat.

WORKS CITED

Ahmed, Sara. *The Promise of Happiness.* Duke UP, 2009.

Amin, Samir. *The Implosion of Contemporary Capitalism.* NYU Press / Monthly Review Press, 2013.

Anthias, Floya. "Thinking Through the Lens of Translocational Positionality: A Frame for Understanding Identity and Belonging." *Translocations: Migration and Social Change,* vol. 4, no. 1, 2008, pp. 5–20.

Ayers, Edward. "What We Talk About When We Talk About the South." *All Over the Map: Rethinking American Regions,* edited by Edward Ayers, et al., Johns Hopkins UP, 1996, pp. 66–74.

Berlant, Lauren. *Cruel Optimism.* Duke UP, 2011.

Brenna, Teresa. *The Transmission of Affect.* Cornell UP, 2014.

Buell, Lawrence. *Writing for an Endangered World: Literature, Culture, and Environment in the U.S. and Beyond.* Harvard UP, 2003.

Castree, Noel, Neil M. Coe, Kevin Ward, and Michael Samers. *Spaces of Work: Global Capitalism and the Geographies of Labour.* Sage Publications Ltd., 2004.

Clough, Patricia. *The Affective Turn: Theorizing the Social.* Duke UP, 2007.

Fiskio, Janet. "Unsettling Ecocriticism: Rethinking Agrarianism, Place, and Citizenship." *American Literature,* vol. 84, no. 2, 2012, pp. 301–25.

Glotfelty, Cheryll. "Big Picture, Local Place: A Conversation with David Robertson and Robert L. Thayer Jr." *The Bioregional Imagination: Literature, Ecology, and Place,* edited by Tom Lynch, Cheryll Glotfelty, and Karla Armbruster. U of Georgia P, 2012, pp. 33–46.

Handley, George B. "Down Under: New World Cultures and Ecocriticism." *The Global South,* vol. 1, no. 1–2, 2007, pp. 91–97.

Heise, Ursla. *Sense of Place and Sense of Planet: The Environmental Imagination of the Global.* Oxford UP, 2008.

Higgs, Robert J., Ambrose N. Manning, and Jim Wayne Miller, editors. *Appalachia Inside Out: Conflict and Change. Vol. 1,* U of Tennessee P, 1995.

Hinrichsen, Lisa. *Possessing the Past: Trauma, Imagination, and Memory in Post-Plantation Southern Literature.* Louisiana State UP, 2015.

House, Silas, and Jason Howard. *Something's Rising: Appalachians Fighting Mountaintop Removal.* U of Kentucky P, 2011.

Jensen, Tim. On the Emotional Terrain of Neoliberalism." *The Journal of Aesthetics and Protest.* Vol. 8, 2011–12, https://www.joaap.org/issue8/jensen.htm#sdendnote4sym.

Jones, Suzanne, and Sharon Monteith, editors. *South to A New Place: Region, Literature, Culture.* Louisiana State UP, 2002.

Lynch, Tom, Cheryll Glotfelty, and Karla Armbruster, editors. *The Bioregional Imagination: Literature, Ecology, and Place.* U of Georgia P, 2012.

Markusen, Ann. "Sticky Places in Slippery Spaces: A Typology of Industrial Districts." *The New Industrial Geography: Regions, Regulation and Institutions,* edited by T. Barnes and M. Gertler, Routledge, 1999, pp. 98–126.

McNeil, Bryan T. *Combating Mountaintop Removal: New Directions in the Fight Against Big Coal.* U of Illinois P, 2011.

Pancake, Ann. "Creative Responses to Worlds Unraveling: The Artist in the 21st Century." *The Georgia Review,* 2013. http://garev.uga.edu/fa1113/pancake.html. Accessed 21 Feb. 2017.

———. *Strange as This Weather Has Been.* Shoemaker & Hoard, 2007.

Santner, Eric L. *On the Psychotheology of Everyday Life: Reflections on Freud and Rosenzweig.* University of Chicago P, 2001.

Scott, Rebecca. *Removing Mountains: Extracting Nature and Identity in the Appalachian Coalfields.* U of Minnesota P, 2010.

Smith, Jon. "Southern Culture on the Skids: Punk, Retro, Narcissism, and the Burden of Southern History." *South to a New Place: Region, Literature, Culture,* edited by Suzanne Jones and Sharon Monteith, Louisiana State UP, 2002, pp. 76–95.

Still, James. *River of Earth.* U of Kentucky P, 2014.

Welty, Eudora. "Place in Fiction." *The Eye of the Story: Selected Essays and Reviews.* Vintage, 1979, p. 119.

Žižek, Slavoj. *Looking Awry: An Introduction to Jacques Lacan Through Popular Culture.* MIT Press, 1992.

Plantation Pasts and the Petrochemical Present
Energy Culture, the Gulf Coast, and *Petrochemical America*

DELIA BYRNES

> If climate scientists have concluded that, based on current trends and best-case
> scenarios, Chicago will soon feel like Baton Rouge, what will Baton Rouge feel like?
> —KATE ORFF, *Petrochemical America*

INTRODUCTION

In early 2017, then-chief executive officer of ExxonMobil, Rex Tillerson, was
confirmed as US secretary of state. Tillerson's appointment came on the heels
of a particularly dire year for the environment: 2016 was, according to NASA,
the hottest year on record; it also marked a global protest against the Dakota
Access Pipeline and the election of a president who has consistently challenged
the scientific consensus on anthropogenic climate change. Amid the gutting
of the EPA and the current discourses of the "war on coal" and "tough oil," the
influence of energy in US life is more apparent now than ever. Indeed, as these
grim terms suggest, our twenty-first-century imaginary is increasingly shadowed by environmental insecurities. Yet despite our awareness of the hazards
of hydrocarbons, "life without oil," as novelist and historian James Buchan observes, "would be so different that it is frightening to contemplate." As debates
about energy and natural resources continue to shape our political, economic,
and environmental landscapes, it is ever more crucial to examine the relationship between energy and cultural practices.

The burgeoning field of environmental humanities reflects the broader
"planetary turn" in cultural studies—an orientation attuned to the significance of global scales in understanding everything from environmental praxis
(for example, locavorism) to broader social, political, and cultural institutions.
Placing increasing pressure on the framework of the nation-state, the planetary turn entreats scholars to engage "the immensity of time and space,"
as Wai Chee Dimock suggests (491). This has served as an influential prov-
ocation across numerous subfields and time periods. However, amidst the

now-prevalent interpretive framework of the local/planetary, Terrell Scott Herring reminds us of the pitfalls of this analytic—namely, that it occludes the "forgotten spaces" of region and microregion that remain crucial to disrupting the "loopy binary" of the local/planetary circuit, which can too easily obscure the multiple scales (the sublocal and the bioregional, for example) that overlap within the "planetary" (628).

The importance of region is a cornerstone of southern studies, which has long illuminated the ways in which regional literature reflects and renegotiates broader social and political structures. Particularly over the past two decades, scholars of the US South have shown how popular ideas of a retrograde and problematic South sustain nationalist and imperialist projects.[1] Understanding the South as a repository into which national problems are tidily displaced, and then reworked and managed as "southern" problems, opens up exciting lines of inquiry for environmental discourse. We might ask, for example, how the disavowal of the South in the US national imaginary contributes to the region's disproportionate toxic burdens, and how writers of the South negotiate this unevenness. Yet even as the environmental humanities has become an academic mainstay, only a modest corpus of scholarship in southern studies engages directly with southern ecologies, examining, for example, the role of agrarianism in southern culture, and southern expressions of nature writing.[2] This focus on the relationship between natural landscapes and southern culture has provided invaluable insight into a region mired in the legacies of plantation capitalism. However, it has tended to preclude engagement with the hyperindustrial environments that shape much of the modern US South—and by extension, with the ways in which the South's industrialized and globalized landscapes interpellate local subjects and reflect broader values and practices. Furthermore, scholarly focus on "natural" environments tends to reflect what Rob Nixon and others term *environmentalisms of the rich,* which ignore issues of industrial toxicity and other examples of environmental injustice.[3] As a case in point, the US Gulf Coast has long been central to North American energy culture and currently produces upwards of 5 million barrels of crude oil per day[4] (in addition to a robust array of petrochemical products and runoff), yet the region continues to escape the attention of literary and cultural scholars.

In order to bring the discourse of the "backward" South to productively bear on the globalized ecologies of the southern United States, it is necessary to rethink traditional regional boundaries and imagine new frames for understanding the relationship between literature and locale. Consequently, I engage a new paradigm for mapping American cultural texts, situating energy as an organizing principle for charting the entanglements of contemporary literature and media, subject positions, national belonging, and global networks. Thus, this essay argues for an *energy regionalism* that brings the fields of southern studies and environmental humanities into dynamic conversation. A concept I borrow primarily from international studies, energy regionalism focuses on the understudied intersections of region and energy policy, the latter of which tends to be examined through national and international frames that neglect the influence of the local and regional.[5] Porting this sensibility into a humanities context illuminates the role of energy in cultural region-making.

From this perspective, the Gulf Coast region—the nation's most robust energy complex—is particularly rich critical terrain. Existing both within and in excess of the discursive "South," the "Third Coast" is emerging with increasing urgency in the US environmental imagination. While the literatures of Texas and Louisiana, for example, have long been the subject of scholarship, analyzing Gulf Coast texts through the prism of energy regionalism offers new access to works that have previously been mapped onto traditional regionalist categories such as "the West" and "the South." These regionalisms continue to offer valuable frames for literary and cultural analysis; however, they can obscure the ecological throughlines in Gulf Coast literature and media, causing us to lose sight of the ways in which a globalized energy industry shapes local imaginations and inspires unique forms of reflection and resistance to issues ranging from coastal subsidence to racial violence to neoliberalism.

This essay thus maintains the urgency of examining what I call the *Gulf Coast imagination:* the corpus of literature, film, photography, digital media, and other imaginative texts that engage with, push back against, and reimagine the region's contemporary energy regimes. Indeed, the Gulf Coast imagination offers invaluable insight into our ambivalent love affair with oil and the ways in which energy shapes—often invisibly—modern life in the United States. In her monograph *Living Oil* (2013), Stephanie LeMenager observes oil's peculiar tendency to "dematerialize as capital" in literary works, thereby escaping critical analysis of its materiality (124). I argue that the intimate proximity of Gulf Coast cultural texts to energy production forestalls the abstraction of oil into metaphor: rather than serving as a metonym for capital, oil emerges as an unruly, volatile material with the ability to permeate bodies, shape identities, and discipline landscapes. Consequently, our ability to disavow the bodily, environmental, and communal violence of US fossil fuel production is disrupted by the crude materiality of oil.

I begin by situating the emerging field of energy humanities in relation to environmental humanities and southern studies, arguing for a southern eco-criticism that is attendant to industrialized environments. As a case study, I examine the ways in which the Gulf Coast oil complex inspires photographer Richard Misrach and landscape architect Kate Orff to engage issues encompassing globalization, climate change, pollution, labor relations, community, and racial justice in their hybrid work of narrative photography and geography, *Petrochemical America* (2012), which traverses the "Cancer Alley" stretch of the lower Mississippi River.

Petrochemical America exposes the stark disparities of energy culture typical to this day in energy-producing regions of the United States, where local communities, particularly in the US South, are saturated by the materiality of petroleum but denied the pleasures of energy wealth and infrastructure. As the text conjures Louisiana's plantation legacies to thematize the exploitation and violence of the modern oil regime, *Petrochemical America* attests to the vital importance of examining the Gulf Coast imagination and its negotiation of energy culture. With the text's overlapping images of opulent plantation houses, displaced African American communities, and poisoned landscapes, *Petrochemical America* grants us intimate access to the ambivalent condition of petromodernity, a term LeMenager introduces to designate the dependence of modern US life on increasingly costly oil-based energy ("Aesthetics" 60). As we further immerse ourselves in the era of "tough oil," our love for the lifestyles engendered by petroleum is shadowed by anxieties about its unsustainability—a condition that LeMenager aptly names "petromelancholia" (*Living Oil* 102). Analyzing *Petrochemical America*'s eco-affects through the framework of energy regionalism thus exposes the Gulf Coast as a liminal space between fantasies of energy exuberance and anxieties of environmental plunder.

ENERGY CULTURE AND THE GULF COAST IMAGINATION

Over the past decade, scholars across a range of disciplines have illuminated the cultural dimensions of energy, uncovering the role of carbon fuels in areas as diverse as suburban expansion and the emergence of the American road novel.[6] Indeed, in her editor's column for *PMLA* in 2011, Patricia Yaeger reflects on the ways in which each new energy resource throughout modern history "instantiates a changing phenomenology" (309). For example, by the twilight of the nineteenth century, the initial excitement over coal as an energy resource par excellence had been replaced by anxieties about its dirtiness, impracticality, and social consequences (Buell 283). As Frederick Buell suggests, it was around this time that the discovery of "black gold" reinvigorated the American discourse of exuberant individualism through the promise of exponential returns on minimal labor, increased mobility, and an emerging consumer culture, among other things (283–90). It is from this perspective that Yaeger imagines reperiodizing literature according to contemporaneous energy regimes, insisting on the relevance of "an energy-driven literary theory" (307).

The emerging field of energy humanities overlaps in important ways with the interdisciplinary field of environmental humanities; however, there are key distinctions between these critical sensibilities that underscore the need for a southern-inflected energy humanities. Where American environmentalism is deeply entangled with ideas of middle-class leisure, escape, and fantasies of unsullied nature,[7] LeMenager, drawing on the work of historian Richard White, reminds us that "environmentalists miss the crucial ways in which work, not leisure, forms our relationship with nonhuman life and force" (*Living Oil* 4). Energy, with its inextricable ties to labor, production, and capital, is nearly impossible to disengage from political and economic contexts. Given the legacy of the agrarian tradition in southern studies (regarding both agriculture generally and the Nashville Agrarians specifically), it is especially important to engage a theoretical framework that refuses the disarticulation of energy (whether manual labor or fossil-fueled) from networks of capital. For this reason, energy humanities is especially well suited to analyze the role of energy systems in cultural practices—especially those that center on industrialized and "contaminated" environments, such as the modern Gulf Coast.

Energy-culture scholars continue to uncover the ways in which the fossil fuel regime interpellates modern Americans through a dazzling range of discourses.[8] Nevertheless, there remains little literary or cultural studies scholarship on what historians Joseph A. Pratt, Martin V. Melosi, and Kathleen A. Brosnan term *energy capitals:* cities and regions with strong ties to energy industries, and specifically, with prominent roles in energy production and distribution (xv). Energy regionalism, this essay suggests, enables deeper engagement with contemporary globalized ecologies precisely because it is grounded in specific sites of extraction and production.

The Gulf Coast is certainly not the only modern energy capital in the United

States—California, Pennsylvania, and Appalachia jump quickly to mind—yet its unique historical and environmental legacies render it an especially productive site for investigation. In addition to its climatic vulnerability, the Gulf Coast is burdened by a long history as a sacrifice zone, in which the region's inhabitants have been systematically denied the infrastructure and safeguards enjoyed by other areas throughout the country. Reflecting on the rapid erosion of Gulf Coast wetlands, LeMenager provocatively asks when exactly "the Gulf Coast fell out of the U.S. territorial imaginary" (*Living Oil* 109).

I maintain that it is this dramatic disparity between energy production and material wealth that defines the modern energy capital of the Gulf Coast. This radical disparity, sustained by rogue forms of capitalism, state complicity, and cycles of violence and displacement, have prompted geographer Michael Watts to designate the Gulf of Mexico an oil "frontier"—a dense space in which new forms of neoliberal accumulation are tested in a climate of elastic laws and violent dispossession (190). These spaces, while terrifyingly material, are also socially constituted through "practice, representation, and acts of imagination" (Watts 191). Positioning energy as a center of gravity in literary and cultural analysis allows these discourses to emerge more fully. Furthermore, it locates Gulf Coast residents on the frontlines of American oil modernity, rendering the Gulf Coast imagination an urgent site of environmental critique.

The importance of attending to the Gulf Coast imagination is made more pressing by the slipperiness of neoliberal industrial pollution—that is, its tendency to evade representation and, by extension, critique. As Watts suggests, the capacity of the global oil complex to "absorb disorder" is a hallmark of contemporary petrocapitalism (207). Similarly, Rob Nixon reminds us that the slow accretions of environmental and bodily damage perpetrated by industry constitute a profound representational challenge due to the vast temporal and invisible cellular scales in which these injuries occur (19). For this reason, it is especially important to develop interpretive strategies that disrupt the neoliberal absorption of disorder and instead allow us to linger in the liminal frontiers of energy production, examining energy's traces in cultural texts.

THE PERSISTENT PLANTATION IN MISRACH'S "CANCER ALLEY"

With its nonlinear narrative and scalar fluidity, *Petrochemical America* is an exemplary text through which to gain purchase on the Gulf Coast imagination. This essay is especially interested in how Misrach and Orff's text invokes the plantation legacies of Louisiana to narrativize the racial and ecological violence lurking within America's dominant energy regime—namely, oil modernity.

In recent years, the heavily industrial stretch of the lower Mississippi River between Baton Rouge and New Orleans has garnered the ominous nickname "Cancer Alley." In the home of the largest concentration of crude oil refineries and petrochemical plants in the Western Hemisphere, the region's predominantly African American residents suffer unusually high rates of disease and disability ranging from emphysema and allergies to carcinoma and other cancers. Although the river's industrial corridor spans less than 150 miles, Orff reminds us that "America's consumption patterns can be traced to the landscape of Cancer Alley" (127). This geography of oil invokes the long relationship between the far-reaching pleasures of energy modernity and the material violence of its extractive regimes, inviting us to consider the ways in which the landscapes of southern Louisiana sustain broader cultural, political, and economic practices.

Indeed, Misrach and Orff trace this geography of oil modernity to the exploitative energy economy that first thrust Louisiana into the global marketplace: plantation slavery. In doing so, they quite literally uncover the historical linkages that connect the signal object of US modernity—oil—to its legacies of exploitation. The Bayou State, among other states of the lower South, has a particularly troubling history of repurposing its former plantations for both commercial and state-subsidized uses. As scholars such as Jessica Adams have observed, Louisiana's "River Road," as it is known in the tourism sector, charts an uncanny topography: some of the numerous plantation homes in the region play host to the state's thriving tourism industry, while others are converted into petroleum complexes, such as the behemoth Dow Chemical, which lays claim to a sprawl of over 1,500 acres across the parishes of Iberville and West Baton Rouge.[9] Descriptions of the Louisiana landscape often invoke the language of opposites, such as "chaotic mixture," to describe the peculiar melding of petro-industry, sugarcane fields, and antebellum plantation houses. Yet the confluence of these features is anything but chaotic: it speaks to a shared genealogy of exploitation and the colonial roots of global capitalism. While a handful of social scientists have documented the Gulf Coast petro-industry's victimization of African Americans,[10] the region's robust oil industry remains profoundly understudied within the humanities.

Petrochemical America maps—culturally, historically, topographically, speculatively—the landscapes of Cancer Alley and traces its entanglements with the broader nation. Part One of the book, "Cancer Alley," consists of Misrach's landscape photographs, spanning 1998 to 2011, which were commissioned for an exhibition titled "Picturing the South" at Atlanta's High Museum of Art. The images encompass plantation tours, roadside attractions, pastoral waterways, and the ubiquitous oil infrastructure that crisscrosses the region. The inclusion of Misrach's photographs in a retrospective titled "Picturing the South" further invites us to contextualize his images within the regional discourse of "the South": here, Cancer Alley emerges not simply as a local peculiarity, but as a poignant reflection of region and nation. Part Two of *Petrochemical America* is Orff's "Ecological Atlas," a series of short-form essays and imaginative maps tracing everything from the prehistory of Louisiana's swamps through the refining process that renders plastic bags from crude oil. Orff's visual strategy is distinctly hybrid and promiscuous, using a "through-line" to layer maps, illustrations, graphs, and images that call backward and forward to other sites in the text. As the authors explain in their introduction, Misrach's photographs showcase the "immediate plight" of beleaguered local communities and the petroscapes that surround them; Orff's "Ecological Atlas" "unravels moments" to reveal the dense interrelation of systems and histories that constitute the landscapes of southeastern Louisiana (17).

In this way, *Petrochemical America* synthesizes temporal inquiry, which links the plantation past to the oily present, and spatial critique, which collapses the entire nation into a 150-mile stretch of toxic landscape. This hybridization suggests that the violent legacies of the past menace our present. Attending to the representation of oil in *Petrochemical America* and its relationship to desire, power, race, mobility, and environment thus positions us to better understand the role of Gulf Coast oil in shaping our social imaginary. Indeed, by examining the haunted landscapes that produce, refine, and distribute modernity's most volatile resource, this essay hopes to implicate the terrifyingly "local" and regional ecologies of the Gulf Coast oil complex in global flows of culture and capital, echoing the ways in which historians and literary scholars of the US South implicate the New World plantation economy in the birth of global capitalism.[11]

As the reader begins Part One of the book, she is introduced to the universe of Cancer Alley through the anachronistic figure of a plantation tour guide, who stands on the veranda of the Oak Alley Plantation in Vacherie, Louisiana. Conjuring the uneasy juxtaposition of past and present that recurs throughout *Petrochemical America,* the white woman appears to be in her sixties and faces the camera, dressed in faux-antebellum attire, complete with a burgundy hoopskirt. A cordless phone rests in her hand, which hangs down by her side. The image reminds the reader of the lucrative plantation tourism industry enjoyed by many of Cancer Alley's wealthy landowners. Further invoking this temporal dissonance, Misrach's adjacent caption observes the "at times pervasive smell of chemicals and the omnipresence of big industry" that hovers around the costumed guide (20). Beckoning the reader into this confluence of industrial effluvia alongside the baroque aesthetics of the resurrected plantation house, Misrach mobilizes an affect of unease and ambivalence, shadowing the nostalgic pleasure of plantation tourism with the uncanny spectacle of toxicity.

Misrach's narrative insists on apprehending Cancer Alley through the legacies of power that have shaped Louisiana's environments. Indeed, the subsequent image shows the opulent, stark-white interior of the restored Nottoway Plantation in White Castle. The viewer is thus initiated into the contemporary landscapes of Cancer Alley through the intimate spaces of a gold-spangled but sterilized house. By introducing his photo series about the hyperindustrialized environments of Louisiana through the decadent space of the plantation house, Misrach suggests that Cancer Alley is inextricable from economies of violence, yet it is also inextricable from our fantasies of luxury, security, and power. In this way, he invites the viewer to reflect on her complicity in the exploitation surrounding the home.

The racial politics of Misrach's narrative emerge further in the subsequent pages of *Petrochemical America*. Though the series opens with the image of a white tour guide gazing into the camera and ready to usher the viewer into the plantation house, Misrach's other photos are notably absent of human subjects, with only a handful of exceptions. One page after the viewer is guided through the Nottoway Plantation and through a jarring subsequent image of slave cabins, she confronts a second tour guide: this time, an African American woman in contemporary dress, who faces away from the camera as she gazes out of the overexposed front window of a plantation house.[12] The juxtaposition of these two tour guides—one, a white woman indulging in historical reenactment as she invites guests into a plantation home; the other, an African American woman whose gaze is turned outward and away from ours—rehearses the leisure/labor binary of the plantation. The white steward invites visitors into fantasies of antebellum nostalgia, while the black guide's outward gaze entreats viewers to investigate the exploitative economies that subtend the plantation house.

Misrach consistently mobilizes tensions such as these, inviting his audience into spaces while thwarting access to them. In a crepuscular image of the Ashland-Belle Helene Plantation in Geismar, the viewer feels almost as if she has been transported into a fantasy of antebellum decadence: a crisp white plantation house draws her eye, its uniform neoclassical columns spreading regally around the building. In front of the meticulously maintained mansion, a stately live oak extends its branches across the width of the frame. The home is one of many restored plantation houses in the area. Yet Ashland-Belle Helene is no longer open to visitors. Indeed, a locked chain-link fence spans the perimeter of the property, emblazoned with signs denying access: "Ashland Belle Helene is closed" (Misrach and Orff 95). An adjacent notice informs visitors that the site is now the domain of Shell Chemical. The uneasy parallel of the nostalgic past and the industrial present confronts the viewer with a sense of dislocation: a voyeuristic desire to travel to an imagined past is thwarted by the threat of trespassing. The image does not portray any industrial infrastructure beyond the assertion of corporate ownership; consequently, the viewer is left to wonder what the site is now used for by Shell Chemical. The fantasy of antebellum nostalgia is ruptured by the utility of energy infrastructure. This image is thus representative of the organizing tensions that structure much of *Petrochemical America:* tensions between security and risk, access and restriction, visibility and invisibility.

VISIBILITY, ERASURE, AND PETROCHEMICAL FUTURES IN ORFF'S "ECOLOGICAL ATLAS"

One of *Petrochemical America*'s most salient visual strategies for confronting the tensions between visibility and invisibility is its emphasis on a radical cartography that privileges alternative knowledges of the environment. As it subverts dominant conventions for representing the relationship between space and politics, Orff's cartography remaps the landscapes of southeastern Louisiana to illuminate current conditions and imagine more just futures. Indeed, the first image following the book's title page is a two-page map: on the left, a small map of the world sits below a map of the United States, which sits below a map of Louisiana. On the right, we see a detailed map of Cancer Alley, which carefully registers the "industrial land use" along the river. This compression of space from the global to the regional to the local further establishes the book's politics of accountability, through which the viewer is never permitted to disarticulate the local from broader scales and is thereby implicated in the region's slow violence.

As Orff explains in the introduction to "Ecological Atlas," the aim of this cartographic project is to reframe contemporary America's oil-based lifestyle and render visible its connections to deep history by "bridging art, research, and action" (115). To disentangle these deep histories, Orff and her team draw on three aesthetic techniques that form throughlines in the atlas: maps, which enable orientation as they layer spatial data, topographical details, and community stories; data narratives, which provide analysis as they decode images through related ecological processes; and "eco-portraits," in which a series of data points and observations merge into an "overall ecology" that joins seemingly isolated phenomena into a "perceptible whole" (117). In this way, Orff's atlas performs a historically engaged ecology that links the deep history of the region with the abstract realm of global capital.

In discussing the "artificial/natural system" of the Gulf Coast, Orff emphasizes the convergence of visible and invisible systems, where a lone pipe peaks out over the levees before it dives back toward its "unknowable" destination (131). In keeping with the theme of invisibility, a series of images represent the clandestine underground caverns where oil, gas, ethylene, drinking water, and other resources are stored, including a portion of the United States' 727-million-barrel Strategic Petroleum Reserve (135). The "unknowability" of these underground networks mirrors the occult workings of global oil capitalism, which, in Nixon's words, "abstract in order to extract" (41).

A particularly striking map titled "Petrochemical Landscape" shows the Mississippi River between Baton Rouge and New Orleans as a black stream. In place of the names of towns, cities, plantations, and landmarks are the names of the various petrochemicals and by-products produced at each site (128–29). From polyethylene in ExxonMobil's industrial expanse to polyisobutylene and paraffin wax in ConocoPhillips properties, the historic River Road emerges as an overwhelming crucible of toxicity that quite literally sits atop the ruins of the plantation. Visualizing toxicity through the epistemological authority of maps offers a compelling strategy for representing the slow violence of industry and its abstract scales. As it appropriates iconic antebellum plantation maps of the Mississippi River, Orff's "Petrochemical Landscape" reminds viewers of the omnipresent authority of industry.

The reimagining of the region's industrial sprawl as the spiritual inheritor of the plantation is vital to contextualizing the continued dislocation of African American communities throughout Cancer Alley. In a map titled "Regional Displacement over Time," Orff acknowledges the numerous black settlements that lined the lower Mississippi River following the Civil War. Constituted of unincorporated areas that do not appear on "official" maps of the region, Orff's expansive two-page map gives a brief description of several historic freedmen communities. She further registers those towns subject to corporate buyouts or payoffs, communities displaced or relocated, sites of legal action on the part of residents, and "industry footprints," all of which crisscross former plantation boundaries (160–61). "On a regional scale," she explains, "the African and Cajun diasporas are repeated" (161). The subsequent map of dislocations is titled "Past and Future Imagined" and gradually dissolves into Misrach's previously discussed photograph of a black tour guide gazing out of the window of a plantation home. This synthesis of Orff's activist cartography and Misrach's evocative imagery gestures to the ways in which black community and kinship in the lower Mississippi region are displaced and subsumed—by both the petrochemical industry and the plantation tourism industry, whose narratives of white loss and suffering displace those of its black descendants.[13] For the African American victims of the region's systematic displacement and toxification, this hybrid image suggests, the plantation repeats itself.

CONCLUSION

The epigraph to this essay, taken from Orff's "Ecological Atlas," underscores the stakes of *Petrochemical America* and the Gulf Coast imagination more broadly: namely, the reciprocal dependency between our global climate system and the US Gulf Coast. Importantly, Orff testifies here to the peculiar position of the southern United States on the fringes of the national imaginary: in the climate-change litmus test she invokes, Baton Rouge becomes the climatic endpoint of global warming—the far reaches of unbearable weather. The changes that will be wrought on Baton Rouge itself are thus inconceivable, unrepresentable, an unanswerable question: What *would* Baton Rouge feel like, if Chicago were to feel like Baton Rouge? The cultural liminality of this southern city, and the US South more broadly, has a long and fraught history and is tied to the ways in which "the South" circulates and sustains ideas of difference, complicity, and disavowal. It is this history, along with the rapidly unfolding futures underwritten by oil modernity, that the Gulf Coast imagination nego-tiates. It is for precisely this reason that southern studies must engage with the energy cultures and eco-affects that constitute the modern Gulf South.

In light of the anxieties about bodily toxicity and environmental devasta-tion that increasingly shape our twenty-first-century lives, this essay has ar-gued for the relevance of an energy regionalism in literary and cultural studies. Specifically, I have suggested that the "Third Coast" offers us crucial purchase on the US environmental imagination, promising insight into our fantasies of energy abundance—and, in the case of Orff's ambitious and imaginative "Eco-logical Atlas," into more just and habitable energy futures. As *Petrochemical America* attests, the contemporary Gulf Coast imagination is characterized by tensions between visibility and invisibility, security and risk, and local versus corporate knowledges. Misrach and Orff's *Petrochemical America* makes its cri-tique of petrocapitalism explicit, and for this reason, it has been an especially salient text through which to argue the importance of Gulf Coast energy in US literary and cultural work. Nevertheless, the constitutive themes and tensions of the Gulf Coast imagination emerge across a range of contemporary texts, both literary and extra-literary, inviting further investigation into these dis-patches from the frontiers of US energy modernity.[14]

NOTES

1. See Duck and Greeson.

2. For example, Wendell Berry remains an influential figure in the southern environ-mental tradition; additionally, Kirby's work is representative of a tradition of environmental exceptionalism in southern studies.

3. See Nixon and Peter Dauvergne, for example.

4. According to the US Energy Information Administration's April 2017 data, this ac-counts for approximately 57 percent of the country's overall daily crude production.

5. See the German Institute of Global and Area Studies' recently convened workshop, "Exploring Energy Regionalism," which brought together a range of international-relations scholars to explore the conceptual and methodological parameters of energy regionalism.

6. See LeMenager, *Living Oil*, for example.

7. See Cronon for a concise articulation of the "trouble" with the concepts of "wilderness" and "nature" in the US environmental imagination.

8. In addition to Buell and LeMenager, see Barrett and Worden's edited collection *Oil Culture*.

9. See Adams for an in-depth discussion of the plantation's myriad afterlives.

10. Most notably, Bullard in his pioneering work *Dumping in Dixie;* additionally, see Allen's more recent study of grassroots activism in Cancer Alley.

11. For example, see Baptist and Greeson.

12. Here, it is worth noting that the only two remaining human figures throughout Misrach's photo series are black men, whose backs are turned to the camera, denying them the power of the invitational gaze conferred to the white tour guide; one is a jogger running alongside a Mississippi River levee as an adjacent caption recounts the horrific execution of nineteen enslaved men, whose heads were displayed along the same embankment (28). The other is a subsistence fisherman standing on the barren banks of the Mississippi, regarding the refinery across the water. The composition of these three images of black Louisianans is a stark reminder of the legacies of brutality that continue to shape the lives of the state's rural African American communities.

13. See Adams's discussion of the systematic erasure of black suffering from the scene of the contemporary plantation tour.

14. Though it is beyond the scope of this essay, we might, for example, ask how the specter of the BP oil spill manifests in literary works; a prime example is Jeff VanderMeer's popular speculative-fiction series, *The Southern Reach Trilogy*.

WORKS CITED

Adams, Jessica. *Wounds of Returning: Race, Memory and Property on the Postslavery Plantation.* U of North Carolina P, 2007.

Allen, Barbara. *Uneasy Alchemy: Citizens and Experts in Louisiana's Chemical Corridor Disputes.* MIT Press, 2003.

Baptist, Edward. *The Half Has Never Been Told: Slavery and the Making of American Capitalism.* Basic Books, 2014.

Barrett, Ross, and Daniel Worden, editors. *Oil Culture.* U of Minnesota P, 2014.

Berry, Wendell. *The Unsettling of America: Culture and Agriculture.* Sierra Club, 1977.

Buchan, James. "Oil: We're Addicted." *NewStatesman,* 17 July 2006, www.newstatesman.com /node/164761. Accessed 17 Oct. 2016.

Buell, Frederick. "A Short History of Oil Cultures: Or, the Marriage of Catastrophe and Exuberance." *Journal of American Studies,* vol. 46, no. 2, 2012, pp. 273–93.

Bullard, Robert. *Dumping in Dixie: Race, Class, and Environmental Quality.* Westview Press, 1990.

Cronon, William. "The Trouble with Wilderness; or, Getting Back to the Wrong Nature." *Uncommon Ground: Rethinking the Human Place in Nature,* edited by William Cronon, Norton, 1996, pp. 69–90.

Dauvergne, Peter. *Environmentalism of the Rich*. MIT Press, 2016.

Dimock, Wai Chee. "Planetary Time and Global Translation: 'Context' in Literary Studies." *Common Knowledge*, vol. 9, no. 3, 2003, pp. 488–507.

Duck, Leigh Anne. *The Nation's Region: Southern Modernism, Segregation, and U.S. Nationalism*. U of Georgia P, 2009.

German Institute of Global and Area Studies. "Exploring Energy Regionalism." *German Institute of Global and Area Studies*, www.giga-hamburg.de/en/event/exploring-energy-region alism. Accessed 18 June 2017.

Greeson, Jennifer Rae. *Our South: Geographic Fantasy and the Rise of National Literature*. Harvard UP, 2010.

Herring, Terrell Scott. "Review: Micro: Region, History, Literature." *American Literary History*, vol. 22, no. 3, 2010, pp. 626–34.

Kirby, Jack Temple. *Mockingbird Song: Ecological Landscapes of the South*. U of North Carolina P, 2006.

LeMenager, Stephanie. "The Aesthetics of Petroleum, After Oil!" *American Literary History*, vol. 24 no. 1, 2012, pp. 59–86.

———. *Living Oil: Petroleum Culture in the American Century*. Oxford UP, 2014.

Misrach, Richard, and Kate Orff. *Petrochemical America*. Aperture, 2012.

Nixon, Rob. *Slow Violence and the Environmentalism of the Poor*. Harvard UP, 2011.

Pratt, Joseph A., Martin V. Melosi, and Kathleen A. Brosnan, editors. *Energy Capitals: Local Impact, Global Influence*. U of Pittsburgh P, 2014.

U.S. Energy Information Administration. "Crude Oil Production." *U.S. Energy Information Administration*, www.eia.gov/dnav/pet/pet_crd_crpdn_adc_mbbl_m.htm. Accessed 2 Apr. 2017.

VanderMeer, Jeff. *The Southern Reach Trilogy*. Farrar, Straus and Giroux, 2014.

Watts, Michael. "Oil Frontiers: The Niger Delta and the Gulf of Mexico." *Oil Culture*, edited by Ross Barrett and Daniel Worden, U of Minnesota P, 2014, pp. 189–210.

Yaeger, Patricia. "Editor's Column: Literature in the Ages of Wood, Tallow, Coal, Whale Oil, Gasoline, Atomic Power, and Other Energy Sources." *PMLA*, vol. 126, no. 2, 2011, pp. 305–10.

Ogling Offshore Oil
Vision and Knowledge in Midcentury Gulf of Mexico Films

ILA TYAGI

In October 1947, the independent Oklahoma oil company Kerr-McGee struck oil ten miles off the Louisiana coast. It was a landmark event—oil drillers had prospected in shallow water immediately off the beaches of Texas and Louisiana prior to the Second World War, but Kerr-McGee was the first to venture beyond wading distance into water out of sight of land (Yergin 429). The early Cold War era happened to be the heyday of industry-sponsored filmmaking, and this exciting new development, offshore oil drilling, soon made its way into educational movies bankrolled by oil companies and subsequently screened at schools, churches, youth and women's groups, and on television. The 1960 television documentary *Progress Parade,* for example, sponsored by the American Petroleum Institute (API), contains a range of sequences designed to inform viewers about how the oil industry devises technological solutions to problems, such as retrieving a drill bit that has accidentally broken off and fallen far down a drill hole, or safely storing liquefied petroleum gas even though it boils well below water's freezing point. The film's "Lifeline to an Oyster" sequence likewise begins with a problem: oysters in the Gulf of Mexico are ailing, and the oyster industry has no idea why. Oystermen blame local oil production for killing off their catches. Oil companies object, but paternalistically agree to look into the matter. They inaugurate what the film's voiceover says developed into a "two-million-dollar oyster research program." Scientists are shown collecting buckets of samples from the oyster beds and placing them into glass tanks at a research laboratory. The oysters are then subjected to a barrage of tests simulating extreme real-world conditions, including pouring crude oil over them and emptying oil-drilling mud directly into their tanks. *Progress Parade* concludes that the test oysters show no ill effects from oil. "As a matter of fact," the voiceover says, "the test oysters were so happy, they brought forth new generations to share their luck. They never had it so good."

Since the oil industry cannot be held responsible for Gulf oysters' sickness, scientists are shown "continuing their progress" by seeking out the real reason for the problem. They harvest oyster tissues and examine them closely under a microscope. The film pays careful attention to the details of this experimental procedure, showing the viewer a series of close-ups of scissors snipping off a tissue sample, a pipette dropping dye onto the sample on a glass slide, and a view through the microscope of greatly magnified *Dermocystidium marinum,* a pathogen known to target oyster populations. The microscope in *Progress Parade,* therefore, solves a problem that has baffled the oyster industry by imparting a superhuman sense of sight to the oil industry, giving it access to more knowledge. *Progress Parade* is joined by other midcentury films—both fictional works and industry-sponsored nonfictional ones—that similarly portray the oil industry as a privileged repository of specialized information as they illuminate offshore oil drilling.

The history of petrocinema aligns closely with the history of the petroleum industry and of the medium of cinema itself. Dating from the turn of the twentieth century, petrocinematic films include the Lumière Brothers' *Oil Wells of Baku: Close View* (1896), Aleksandr Mişon's *Oil Gush Fire in Bibi Heybat* (1898), and Thomas A. Edison's *Burning of the Standard Oil Co's tanks, Bayonne, N.J.* (1900). These pioneering films, each only a few seconds long, are fascinated by the ever-present risk of fiery catastrophe that dogged the oil industry in its freewheeling early years. Midcentury petrocinema reflects the fact that the postwar American oil industry had overcome the growing pains of prior decades and was now efficiently managed and technoscientifically advanced. As a result, the industry was supremely confident in its own expertise, as well as in the righteousness of its mission to fuel the economic growth of the United States while enriching itself. Crude oil derivatives were used to create a flood of commodities, from plastics to cosmetics to electronics, that kept the American standard of living the highest in the world. Midcentury petrocinema mirrors the industry's aplomb at the time, enjoying as it did easy dominion over economics, politics, and the environment. Highlights of midcentury petrocinema include Robert Flaherty's Standard Oil–sponsored *Louisiana Story* (1948); *Thunder Bay* (1953), a Hollywood film released by Universal Studios starring Jimmy Stewart and Dan Duryea; *Muddy Waters* (1954), sponsored by Humble Oil; and *Hellfighters* (1968), another Universal film starring John Wayne and Vera Miles.

In *Thunder Bay,* the penniless oilman played by Stewart tries to persuade a rich one that there is oil under the Gulf of Mexico worth building a rig to drill. "Now look down there," he tells his prospective investor. "All you can see is water, but if you dream real hard, you can smell the oil." He takes a deep sniff. "There, can't you smell it?" The rig does get built, striking a powerful gusher by the end of the film that shoots out of the ground and soaks everyone in sticky crude. Oilfield operations offer hyperabundant stimuli for the eye, nose, and skin. Petrocinema often foregrounds these stimuli, lingering on how spectacular oil-well fires look, or on the smell of crude, or how gin washes oil off the body more easily than water. The films I will examine in this essay are no different. They are united by a mutual interest in the relationship between sensory perception and the acquisition of knowledge, particularly in the power that seeing and smelling better than the average person affords. I argue that in midcentury films featuring drilling in the Gulf, the oil industry and its representatives see and know more than other agents by interacting closely with a hardy nature that keeps their perception sharp. The oilmen in *Thunder Bay* and *Hellfighters* love being outdoors, because interacting closely with nature and bringing it under their control hone their eyes and noses, giving them the ability to locate oil reserves or manage oilfield accidents more adeptly than anyone else. Additionally, the pilots and scientists in films like *Muddy Waters* and *Progress Parade* easily find the root of problems that have baffled others with the aid of technological enhancements for the naked eye, like polarizing filters and microscopes. Superior sensory acuity yields superior knowledge, which the oil industry shares with others, ostensibly for their benefit but ultimately for its own. Focusing on technologically advanced eyesight in films dating from the inception of offshore oil exploration yields fresh insights into the interlacing of energy and ecology in the American visual imaginary. *Louisiana Story* and *Thunder Bay* both depict oil-industry workers blasting dynamite underwater in order to carry out geologic surveys. Richard Leacock, *Louisiana Story*'s cinematographer, later described the process by which the film's crew shot its geologic-survey sequence. "We started filming a seismograph crew in the marsh grass exploding charges of dynamite and recording the echoes from down under on graph paper rolls," he said. "We did everything we could think of but the results were dismally dull" (Leacock). Taking a different, more visually compelling approach, the crew decided to root the sequence to the perspective of the young Cajun boy, Alexander Napolean Ulysses Latour (Joseph Boudreaux), who serves as the film's protagonist. While rowing through the backcountry bayou he calls home, Alexander sees and hears the dynamite charges going off through the tall surrounding grass but does not understand their significance. Instead of explaining the seismographic survey process, *Lou-*

isiana Story turns it into a mystery glimpsed through juvenile eyes. Alexander's youth—he does not seem much older than ten—as well as his poverty and rural provenance mean that the oil-industry workers he encounters treat him in a pleasantly patronizing manner, chuckling indulgently, for instance, when he drops salt and spits into their well in the superstitious belief that doing so will make the well come in (industry-speak for successfully striking oil).

Alexander's father Jean Latour (Lionel Le Blanc), a fisherman, is similarly infantilized, which works to justify corporate colonization of southern Louisiana and the exploitation of locals' resources in the national imagination. Jean is shown scrawling his signature on a lease agreement as painstakingly as a child just learning how to write, as well as asking, with childlike innocence, whether the dynamite blasts can really locate oil. Once again, seismographic surveys are rendered as something only the oil industry properly understands. The Latours' infantilization in *Louisiana Story* makes the oil-industry representatives in the film, and, by extension, the oil industry as a whole, seem like a wise parent who knows things these babes in the bayou do not: the dynamite can tell where the oil is, and the industry knows just how to get it out, too.

The Latours' infantilization in *Louisiana Story* is mirrored by the fishermen's infantilization in *Thunder Bay*. Stewart's and Duryea's characters, Steve Martin and Johnny Gambi, arrive in a coastal Louisiana town called Port Felicity to demonstrate an offshore drilling strategy they have devised, hoping to persuade a rich oilman to invest in their scheme. Erroneously thinking that the newcomers actually plan to set up a fish cannery, Port Felicity's fishing community helps Martin and Gambi at first. Swarthy shrimper Teche Bossier, played by Gilbert Roland, accompanies them out to the bay in his boat to conduct seismographic surveys. When he sees what seismographic surveys entail, however, he is horrified at the damage the dynamite charges will cause to his livelihood, the bay's shrimp beds. "*Mamma mia!* The shrimp beds!" he cries, aghast. "The shrimp beds! The shrimp beds! No!" In a fit of pique, he breaks Martin's seismic equipment and turns his boat around back to shore. Bossier, like his fellow fishermen, comes across as ignorant, petulant, impulsive, stubborn—in a word, childish. (This may also have something to do with the fact that he is coded as "foreign," being dark-skinned, pencil-mustached, and accented: the Mexican-born Roland specialized in playing Latin-Lover types.)

Stewart's unimpeachably white Martin, in contrast, is portrayed as a grownup. He explains patiently, insistently (and not a little condescendingly) to Bossier and the other fishermen that "those shrimp were built to stand 50 times the force of those blasts" and "that dynamiting doesn't do any harm. If it hurt the shrimp, I'd stop it." Martin's love interest Stella Rigaud (Joanne Dru) and Bossier eventually come round to believing his claim, and the film rewards them by granting them some of the dignity of adults. "We know now that our people are acting like children," Rigaud says to Bossier and the members of their community still resisting Martin, and Bossier later echoes her line by exclaiming to Martin, "These people are like children!" The film vindicates Martin's supposedly specialized knowledge that shrimp are immune to dynamite blasts by having shrimp swarm so densely around his drilling rig that they clog its intake valves. These rather large creatures, it turns out, are the mythical "golden shrimp" that Port Felicity's fishermen have fruitlessly sought for years. Thus, the offshore oil industry is shown not just to have had no adverse ecological impact on the bay; it is shown to improve the fishermen's lot.

Of course, *Thunder Bay*'s assertion that offshore oil drilling does not simply coexist with fishing in the Gulf of Mexico but can actually *boost* shrimp catches strains credulity. Joseph K. Heumann and Robin L. Murray have noted that two myths run through *Louisiana Story* and *Thunder Bay:* the myth that oil drilling can leave the natural world unpolluted, and the myth that oil drilling and fishing can coexist interdependently. This ideology is explicitly spelled out at the end of *Thunder Bay,* when Martin exasperatedly schools a recalcitrant fisherman: "we won't hurt you. We never will. You and I ought to be friends, Dominique. We have the same kind of a job. You look for one thing here in the Gulf. I'm looking for something else. That's the only difference." This dialogue ostensibly pits offshore oil drilling and fishing as two industries equal to each other, but a power imbalance is nevertheless at play. Martin's assurance that "we won't hurt you" sounds oddly like a threat: we *could* hurt you if you do not cooperate, it seems to suggest, as we are much more powerful than you are.

The oil industry in *Thunder Bay* is portrayed as all-powerful, partly because Martin, its personification, is the keeper of specialized knowledge to which ordinary fishermen are not privy (such as the fact that golden shrimp come out at night, and are unharmed by dynamiting), and partly because he is the fortunate possessor of seemingly superhuman sensory perception. Martin both knows more, and sees and smells more razor-sharply, than anyone else can. Port Felicity fishermen, baffled by his and Gambi's keen interest in the bay, assure them that "there's nothing here but fish." Films sympathetic to the oil industry like *Louisiana Story* and *Thunder Bay* delight in proving scoffing laymen wrong, valorizing their oilmen as visionaries who deserve to be commended for having enough foresight and initiative to mine southern Louisiana's environmental resources for the greater national good. After signing the lease agreement in *Louisiana Story*, Alexander's father laughingly wishes the oil-industry employee luck, because "you're gonna need it!" His skepticism is overturned when the bayou well comes in. *Thunder Bay*'s misguidedly confident fishermen are also proven wrong when Martin's well finally erupts in a spectacular gusher at the end of the film. This climactic ending has never been in any doubt, despite Martin's many trials and tribulations over the course of the film, because Martin most assuredly knows better than the fishermen. He is certain, as he says, that the "Gulf out there is hiding enough oil to make an inland field dry up in shame." He knows what the others do not because his eyes and nose are represented as unusually acute. As I have shown, he pretends he can actually smell the oil lying beneath the Gulf when courting his prospective investor, a skill the investor does not share. "Maybe you've got a better nose than I have," the older oilman says admiringly. "Maybe you've been cooped up in that office too long," Martin replies. "Twenty years ago, I'll bet you could smell it in the middle of a wheat field in Oklahoma. The only difference here is 48 feet of water, and my platform will take care of that." Other people dimly glean only an ordinary bayou or wheat field, but oilmen like Martin, gifted with a kind of X-ray vision, see clearly through these obstructions straight to the oil. Keeping that special X-ray vision finely honed is portrayed as a product of remaining in the rough-and-tumble world of the great outdoors. Martin gently criticizes the investor for having been confined to his office for too long. A real oilman, he implies, stays in the field, taking risks, sometimes failing, but always doing his bit at the frontline of America's energy needs instead of opting for cushy comfort indoors.

The prospective investor in *Thunder Bay* is played by Jay C. Flippen, who also plays one of Wayne's close friends and advisors in *Hellfighters*. Wayne's character, Chance Buckman, is a lightly fictionalized version of real-life daredevil oil-well firefighter Paul Neal "Red" Adair. We first see Buckman being called upon to blast a flaming gusher with nitroglycerine in Baytown, on the Texas Gulf Coast. A process originally devised in 1913 by firefighter Myron M. Kinley, the nitroglycerine explosion sucks oxygen away from the fire, extinguishing the flames long enough for Buckman to cap the spewing well ("The Fire Beater" 86). One false move, however, and he could be blown to bits. Later in the film, Buckman briefly tries renouncing the thrilling danger of battling blowouts by taking up an executive role at Lomax Oil's Houston headquarters. The company is named after Flippen's character, Jack Lomax. Knowing that Buckman belongs outdoors and is chafing at his new desk-bound life, Lomax encourages his friend to skip a meeting at one point, as it is all "fiscal stuff—you'd hate it." At an earlier corporate meeting that Buckman does deign to attend, the subject under discussion is the color of restroom tiles in Lomax Oil gas stations. The suits who present the various tiling options—"soft willow green," "lovely royal blue," and "flaming-heart red"—to their fellow executives are bespectacled, balding, pudgy, ineffectual. Their fussy attentiveness to the different effects produced by the three colors and the flowery adjectives used to describe them are intended to make these pen pushers seem effete, a striking contrast to the virile outdoorsman Wayne usually played onscreen. Being stuck indoors, the traditionally female, domestic sphere, is thus portrayed as emasculating, a tiresome antithesis to the freedom he enjoys outside. Buckman, to his relief, is soon back wrestling well fires amid stunning mountain scenery.

Like *Thunder Bay*, *Hellfighters* implies that being trapped indoors for too long dulls the senses—a good oilman has a nose for finding the stuff, but only if he stays physically close to the ground, or actually out on the water. Later, in the restroom-tile meeting, a craven executive tries to dissuade Lomax from entering a deal with "the Jansen brothers" that would contravene company policy by not allowing him to control drilling operations. "Thompson, I don't know too much about policy around here, but the Jansen brothers were smellin' out oil before you were born," Buckman says. "Check the fields they've brought in. You can call it luck, or seat of your pants, or whatever. They find oil." Since finding oil is an inexact science, seemingly as dependent on luck as it is on seismographic surveys, Buckman and his ilk revere a good oilman's intuition. That intuition is informed by sensory familiarity with the natural environments from which oil springs, knowledge that boardroom executives have either lost touch with or never had. That sensory familiarity with nature comes, in turn, from initially having too little money to have any choice but to face the elements outdoors. In *Thunder Bay*, Martin and Gambi are first seen trudging along a seashell-encrusted road thickly fringed with shrubs and trees as they make their way to Port Felicity, too poor to travel within the comfort of a car. Martin pauses to prise a shell out of his disintegrating shoe, examining it carefully in his hand and turning it over to Gambi to look at as well. In a speech reminiscent of Buckman's praising the Jansen brothers' preternatural ability to find oil in *Hellfighters*, Flippen's character in *Thunder Bay* responds to another craven executive trying to discourage him from partnering with "penniless wastrels" Martin and Gambi by saying:

> You've never been one, have you, Rawlings? Never had to talk yourself out of a jam. Never had the privilege of gambling your last penny on a dream. I feel sorry for you. You lost a lot of education by going to college. And I'll tell you another thing. If this penniless wastrel hadn't called me, I would've looked him up, because I know he's the only man in the country that can lick this offshore problem.

Classical Hollywood petrocinema regards eventually accumulating fabulous wealth as an oilman's rightful reward, a happy ending he is ineluctably entitled to in exchange for the hard knocks and risky gambles he takes when he is starting out. Flippen's character's nonchalance about his fortune in *Hellfighters*—"I'm just another Texas oilman with his own building"—speaks to how, according to the logic of the film, just about any reasonably successful oilman can expect to end up with his name on a skyscraper. Films like *Thunder Bay* and *Hellfighters* romanticize wealth, such as in the casual way characters in *Hellfighters* fly around in private planes and inherit department-store empires and hobnob with presidents, but they also romanticize poverty. While one works up to wealth and professional success, they suggest, something gets lost along the way. That something is the excitement of "gambling your last penny on a dream," of walking along a seashell road with your best friend, hoping that a knack to smell out oil will see you through. Wealth brings ease, but it also mollycoddles, cutting the rich off from raw sensory experience.

As a result, the rich in *Thunder Bay* and *Hellfighters* yearn for the raw sensory stimuli to be found outside their gilded offices—at sea, in jungles, or along mountain ranges. In doing so, they join a long tradition of urban elites who yearned for the vigorousness of the frontier. William Cronon has shown how the very individuals who "most benefited from urban-industrial capitalism," such as Owen Wister and Theodore Roosevelt, were most eager to seek out "the regeneration and renewal that came from sleeping under the stars, participating in blood sports, and living off the land" (222). Films like *Thunder Bay* and *Hellfighters* cast their oilmen in the rugged Roosevelt mold, sufficiently in tune with nature to, say, understand shrimp better than shrimpers do themselves. Shrimping is shown to be something anyone can do, whereas only oilmen like Martin can pull off the feat of building the world's first offshore oil platform and then subsequently finding oil. He is a master of two skills, oil drilling and shrimping, whereas the shrimpers can barely manage one.

The idea that the oil industry knows better, and is simply more competent than everyone else, is similarly foregrounded in propagandistic documentaries like Humble Oil's *Muddy Waters* and the API's *Progress Parade*. Their tone unites didacticism with technoscientific triumphalism. *Muddy Waters,* which predates *Progress Parade* by six years, was designed to settle a "long feud" between oilmen and oystermen in Louisiana's "mysteriously murky" Barataria Bay ("Unusual Humble" 45). Oystermen had been claiming that oil-industry channel-dredging operations were stirring up this shallow bay's fine silt, smothering their oysters. The oil industry, on the other hand, claimed that turbidity tests of the water around the dredge had shown it to contain no more silt per cubic inch than was found in other reaches of the bay. According to them, the dredges pushed through the bay bottom and sucked up the loose silt through pipes which emptied at a distance from the oyster beds, forming an island of silt that was gradually washed downstream, even farther away.

An eighteen-minute color film, *Muddy Waters* set out to definitively prove the oil industry to be correct by using more advanced optical technologies than those available to the oystermen. The company Humble Oil hired the Houston firm Channing Productions to shoot aerial footage of the silt island at varying altitudes, first fifty feet and then seven hundred feet, showing it to be tightly confined to a small area and the blue water around it to be silt-free. Channing's cameramen, working from helicopters and amphibian planes, were also rewarded with what *Business Screen* called "ironical evidence" ("Unusual Humble" 45). Scanning the bay from above using a polaroid filter, they "discovered" that oyster boats' propellers and dragnets were scraping the bay bottom where oyster beds lay and thus churning up dense clouds of silt. Polarizing camera filters reduce glare from reflective surfaces like water, allowing natural color and the details of what is beneath to come through. Thanks to flight and filters, shrimp boats were likewise exposed as "silt-villains" as they were "mugged in motion" dragging heavy seines over the bottom of the bay while trawling for shrimp ("Unusual Humble" 45). "Due to the oblique angle of view and the widening action of the silt trains," *Business Screen* added, "this muddying of the waters is not visible at water level or from an altitude under 100 feet" ("Unusual Humble" 45).

Restricted vision equals restricted knowledge. Their view limited to water level, oystermen cannot hope to grasp all the facets of a complex problem. "The island of silt streaming from the discharge pipe was enough evidence to convince the oystermen that the oil operations were at fault," the *Business Screen* article says, deriding them for misguidedly fixating on a single detail and holding it wholly responsible. Access to an all-seeing eye in the sky makes the oil industry omniscient. In contrast to the blinkered oystermen, its expanded view permits it an all-encompassing perspective of the turbidity problem. This God-like knowledge handily allows it to turn the tables on its adversaries. In the same tradition of the white man's burden, however, or noblesse oblige, the oil industry cannot begrudge them their wrongheadedness. Its superior knowledge makes it incumbent upon the oil industry to show muddled oystermen their error. It does so using tools even a child can understand: pictures. "To make the actual situation clear to the oystermen," explains *Business Screen,* "the oilmen decided to make it graphic" ("Unusual Humble" 45).

In another conciliatory gesture, *Muddy Waters* tries to show that both oystermen and oilmen are united against a shared opponent: nature. In the same way that Martin seeks to find common ground with Dominique (Antonio Moreno) in *Thunder Bay* by pointing out that both oilmen and fishermen are searching for their livelihood in the Gulf, *Muddy Waters* argues that both oystermen and oilmen there endure the machinations of obdurate nature, the "master rogue of the silt drama" ("Unusual Humble" 45). While shooting the film, the cameramen supposedly found that the quantity of silt choking the bay was too great to have been stirred up by oyster and shrimp boats alone. Flying out over the Gulf, they filmed silt pouring into the bay via tides invading through narrow inlets. The silt, in other words, had traveled to the Gulf from along the length of the Mississippi River and was now being cast into its shallows, a process that *Muddy Waters* alleges is the product of natural forces rather than human activity. This conclusion conveniently absolved both the oystermen and the oil industry of any significant culpability for the problem.

Just as *Muddy Waters* scapegoats nature, *Progress Parade* smoothly deflects the blame for oyster mortality to nature rather than oil-industry activity in the Gulf. Besides the natural *Dermocystidium marinum* pathogen, the film says that natural climatic changes altering the proportion of fresh water and saltwater on the Gulf Coast are causing oyster mortality. Once again, the oil industry manipulates viewers into believing that nature is the true culprit for the problems bedeviling oystermen. By shifting blame for a silted bay and dying oysters to "nature," the films portray it as a malevolent entity deserving to be dominated by technology and science, a prevalent midcentury point of view.

A biochemist named Dr. Robert White-Stevens, for instance, went head-to-head with Rachel Carson following the 1962 publication of her ground-breaking book *Silent Spring*. In a CBS interview, he declared, "Miss Carson maintains that the balance of nature is a major force in the survival of man, whereas the modern chemist, the modern biologist, the modern scientist, believes that man is steadily controlling nature" (Brulle 124). White-Stevens is filmed wearing a white lab coat inside a laboratory, looking much like the scientists in *Progress Parade*. Far from trusting implicitly in scientific author-ity, Carson argued that controlling nature was "a phrase conceived in arro-gance," an outlook that gained growing currency in the second half of the twentieth century (297). *Silent Spring* deliberately focuses on nature's benevo-lent aspects, such as birds and berries, making the reader's heart bleed all the more profusely when contemplating the destructiveness of pesticide overuse. White-Stevens held a grimmer view of nature, insisting that "if men were to faithfully follow the teachings of Miss Carson, we would return to the Dark Ages and the insects and diseases and vermin would once again inherit the Earth" (Elliott).

Unlike midcentury films, twenty-first-century films set in the Gulf have been shaped by the legacy of the environmental movement of the 1960s and 1970s that *Silent Spring* helped spawn. Because petrocinema usually responds to major events in the oil industry, if we were to track the number of films revolving around Gulf oil, we would see two spikes, one at midcentury when offshore exploration in the region was taking off, and one again after 2010, the year of the catastrophic Deepwater Horizon disaster (to date the largest oil spill in US history). *Vanishing Pearls* (2014), a documentary centering on Afri-can American oystermen in the Louisiana village of Pointe à la Hache, diverges sharply from *Progress Parade*'s take on the effect of drilling in the Gulf. *Progress Parade* and the other midcentury films I have discussed were all made from a standpoint amenable to oil-industry interests. *Vanishing Pearls* as well as other films released after Deepwater Horizon like the documentary *The Great Invis-ible* (2014) and the narrative feature *Deepwater Horizon* (2016) are appalled by the devastation it wreaks.

BP initially tried to turn the area over the oil spill into a blind spot for media and the public, issuing a moratorium on aircraft flying overhead and delaying the release of the first images of the spill until three weeks after it oc-curred. "What was just shocking was the expanse of it," says Bonny Schumaker in *Vanishing Pearls*. "Even when you would go as high as 3,000 feet, it was as far as you could see." Schumaker is introduced as a pilot and the founder of On Wings of Care, a nonprofit organization that aims to protect natural ecosystems through constant visual surveillance. Footage of the Deepwater Horizon spill gathered by On Wings of Care and included in *Vanishing Pearls* punctures BP's blind spot, making plainly visible what the company sought to hide.

The number of films produced, distributed, and exhibited by the oil industry has declined since its postwar heyday, which means the industry cannot control its image as carefully as it once did. Other filmmakers unaffiliated with the oil industry have gained access to the vision-enhancing technologies that it used to make its films, such as helicopters and amphibian planes for aerial perspectives on the Gulf, polarizing filters, and microscopes, which means that they can now unveil for audiences what the oil industry would have preferred to keep hidden. Twenty-first-century films set in the Gulf help level the visual playing field between the oil industry and everybody else, allowing us to see, and therefore know, as much as it does, better enabling us to hold it accountable for the damage it causes.

WORKS CITED

Brulle, Robert J. *Agency, Democracy, and Nature: The U.S. Environmental Movement from a Critical Theory Perspective.* MIT Press, 2000.

Carson, Rachel. *Silent Spring.* 1962. Mariner Books, 2002.

Cronon, William. "The Trouble with Wilderness, or, Getting Back to the Wrong Nature." *American Environmental History,* edited by Louis S. Warren, Blackwell Publishing, 2003, pp. 213–36.

Deepwater Horizon. Directed by Peter Berg, Summit Entertainment, 2016.

Elliott, Debbie. "Carson's 'Silent Spring' Still Making Noise." NPR, 27 May 2007, www.npr.org/templates/story/story.php?storyId=10486240. Accessed 25 July 2017.

"The Fire Beater." *Time,* 9 Feb. 1953, pp. 85–86.

The Great Invisible. Directed by Margaret Brown, Gigantic and Motto Pictures, 2014.

Hellfighters. Directed by Andrew V. McLaglen, Universal, 1968.

Heumann, Joseph K., and Robin L. Murray. "Oil Drilling and the Search for the 'Golde Shrimp': The Myth of Interdependence in Oil Drilling Films." *eJumpCut,* www.ejumpcut.org/archive/jc53.2011/ThunderBayLAstory/index.html. Accessed 17 Oct. 2016.

Leacock, Richard. "The Making of *Louisiana Story.*" Richard Leacock, www.richardleacock.com/Louisiana-Story. Accessed 17 Oct. 2016.

Louisiana Story. Directed by Robert Flaherty, Standard Oil, 1948.

Muddy Waters. Sponsored by Humble Oil, 1954.

Progress Parade. Sponsored by the American Petroleum Institute, 1960.

Thunder Bay. Directed by Anthony Mann, Universal, 1953.

"Unusual Humble Film Answers Industry Problem." *Business Screen,* vol. 7, no. 15, 1954, p. 45.

Vanishing Pearls: The Oystermen of Pointe a la Hache. Directed by Nailah Jefferson, Perspective Pictures, 2014.

Yergin, Daniel. *The Prize.* Simon & Schuster, 1991.

II

ROUTES, ROADS, &
THE RHIZOMATIC
SOUTH

"So Many Strange Plants"

Race and Environment in John Muir's *A Thousand-Mile Walk to the Gulf*

SCOTT OBERNESSER

While notions of regional and environmental distinctiveness have been widely debated within southern studies, early naturalists and ecologists—often northerners or Europeans—were nonetheless fascinated with the otherness of southern landscapes.[1] The swamps, wildlife, and grandiose flora made for adventurous studies and unique discoveries both before and after the Civil War. The South's allure drew the attention of Scottish-American conservationist John Muir, who set off southward from Indianapolis, Indiana, in 1867. Published posthumously and comprised of journal entries, sketches, and tracings, *A Thousand-Mile Walk to the Gulf* (1916) recounts Muir's six-month journey "by the wildest, leafiest and least trodden way" from Indianapolis to Cedar Keys, Florida (2). *A Thousand-Mile Walk to the Gulf* complicates notions of southern otherness via two primary textual threads: first, the major environmental ethic developed throughout the work, which begins to break down strict North/South binaries through local and holistic ecological contact, observing contiguous biomes as both individual ecosystems and contributors to a larger environmental body; and second, through commentary (or lack thereof) on the interconnections of race, class, and environment in the wake of slavery. While Muir is committed to common regional identifications and even stereotypes, the text itself conveys a South of ecological and cultural variance,[2] and the most productive work comes in his attempt to fully engage individual biomes. In so doing, Muir draws attention to local and even minute details and away from regional distinctions. Strangely, it is this kind of attention that eventually draws Muir farther into wilderness spaces, away from modes of infrastructural conditioning migrating south from more industrialized states. Finally, though the text imagines progressive futures for American conservation, Muir's problematic depictions of race demonstrate the need for "progressive" northerners to continue rethinking and upending social conventions after the war.[3] *A Thousand-Mile Walk to the Gulf* reveals a productive space within southern studies and ecocriticism to consider moments when race and environment intersect, particularly amidst national narratives of westward expansion or racial and class discrimination that have shaped national land-use ethics throughout the twentieth century.

As Scott Romine notes in *The Real South*, "stories that *use* the South by purporting to *map* it are no new thing" (8, emphasis in original). Ecologists and botanists generated their own regional representations of the US South. The subtropic climate and exotic plant species—particularly the palm tree and citrus fruits—were especially attractive to those in colder climates. European colonists used parts of Georgia and Florida to cultivate crops that would eventually fill hothouses with "New World curiosities" throughout Europe (Fishman 35).[4] Eighteenth-century botanist John Bartram collected seeds from various American plants for European merchants, recording and classifying the species at the same time. Years later, John Bartram's son William penned *Bartram's Travels* (1791), a lengthy record of his explorations throughout Florida and the Carolinas. A "link between colonial and early national science," *Bartram's Travels* serves as a precursor to Muir's own work, blending elements of empirical science with the language of romantic experience (Hallock 149).[5] The French botanist André Michaux also traveled the South, and he planted and maintained impressive gardens in South Carolina, including many species of orchid especially attractive to Europeans (Fishman 72). Muir's journey thus follows a long tradition of classical botanists fascinated with the South. In part, the attraction stems from the region's climate; however, many of these explorers were interested in the South simply because it promised difference (Sutter 3).

The South—even into the years of Reconstruction—was routinely imagined as the rural, conservative foil to the industrialized, liberal North.[6] These cultural precepts allowed for the kind of scientific distance needed to observe without action. In *Bartram's Travels*, William Bartram archives a range of flora and fauna and spends time with Native tribes, but his distance as a scientist allows him to observe and leave with ease. Following suit, Muir describes the South as "a meeting [of] so many strange plants" (91). This strangeness, which could be extended to culture as well as ecology, was further accentuated throughout the Civil War and Reconstruction, despite national narratives unifying "different" regions. Jennifer Rae Greeson explains this same divide via the colonist and colony, namely that the South during Reconstruction was discursively rendered a colonized region (230–37). Muir, a Scottish immigrant who did not fight in the Civil War, showed very little interest in the politics that separated North and South. In fact, Muir had traveled to Ontario with his brother to avoid being drafted into the Civil War. Despite his aversion to American politics, Muir was invested in American botanical history, much of which had been historically framed through the lens of a North/South divide.

This is not to say Muir is completely divested from sociocultural constructions that polarize North and South, but it is clear that Muir's environmental praxis is still developing throughout *A Thousand-Mile Walk to the Gulf.* The impulse to categorize—judging the nobility of the hemlock or rank of the palm—and personify—vines with "toothed arching branches" that wrap like "cruel living arms" (27)—concedes an undeniably anthropomorphic rhetorical taxonomy. Likewise, Muir relies on comparison to northern fauna when his method is interrupted or he is unable to spend necessary time in a place. When this occurs, he almost systematically compares all oak and pine forests to those in Wisconsin. He even explains southern climate through a northern comparison: "The climate . . . is simply warm summer and warmer summer, corresponding in time with winter and summer in the North" (133). Muir's comparisons are problematic because the North becomes standard in these instances. Northern seasonal progression is "normal," and warmer climates in southern spaces become abnormal. Troubling as these moments can be, it seems Muir reverts to these strategies for two reasons. First, he is only familiar with northern plants, making his comparisons more a function of instinct than of regional bias. Second, Muir's developing praxis requires time spent in contact with place. In much of his work, Lawrence Buell notes that one's identification with place depends upon a number of factors—race, class, or gender, for instance—all of which stem from experience. Buell explains the physical environment as a "destabilizing force," meaning deep ecological engagement transforms "first impressions" into a more "complicated sense of engagement" (*Writing* 17).[7] At least one consequence of Muir's fast-paced travel southward was that he often failed to attain substantive connections to place.[8]

Despite his trouble overcoming historical North/South binaries, Muir's objective throughout the text is to develop understandings of—both ecologically and spiritually—the various bioregions he contacts. Muir works within a spectrum of evaluation wherein the "happiness" of plants and animals is placed above their value as material resource (139). These more nuanced contemplations, rationalized through Christian theology, anticipate deep ecology in the twentieth century: "Why should man value himself as more than a small part of the one great unit of creation?" (139). Buell explains that Muir imagined

"God as having created the universe as a vast interwoven fraternity of abso-
lutely equal members" (*The Environmental* 193). These moments—wherein nature writing and religious philosophy merge—allow Muir to conceive a biocentric cosmology that rises above cultural and political boundaries. Muir borders
early notions of biocentrism—an approach to ecology that negates anthropocentrism and exists beyond culturally and geographically constructed binaries
such as North and South. Furthermore, biocentrism suggests a wide-ranging
egalitarian ecosystem within which humankind is merely one component.

Throughout *A Thousand-Mile Walk to the Gulf,* Muir chronicles nearly every
species he encounters. For example, he carefully measures the dimensions of
various palm trees: the crown "about six to twelve inches in diameter," the clus-
ter of leaves arching in a "sphere about ten or twelve feet in diameter" (117). The
"remarkable" long-leafed pine is "sixty to seventy feet in height, from twenty
to thirty inches in diameter, with leaves ten to fifteen inches long" (54–55).
This process of observation reflects Enlightenment-era botany (similar to Carl
Linnaeus or Bartram), but Muir uses scientific observation as an accompa-
niment to his own spiritual doctrine (*The Environmental* 193). He personifies
nature through "spontaneous pantheism," and he reframes Christianity as
a broader spiritual experience (192). "They tell us that plants are perishable,
soulless creatures," Muir writes, ". . . but this, I think, is something that we
know very nearly nothing about. Anyhow, this palm was indescribably impressive and told me grander things than I ever got from human priest" (92).
In the vein of Emerson and Thoreau, Muir's nature provides direct access to
truth, rather than relying on a human interpreter. This not only destabilizes
anthropocentrism, but it places plants, animals, and people—all of "creation,"
Muir says—within the same spirituality. When Muir writes of Kentucky, "Here
is Eden, the paradise of oaks," he does not limit paradise geographically (15).
Those oaks in that particular Kentucky forest are a paradise amongst many
other natural spaces. This complex acknowledgment of religious sentiment
amidst a larger spirituality represented by nonhuman nature garnered great
audience appeal and set a precedent for American nature writing.

The contact with deep ecology elicits experiences of place that reorient human relationships with nonhuman nature. As those encounters accumulate
within the text, Muir's understanding of the South becomes more experiential
and less based within preconceived notions of region, such as those based on
North/South binaries. While late nineteenth-century nature writing is characterized by the Romantic distance "to return or realize their object," so much

of Muir's experience is directly impacted by natural landscapes (*The Environmental* 11). His trails are guided by vines and thorns, his sleep affected by the sound of the wind, his science influenced by microclimates. Nature is never simply "a screen for something else" (11). Muir experiences "confrontation with an actual landscape," encounters that inspire partnership with varying bioregions (12). These experiences complicate the more simplistic anthropocentric frameworks that typify Muir's earlier observations. "The whole world was not made for him," he explains; rather, humans ought to conform "with the rest of terrestrial creation" (142). As a fledgling philosopher, this moment is imperative for Muir because it starts to deconstruct notions of constructed difference. Instead of relying on the predominant nineteenth-century belief that the earth was created for humans, Muir attributes vitality to nature beyond human manipulation. Similarly, rather than relying on what he has been told about southern plants, Muir begins to observe the different "motions" and "gestures" of each species for himself (116). The palm tree, for instance, is "not very graceful" and appears "to best advantage when perfectly motionless" (116). As if the tree worked to make its uniqueness perfectly clear, he recognizes that the motionless palmetto hummock is strangely utopic, almost alien; unlike the pine and oak forests Muir is accustomed to, there is "no jostling, no apparent effort to outgrow each other" (115). The forests of the North are ordered, in direct contrast to the "vine-laden" swamps throughout Florida or the looming oak stands in Kentucky. He stands "enchanted in their [palm trees'] midst," but it takes time for him to fully consider this biome (115). Most notably, Muir cannot settle for Linnaeus's descriptions of the palm; rather, he must experience the ecological implications of the materials themselves—the trees, plants, animals, and people.

In encountering the palm, Muir develops an entirely different interpretation of the object—and therein nature itself. This type of contact spans different classical divides: social, cultural, historic, geographic, even textual. Whether in the North, South, or West, this is where Muir begins to engage place with "immersion and *discipline*" (*The Environmental* 14). Muir's evolving environmental contact is more prominent in later works but is particularly evocative in an early piece like *A Thousand-Mile Walk to the Gulf.* Perhaps the most notable part of this text is the failure of his preconceived notions, which had tied him to projections of southern otherness. Despite attempts to engage different ecosystems, Muir must reconcile the social and political forces that interrupt "untouched nature" and the botanical histories of an empty, other

South, which he admires. When Muir arrives at other western ecosystems, he achieves "immersion" more readily; however, in the South, the history and development of the region suspend much of Muir's—perhaps naïve—initial objectives. For places like the South, "deep [and] rich with layers of human time and history," rewriting ecological history depends upon reformation (Bass 146). Though Muir considers different forms of reformation, he is often unable to fully divest himself from projections of the "backward" South. Again, Muir most effectively reforms notions of region and ecology when he is able to stop and take the time to truly consider place. This kind of engagement complicates how Muir sees and experiences the place, but alters temporality. Muir's entire walk to Florida spans roughly two months, leaving very little time to plunge into specific places.

If we consider Muir's time in the South as one in a series of experiments contributing to his tenets of environmental praxis, it becomes apparent how influential these few months are to his later conception of conservation and preservation.[9] In the Sierra, he delves into the environment with a longevity he cannot equal in the South, not only because he commits more time to the West, but because he sees the Sierra as more pristine. Still, A Thousand-Mile Walk to the Gulf recounts one of Muir's earliest explorations of wilderness spaces. Throughout the text, it is readily apparent that he pursues the leafy woods above the cityscape. He automatically seeks out the wild landscapes and avoids the cultivated spaces. This can be seen in Muir's admiration of Kentucky's "virgin" forests and in his arduous movement through the thickest vine-laden swamps in Florida. The pursuit and preservation of undisturbed places is perhaps the most lasting tenet of Muir's environmental legacy, the seeds of which we see in A Thousand-Mile Walk to the Gulf.[10] Muir pursues his method of deep ecological contact when possible, yet it is clear the West represents a vast acceleration of preservationist environmental and philosophical vision, an acceleration impeded by social histories in the South. However, it is ultimately not regional distinction that drives Muir west but rather encroaching industrial modernity. Muir, who had left the North in search of wilderness spaces, finds the South a much closer reflection of the North than he anticipated.

Here we encounter the most significant and dramatic irony within the text: that Muir, despite his avowal to the South's strangeness, goes west because the South is too much like the North. Though initially invested in the image of an exotic, "strange" South, what Muir predominantly encounters is a populated, diverse, political region committed to the same modern trajectory as the North—a national modernity. Muir does not always consciously recognize this; though his experiences ought to transform his overly simplistic view of the South, he continuously works to reaffirm that simplicity rather than confronting a more complex network of national interrelations. Sailing to New York and reflecting on his journey, he insists he felt himself a "stranger in a strange land" while traveling in the South (176). Despite his protests, the people Muir interacts with reflect a strong congruity with national modernity. Take, for example, Muir's conversations with an old mountaineer, who "speaks of the 'old-fashioned unenlightened times' like a philosopher in the best light of civilization":

> "I believe in providence," said he. "Our fathers came into these valleys, got the richest of them, and skimmed off the cream of the soil. The worn-out ground won't yield no roastin' ears now. But the Lord foresaw this state of affairs, and prepared something else for us. And what is it? Why, He meant us to bust open these copper mines and gold mines, so that we may have money to buy the corn that we cannot raise." A most profound observation. (38)

Muir finds the old man's logic lacking—trading agriculture for extraction—but is predominantly alarmed by the ready welcome of the industrial modernity Muir is looking to escape when he leaves Indianapolis. The man's use of divine sanction as justification for industrial enterprise is further troubling, as it runs counter to Muir's aesthetic and spiritual vision (one that equates holiness with nature's beauty). The sarcastic response—"A most profound observation"—conveys a certain contempt for what Muir regards as poor logic. However, the mountaineer observes a national trajectory that Muir either initially misses or wishes to run away from.

Later, a wealthy planter in Georgia named Mr. Cameron explains his hobby, "e-lec-tricity," a "mysterious force" that "will do all the work of the world" (63). Muir admits, "nearly all that he foresaw has been accomplished, and the use of electricity is being extended more and more every year" (63). Moments such as these subtly signal the economic and environmental future of the South, which is integrally connected to the industrial future of the nation. The value of gold and copper is highly dependent upon the commercial production of northern commodities. Developing national industries *must* have the raw materials to produce competitively within global commerce. By supplying the nation with these raw materials, the South firmly ties itself to the nation and commits its natural spaces to extraction. Similarly, there is at least some recognition on Muir's part that the spread of electricity throughout the South is only a matter of time, as in the North.

Muir's text seems to presciently anticipate the economic and industrial reforms of Reconstruction. In the interest of sectional unification, these changes are meant to bind the future of the South to the trajectory of the nation: a modern, imperial vision of American expansion. Muir's movement west is about finding untouched spaces. Other explorers and botanists like Bartram displayed the South as an othered space, wild and unexplored. And while Muir himself might remain attached to such projections, the text itself shows a very different space. In the South, even the most rural places are inhabited by varieties of peoples, from planters to poor whites to newly freed blacks. Much of the land is cultivated, not the urban factory-scape of the North but an equally curated agrarian space. Additionally, the Civil War left its mark on nearly every facet of the landscape. "Traces of the war," writes Muir, are "apparent on the broken fields, burnt fences, mills, and woods ruthlessly slaughtered" (84). Deep in the forests, Muir finds evidence of the fighting, with new forms of warfare increasingly damaging natural landscapes.

The more Muir observes, the more the "strange" South seems a reflection of national trajectories. Muir's conception of what Romine calls the "natural" South and the "national" South at once periodizes his perception of region during Reconstruction and forecasts a longer infrastructural future of "projects . . . decompressing space and time against modernity's late encroachments" (9). In other words, the boundaries—whether ecological, geographical, or political—have always been (and continue to be) porous constructions, networked within national trajectories in as much as one might perceive the "strange" South as separate: "As deterritorialization proceeds apace, efforts to reterritorialize—to reproduce place and locality—are increasingly mobilized under the aegis of tradition, heritage, culture, and identity. Put another way, we are still reproducing and naturalizing the South *as place* in an age defined, according to one story (Jameson's postmodern one), by 'nature' being 'gone for good'" (Romine 9). Muir's text, then, embodies the conflict between sociopolitical influence and observational reality. Romine sums up the disconnect, writing, "To suggest that the South isn't going anywhere is not to say that it is impervious to motion" (9). The "motion" of industrial modernity set against Muir's desire for pristine natural spaces further reinforces Muir's commitment to the environment, even as that commitment is fundamentally skewed. The kind of infrastructural conditioning instigated during Reconstruction is the very segmented, mercantile economy that initially sparks Muir's walk. Prior to his departure from Indianapolis, Muir worked in a machine shop where he injured his eye. After several months of recovery, he regained his sight and the determination to pursue botany. A similar kind of experience occurs at the conclusion of his walk at Cedar Keys. Muir arrives there looking for a boat to Cuba and, if possible, some money. He finds work in Mr. Hodgson's sawmill, but promptly contracts malarial typhoid. Bedridden for three months, he misses his ship to Cuba and finds himself in Mrs. Hodgson's care. Muir describes this as "a weary time" (129). Tellingly, when healthy again he does not make for the sawmill; instead, he gravitates back toward the woods, sitting "day after day" staring at the oaks draped in Spanish moss (130).

I do not mean to imply that Muir himself made a conscious connection between these two experiences—the machine shop and the sawmill—which then compelled him to the Sierra Mountains. However, it seems likely that both incidents elicited the same reaction: to move further into wilderness, a designation the South no longer fulfilled, if it ever did. Muir's notions of preservation became more prevalent in spaces where he could witness a seemingly pristine ecosystem, where he could battle for the "virginal" wilderness. In the South, those movements of modernization were more than a foregone conclusion: they were already in place, augmented by the war and accelerated throughout Reconstruction. Despite national projections about what the South is or what southernness entails, the text conveys a complex regional narrative—one that Muir himself often misses. As a northerner, Muir separates himself from the "backwardness" he records, as if notions of travel or scientific method release him from complicity. The racism, rampant material extraction, and subjugation of natural space the text chronicles are problems Muir and others attribute to the South, when in reality these are national problems that cannot be adequately addressed without the full nation's attention.

In "If John Muir Had Been an Agrarian: American Environmental History West and South," Mart Stewart explains the importance of race in shaping southern landscapes: "For most of the history of the South, significant social and political relationships cannot be separated from the agricultural landscapes in which they are embedded" (198). Stewart goes on to argue that environmental history in the South is far less about notions of wilderness than it is about the politics of race, gender, ethnicity, and class that shape landscapes (213). The increased scholarly and activist attention to ecojustice has strengthened this notion: in seeking justice for those subject to toxicity and environmental devastation, the social and political become indivisible from the environmental. Throughout *A Thousand-Mile Walk to the Gulf,* Muir encounters newly freed African Americans, poor white laborers, former Confederate soldiers, roaming vigilante rebels, ministers, doctors, lawyers, planters, and farmers. For Muir, such encounters are merely what happen in between his more important work. They are, in other words, the travel narrative Muir sees as secondary to his botanical science. Yet Muir's social encounters reveal something about environments that his otherwise scientific observation misses. Whether he recognizes it or not, those social influences shape the biomes he observes and direct his movements.[11] Muir's refusal to acknowledge the impact of slavery and slave culture in both shaping southern landscapes and his own interactions with space is the most problematic sociocultural and ecological issue throughout the text. That Muir avoids the topic indicates a failure to rethink social convention concerning race. The end of the war does not—as some Americans imagined—end national racism or erase the effects of slavery. Racial conflict remains relevant throughout Reconstruction and the late nineteenth century and continues to shape southern and national environments today.

Muir is happiest in the woods on his own, and the majority of the text chronicles such moments. However, Muir cannot entirely erase those portions of his travels that bring him in contact with diverse peoples. Though he actively avoids other people—walking through the entirety of Louisville "without speaking a word to anyone"—he admits to being lonely and tired (1). He is scared when he witnesses vigilante ex-Confederates roaming the edges of the woods (29). More often than not, southerners are suspicious of Muir. He repeatedly has to justify why he has come "down through the South, so soon after the war," and occasionally he has trouble negotiating his way through the social contexts he encounters (62).

As a northerner and "outside" observer, Muir does not see himself as part of the South's racial history, nor does he acknowledge the prevalence of race in shaping southern environmental history. For Muir, slavery, interpreted as solely a southern phenomenon, receives scant attention throughout the text. Consequently, he is unable to recognize the impact of slavery and Emancipation upon his own developing environmental ideas. After setting off into the deepest woods, the first people Muir encounters are freed African Americans.

As Stewart notes, slaves and freedmen used uncultivated lands throughout the South for a variety of reasons: to escape the heat, to congregate with family, or perform religious ceremonies (202). The woods grant African Americans temporary respite from the world of white oppression—oddly reminiscent of the alternative to industrial modernism the woods represent to Muir. In parts of Kentucky, Muir finds the drinking water "intolerable with salt" (5). Though Muir states that a black man tells him where and how to get drinkable water, he does not explain why this man knows this forest so well. These sections of Kentucky are largely populated by African Americans, where white plantation owners had relegated slave quarters to less desirable lands—places with undrinkable water or untillable soil. Despite Emancipation, Muir still describes black laborers as "slaves," observing that some freedmen still working plantations continue to call employers "Massa" (60). In Georgia, he describes cotton pickers, noting "the negroes are easy-going and merry, making a great deal of noise and doing little work" (51). This particularly troubling passage reveals Muir's naïveté and his inability to recognize the need for further racial reconciliation after Emancipation. Muir, who had always been industrious, equates labor with payment. "One energetic white man, working with a will," he writes, "would easily pick as much cotton as half a dozen Sambos and Sallies" (51). Of course, what Muir fails to acknowledge is the obvious: that slaves were not paid and even after Emancipation were paid exceedingly poorly, if at all. He notes that black laborers are paid "seven to ten dollars a month," as if to solidify the successes of Emancipation, yet just days later a wealthy planter named Mr. Cameron brags that labor now "costs him less than it did before the emancipation of the negroes" (53–60). Thus, Muir not only continues to "other" the South via this narrative, but dangerously oversimplifies race during Reconstruction.

What remains apparent is Muir's inability to transfer his precursory notions of deep ecological contact beyond the natural world. Stewart contends that Muir does not spend the time necessary to effectively connect issues of race, labor, and environment that are central to southern environmental history. For all the contact Muir experiences with ecosystems, he spends little time or effort evaluating the sociocultural influences that inevitably impact the lands with which he interacts. Textual conflicts occur in those instances when social issues alter Muir's utopic vision of nature. Perhaps most disconcerting is an encounter with a black family in the woods of Florida. Muir approaches a distant campfire in hopes of finding some food or water. He creeps

up "cautiously" being afraid of "robber negroes," but instead finds a family living in one of the "most primitive of all the domestic establishments I have yet
seen in town or grove" (105). Initially, Muir seems to romanticize the scene: he
is drawn "forward to the radiant presence of the black pair" and handed some
water after withstanding their stare of "desperate fixedness which is said to
subdue the lion" (106). Echoing Thoreau, he seems to admire the "simplicity
of the establishment," as if this man and woman exist as one with the forest
(106). However, a clear turn occurs when Muir notices the pair's child, "a black
lump of something lying in the ashes of the fire" (106). The boy moves out of
the ashes, "rising from the earth naked as to the earth he came" (106). Muir
continues, "had he emerged from the black muck of a marsh, we might easily
have believed that the Lord had manufactured him like Adam direct from the
earth" (107). Despite the biblical allusion, he is troubled by the child's naked-
ness and the ash and dirt. "This fashion is sufficiently simple," Muir explains,
"but it certainly is not quite in harmony with Nature. Birds make nests and
nearly all beasts make some kind of bed for their young; but these negroes
allow their younglings to lie nestless and naked in the dirt" (107).[12] The child's
dirtiness is equivalent with disharmony. In fact, uncleanliness not only questions one's harmony with nature, but one's humanity: "Man and other civilized animals are the only creatures that ever become dirty" (110).

This encounter in the Florida woods fully realizes Muir's inability to recognize the persistence of racial inequality, and it also interrupts his utopic
vision of nature. Emancipation promised forty acres and a mule, but the reality is that many freed slaves were either forced into employment with former
owners or made to survive through other means—in this case, a "primitive"
shelter in those uncultivated lands. What Muir first romanticizes is the failure of Reconstruction to adequately accommodate Emancipation and reconcile
centuries of slavery. This moment offers Muir an opportunity to acknowledge
the structures of racism that have relegated this family to the woods. However,
he does not. At no point does he realize that slavery and national racist politics are responsible for interrupting his utopic vision of nature. Herein lies the
foundational problem: Muir's inability to balance this space as both nature and
a site of social, cultural, and political contest.

Muir's praxis—"biocentrism"—deconstructs projective fantasies of the
South, but it is important to expand that framework. Highlighting the tensions
in Muir's own writing makes it clear that—even in the nineteenth century—
an active environmentalism could not wholly remove the human from the bi-

ome. We must be able to trace those cultural factors (often based in racial, gender, or class discriminations) that shape physical spaces. At the same time, *A Thousand-Mile Walk to the Gulf* conveys the value in considering the "happiness" of plants and animals, all made "from the same material" as every other creature (138–39). In fact, it is this kind of depth and understanding that makes it possible to alter popular and cultural perception. If a text like *A Thousand-Mile Walk to the Gulf* conveys the dissolution of an overly simplistic regional binary through the depth of natural consideration, then the same consideration can reveal and break down racial barriers as well. Muir's deep ecological method is not wrong, but he fails to apply that method to the human, to consider cultural and social forces that also shape environments. Too often we assume nature writers and ecocritics share these sympathies; however, the future of ecocriticism lies in making implicit assumptions explicit realities.

NOTES

1. The US South has often been represented "as backward, wild, uncivilized, and dangerous" (Cox 2). Leigh Ann Duck notes in *The Nation's Region* that the South became a region of "projective fantasies" (Duck 3). In the collection *Environmental History and the American South* (2009), Paul Sutter explains that although many southern environmental scholars acknowledge the South's "distinctive regional dimensions," they "often have other fish to fry" (2).

2. Muir makes comparisons between North and South, East and West throughout his career.

3. The environmental praxis—the environmental method Muir details through both language and action—within *A Thousand-Mile Walk to the Gulf* acts as a precursor for later modes of conservation that writers such as Aldo Leopold and Wendell Berry continue to refine throughout the twentieth century and the early twenty-first century.

4. Hothouses are essentially greenhouses where planters would keep species that could not survive British climates. Often these hothouses were heated by coal furnaces.

5. Pamela Regis describes these two styles as the convergence of "natural history and the sublime" (41). She notes the two methods "complement each other," as either method "compels notice of a different selection of creation" (41).

6. In *The Nation's Region,* Duck explores the South as a region made distinct within the larger nation as a way to contain antiliberal ideals that might run counter to the image of a progressive, democratic United States (7). In carving out such regional distinctions, the South was shaped by "projective fantasies," which necessitated that the South was different from the North—at once a part of the nation, yet other as well (Duck 4).

7. Deep ecologists support an ethical rendering of the environment that claims the human and nonhuman have equal value.

8. Muir was known for his vigorous hiking pace.

9. Conservation and preservation signify differing levels of environmental stewardship and human presence; the former usually indicates the sustainable use of natural resources, while the latter indicates natural resources wholly protected from human use.

10. Of course, this is also one of the most debated. As ecocritics Buell, Neil Evernden, and Bill McKibben have addressed, the idea of an "undisturbed" environment is fundamentally flawed.

11. This comes full well knowing that Muir himself feels that by avoiding "society" and "culture," he is the one in fact directing his own movement, when we can just as easily say his movement is directed by the presence of those places he works to avoid.

12. In "John Muir's Evolving Attitudes Towards Native American Cultures," Robert Fleck notes that Muir expressed "ambivalent," even disapproving views of Digger Indians in the Sierra. He spoke of their "uncleanliness," particularly confusing for Muir since the Native Americans "lived in the pure and fresh wilderness" (21).

WORKS CITED

Badè, William Frederic, editor. "Introduction." *A Thousand-Mile Walk to the Gulf*. Houghton Mifflin, 1998.

Bartram, William. *Travels through North & South Carolina: Georgia, East & West Florida, the Cherokee Country, the Extensive Territories of the Muscogulges, or Creek Confederacy, and the Country of the Chactaws*. James & Johnson, 1791.

Bass, Rick. "Losses and Gains." *Elemental South: An Anthology of Southern Nature Writing*, edited by Dorinda G. Dallmeyer, U of Georgia P, 2004, pp. 15–19.

Buell, Lawrence. *The Environmental Imagination: Thoreau, Nature Writing, and the Formation of American Culture*. Harvard UP, 1996.

———. *The Future of Environmental Criticism: Environmental Crisis and Literary Imagination*. Blackwell, 2008.

Cobb, James C. *The Most Southern Place on Earth: The Mississippi Delta and the Roots of Regional Identity*. Oxford UP, 1992.

Cox, John David. *Traveling South: Travel Narratives and the Construction of American Identity*. U of Georgia P, 2005.

Duck, Leigh Anne. *The Nation's Region: Southern Modernism, Segregation, and U.S. Nationalism*. U of Georgia P, 2009.

Finch, Robert, and John Elder, editors. "Introduction." *Nature Writing: The Tradition in English*. Norton, 2002.

Fishman, Gail. *Journeys Through Paradise: Pioneering Naturalists in the Southeast*. UP of Florida. 2017.

Fleck, Richard F. "John Muir's Evolving Attitudes toward Native American Cultures." *American Indian* Quarterly, vol. 4, no. 1, 1978, pp. 19–35. Web.

Gifford, Terry. *Reconnecting with John Muir: Essays in Post-Pastoral Practice.* U of Georgia P, 2006.

Greeson, Jennifer Rae. *Our South: Geographic Fantasy and the Rise of National Literature.* Harvard UP, 2010.

Hallock, Thomas. *From the Fallen Tree: Frontier Narratives, Environmental Politics, and the Roots of a National Pastoral, 1749–1826.* U of North Carolina P, 2004.

Lane, John, and Gerald Thurmond. *The Woods Stretched for Miles: New Nature Writing from the South.* U of Georgia P, 1999.

Muir, John. *A Thousand-Mile Walk to the Gulf.* Houghton Mifflin, 1916.

Norman, Charles. *John Muir, Father of Our National Parks.* Messner, 1957.

Romine, Scott. *The Real South: Southern Narrative in the Age of Cultural Reproduction.* Louisiana State UP, 2008.

Scheese, Don. *Nature Writing: The Pastoral Impulse in America.* Twayne, 1996.

Stewart, Mart. "If John Muir Had Been an Agrarian: American Environmental History West and South." *Environmental History and the American South: A Reader,* edited by Paul S. Sutter and Christopher J. Manganiello, U of Georgia P, 2009, pp. 196–219.

Sutter, Paul S. "Introduction: No More the Backward Region: Southern Environmental History Comes of Age." *Environmental History and the American South: A Reader,* edited by Paul S. Sutter and Christopher J. Manganiello, U of Georgia P, 2009, 1–24.

Country Roads

Mountain Journeys in the Anthropocene

JIMMY DEAN SMITH

THE GRADED GRAVELED

Among the artifacts signifying humanity's will to dominate the Appalachian landscape—reservoirs, mountaintop-removal sites, strip mines, tunnels—are roads. Like those other technofossils, roads are "the preserved remnant" of the "[c]urrent evolution of the technosphere" (Haff 301), the signature humanity has inscribed on the environment to denote ownership of a region whose history and literature have been characterized by successive, accelerating attempts to exploit its resources, as well as acts of resistance against that exploitation. Roads, as well as less benign technofossils, are nonverbal utterances in the master narrative of Western culture, through which agents of domination identify and remedy problems that may, after all, exist only in this one, albeit all-consuming, narrative. Thus, the colonizers of a "primitive" place rely on a rhetoric, both verbal and nonverbal, that designates and denigrates places and people as "wild," while promulgating a rationalizing, progressive solution to problems that may not, in fact, have existed before civilization appeared and ensnared nature in the rationalist master narrative. Roads signify that human beings have encountered nature and defeated it.

Roads not only designate the imposition of the reasoning mind on nature but, by greatly facilitating the egress of human agents, also allow a much faster rate of anthropogenic change. In 1750, the explorer and land speculator Thomas Walker found and used buffalo trails and Native American roads leading into Kentucky, but he yearned for more: "[March] 13th. . . . [we] took the main wagaon (sic) road leading to . . . the New River. It is not well cleared or beaten yet, but will be a very good one with proper management." In a mere instant of geological time (twenty-five years), he got his wish when others, prominent among them Daniel Boone, cleared the Wilderness Road (Filson 46). Thus, within fifty years of Walker's passage through the Cumberland Gap, thousands of Euro-Americans had traversed a much better road, purportedly

bringing reason to the wilderness. The march of civilization has since accelerated. "Stand at Cumberland Gap and watch the procession of civilization,"
wrote Frederick Jackson Turner (12). With each wave of immigration—from
buffalo to Native to white hunter to "pioneer farmer"—the road improved
and, per the master narrative, humanity set itself further apart from the environment. It took Walker most of a day to traverse the Cumberland Gap; today,
it takes about two minutes to drive through a well-lit tunnel.

One prominent midcentury writer's novels and social histories persistently
focus on roads as anthropogenic signatures on the broken wilderness. For
most of her life, Harriette Simpson Arnow lived in or near Ann Arbor, Michigan, but nearly all her books are set either completely or partly in her native
southern Kentucky. The Upper Cumberland watershed is the focus of her social histories (*Seedtime on the Cumberland* [1960] and *Flowering of the Cumberland* [1963]) and her memoir (*Old Burnside* [1977]). While Arnow's three books
of nonfiction celebrate the Upper Cumberland River Watershed and mourn
its death-through-damming, her early novels, although certainly not ignoring
waterways, more thoroughly scrutinize roads. "At an early age I saw my work
as a record of people's lives in terms of roads," Arnow told Barbara Baer. "At
first, it was only a path, then a community at the end of a gravel road that
took men and families away, and finally, . . . a highway [that] destroyed the
hill community" (53). Set in the present but rooted in Arnow's close attention
to historical and geological fact, *Mountain Path* (1936), *Hunter's Horn* (1949),
and *The Dollmaker* (1954) thus comprise an unofficial study of "locomotion
traces"—roads, but also rivers and railways—(Zalasiewicz et al. 40) and their
evolution in contemporary Appalachia.

The Dollmaker "beg[ins] where the graveled road [leads] onto the highway"
and ends up in "a wartime housing development in Detroit" (*Introduction* 248),
her region's demise told in miniature: with massive outmigration, notes Arnow, "The hill community . . . was gone" (*Introduction* 248). On the first page of
The Dollmaker, Gertie Nevels emerges from scrub pines onto "a road fer automobiles" (1–2). She is on muleback. Arnow's scene thus mirrors that depicted
in George Caleb Bingham's painting *Daniel Boone Escorting Settlers through the
Cumberland Gap* (1851–1852). In the painting, "Rebecca Boone, atop [a] horse,
suggests the Virgin Mary, symbolizing the courageous spirit of pioneer
women" there at the Gap (Bingham). Gertie is at the point of the Appalachian
journey that follows modern highways out of hill communities and into the
industrial Midwest. Her mule immediately loses a great deal of its usefulness.

The setting is fraught with rhetorical value; in Detroit, mules will not get Gertie around, while the automobiles manufactured there would be of little use in the Cumberland's roadless valleys.

Roads signify in Arnow's earlier novels as well, with paving materials juxtaposed to suggest alternatively how well such roads complement the environment and how insistently humanity has forced a rationalist narrative onto the wild. Another allegorical crossroads appears in *Hunter's Horn*. In Chapter 8, its protagonist, Nunn Ballew, emerges from his own hill community to sell his stock. In town, "among all the rich farmers in fine big trucks and the trucks full of fine fat cattle" (68), he is fleeced by urban sharpies. On the way home, Nunn takes out some of his anger on the bus driver who stops to let Nunn out in "ankle-deep snow." This stop makes no sense to the driver, who is used to highways, to Western reason and technofossils. "Are you sure, buddy, this is where you want off?" he asks. "There's nothen here, no light, nothen." Nunn, who has had enough of buses and "fine big trucks," responds, "It's th beginnen a th graded graveled, an I recken I know my own way home" (78). Later, Nunn pursues an *ubi sunt* reverie down one of those gravel roads:

> At intervals . . . were smooth open patches of snow bordered by old twisted-limbed and black-trunked apple trees half smothered in young forest growth and briars. Sometimes in the middle of the plot . . . would be a chimney where in summer the chimney swifts still came. . . . Nunn . . . pondered with a mixture of wonder and sadness on the lost people. Where were they and their children and grandchildren? . . . Where had they gone, those lost people? What were they doing? (268)

Where have the lost people gone, and what are they doing? The likely answers—to Detroit, making cars—are not the only ones; these questions are ultimately unanswerable. But another is not: How did those lost people leave this place? On this, the old wagon road that eventually comes to a highway. From the road, Nunn easily discerns artifacts—chimneys, apple trees, cleared land—that signify how the people of Little Smoky Creek attempted to dominate nature and how nature, with infinite patience, has rejected its attempted subjugation to human reason: birds fly in and out of the chimneys, briars entangle the cultivated trees, and snow covers the carefully cleared plots. The road Nunn walks is the most significant technofossil of all, a monument to the desire that brought people to instrumentalize wildness and that allowed them to retreat when their human plans failed.

ROADS THAT GLIMMER IN THE NIGHT

The significance of roads as anthropogenic markers had been on Harriette Simpson Arnow's mind from her beginnings as a writer. "When I went out to teach in 1926 there were hundreds of roadless creek valleys all through the Southern Appalachians, and almost no roads at all in Eastern Kentucky," writes Arnow in an introduction to her first book *Mountain Path* (242). The earliest of her "roads trilogy" may be her most perceptive investigation of locomotion technofossils. In the novel, a Lexingtonian and University of Kentucky student, Louisa Sheridan, has had an education steeped in Western values: "Sentiment has little or no place in this our modern civilization," says one of her professors; "[you] must learn to reason" (175). In the potboiler Arnow's editor demanded, Louisa finds love and moonshine and feuding and eventually gets over a lonesome ache—"The long vistas of uninhabited ridges and hills made her too acutely aware of how far away the world was—her world" (112), when she rejects "modern civilization" for the simple life: "She was happy. Happier than she could remember ever having been before, and all because a handful of people, their illiteracy exceeded only by their poverty, had this day shown that they liked her and were pleased that she was among them" (175).

Path can, of course, be read as an allegorical title—i.e., Louisa is "finding her path in life"—but the more thoughtful, slower book hiding inside the page-turner asks why people build roads and whether Western reason can come to an understanding with nature. A smart but impoverished student, Louisa has no choice but to teach for a year on the Cumberland: "One studied three years, and learned things, and ranked in the upper two percent in achievement and intelligence, and then came out into the world for a job, and learned that the ability to ride a mule counted for more than an Einstein's knowledge of trigonometric formulae" (3). She is not kidding about the mule. After a lengthy bus ride from town, the "leetle stranger woman" (11) meets the local who will guide her from the highway into Cal Valley. He furnishes her with a mule. As it happens in the mountains, it is indeed more important to know how to ride than to work formulae. After an uneventful trip on fairly flat paths, her guide says,

"'This is th' jumpin' off place'" (18), and the earth falls out from under Louisa. Fortunately, she is in the care of a creature that, though known for its irrationality, is well suited to the valley's physical and metaphorical terrain: "The road was steeper than she had dared think it could be. . . . [The mule] skidded a bit, and sat for a time on her hind quarters, but soon righted herself and went on carefully enough" (18).

Louisa's muleback journey reverses that of Gertie Nevels up backcountry trails and onto the highway. But Arnow, anticipating Gertie's connection with Rebecca Boone in Bingham's allegorical painting, invokes the pioneer woman/Virgin Mary archetype in a later scene. Feudists have tussled, and civilized Louisa is retreating from that irrational event. Once more, she is riding a mule, and even has a babe in arms. The baby is not hers, but still she reflects maternally:

> The mule stepped slowly and carefully. . . . It was pleasant to be riding in the dark wrapped in a feeling of safety, hearing nothing but the squeak of saddle leather and the breathing of the mules. Odd and disconcerting to feel so completely at ease on a mule's back with a baby in your arms and a man by your side. . . . She thought of the other women with children in their arms who had come over this road before her a hundred years ago. . . . (134–35)

Louisa toys with the idea of identifying with mountain women. She is also getting used to the slow pace of traffic on unpaved valley roads.

That slowness and Louisa's acclimation to it denote the fact that sometimes backcountry roads are made *from* and *for* the environment, not to signify its defeat or hasten its despoliation. The mountain paths are steep and slippery; the "'big road' [is] filled with large, uneven pieces of blue-white limestone" (38–39). Limestone is all over Cal Valley—hardening wash-water (29), looming in bluffs over the river (10), collapsing into sinkholes (52), forming caves and "[w]hite feathery stalactites [that] glitter" from the roofs of caves (76). Limestone provides stepping stones for cabin dooryards (56) and the hearthstones of the house Louisa boards in (19). Louisa comes to the valley with a watch that she, with her faith in reason and technology, considers the most accurate measure of time. But in the valley's enormous limestone cave, listening to "the musical note of a single drop of water" resets her to nature's time: "[F]or lack of anything else to do she fell to counting between each drop. She counted for some time—one, two, three, four, five, clink. Always five counts and then the single note. . . . The water, she reasoned, had dropped in just that measured fashion for hundreds, perhaps thousands, of years" (77). The limestone that forms the cave and through which the valley's creek water flows (14) also paves the "big road" well enough for foot and mule travel. While cars and buses require modern industrial paving, the pace of time in the valley allows roads to be constructed of what wildness itself provides. The dualistic separation between civilization and nature does not seem so strong. On the dark night of her muleback escape, Louisa notes that "nowhere was there light except the bright points overhead and the faint glimmering of limestone rocks"—as if the ground beneath her, conscious of its ancient affinities, is in conversation with the stars. "A smattering of geology had given her an interest in rock formations" (76); that is, the university had made her think like an amateur geologist. But the steep and slippery paths have inspired Louisa to think like a creek valley.

MONSTERS AND MASTERS OF THE PLACE

A later-arriving novel chronologically places roadbuilding much earlier in the European colonization of Appalachia. Set in western North Carolina in 1779, John Ehle's *The Land Breakers* (1964) is the first of a seven-novel series focused on the settlement of that area of Appalachia. It begins with a genesis story when a young couple claims their share of American Eden and continues with further attempts to subdue wildness. (The word *breakers* in the title suggests the vehemence with which they and their descendants impose their will on nature.) Recently arrived from Philadelphia, Mooney and Imy Wright have followed the Great Valley south to Morganton, "little more than a long muddy street with poles stuck in the mudholes" (3). Scots by way of Ulster and recently freed from indenture, they are anxious to be their own masters. So, not only chasing a romantic ideal but also making a political statement like many others in the Appalachian migration, the Wrights are looking for "good land they could work on their own" (4). They seem to find it when a storekeeper sells them "six hundred forty acres of bottom land" (8) on a "little river [that] is fresh and fish-filled, with a valley as flat as God's palm" (5). But their own Eden is at the end of a hard road. The path leading toward their place is terrifying: "As they climbed the trail . . . , they entered a misty spot, then walked into a cloud. They were in that cloud all day. . . . [T]he whole place looked like a ghost world to them" (8). After two days on "the narrow road that led from Old Fort to Watauga," they locate "a hickory tree marked with three deep gashes, . . . the sign of the trail that led to their land" (10). Blazed thus, the trail evinces the human desire to rationalize and thus subdue nature. But Ehle takes pains to emphasize this road's roots in nonhuman activity. The trail "twist[s] in and out around the trees, a trail made by animals, most likely" (11)—in other words, that trail is probably nature's own, as so many human highways in the mountains originally were. Later, Ehle depicts roadbuilding as a proto-industrial capitalist enterprise ("three Negro male slaves worked to hack a wider trail for oxen and carts" [20]), reminding us that the apparent ecological sensitivity of unpaved roads can still be balanced on the backs of the oppressed. (Convict labor builds a railroad in Ehle's *The Road* [1967].) But Mooney and Imy's turn at the tree marked with three gashes indicates a world-altering shift, as human reason arrives to put nature in its place: "Not even a savage's footprint was on the moss of the forest, nor the sight or sound of another person was found anywhere. This was the land of the wolf and the bear, the panther, the snake, the eagle high above them, the buzzards following them—or so it had been until they arrived" (11). However, settling—breaking—the land seems to drain and then break Imy as well, albeit the symptoms of her fatal illness (exhaustion; "coughing and restlessness" [16]) also suggest a wasting disease (16–9). In any case, to Mooney, it seems that "the pained spirit of this place" (19) has taken her away. Nature, either by beating her down with its immense toughness or by metastasizing a few aberrant cells, has won.

In *The Land Breakers,* the wildlife of western North Carolina is not cuddly. "'Have you got a gun? You'll need one up there," says the storekeeper who sells the Wrights their property. "[I]t's land a person will have to fight beasts for" (6). And along the trail they encounter every indication that they will indeed have to do battle with beasts. Nights in the howling wilderness, they cower to a "current of cries . . . , a babble of screeches, screams, calls" (9), attributing the terrifying cacophony to "'Panthers, most likely. Wolves. Lord knows what all" (10). One day while clearing land, Mooney finds a "great footprint in the ground, one far larger than his own" (13), and he and Imy puzzle over what made it. The banality of her question—"What in the world?"—disguises its acuity. In the world as they understand it, such things simply do not exist. Later, when Mooney is kneeling at a spring and drinking, the creature reveals itself to be "a great bear, almost twice as tall as a man" (15) that has come there to drink, too. It incarnates what Val Plumwood refers to as the "monster myth" (86) whereby nature's most formidable beasts must be absorbed into the rationalist master narrative as monsters. Terrified but logical, Mooney tries to strike a bargain with "the beast": "We didn't come here to harm you. I know we cut down enough trees for a cabin, and we'll girdle trees to clear a path for planting crops, but we didn't aim to harm you or this place" (15). The old bear is unimpressed with Mooney's offer: "The bear . . . was a lonely superior figure, *the master of the place,* of the spring, of the mountain, of the wood, of whatever his red eyes saw" (15, emphasis added). The bear regards Mooney with a look of "dumb-minded contemplation" (15), but if it were capable of responding to human argument, it would likely have an impressive response. Mooney (and, in decades and novels to come, countless other settlers) says that he means no harm to bear or place—to wildness—claiming that he is only killing enough trees to "clear a path" for agriculture. He and Imy aim to build the first of many roads that will instrumentalize the North Carolina mountains for ensuing generations, roads that will open the region to settlement while chasing off the land's nonhuman inhabitants. Despite his diplomatic words to the bear, Mooney is not offering genuine peaceful coexistence. He does not seem even to consider that the path that brought him to the creek had already been there when he and Imy first ventured into wildness.

THE WORLD IN ITS BECOMING

Increasingly, the literature of Appalachia—a region that is synonymous both with nature-in-its-rawness and the instumentalizing of wildness—explicitly dramatizes the climatological precarity of its local and global setting. In their brief but seminal article "The 'Anthropocene,'" Paul J. Crutzen and Eugene F. Stoermer argue that "human induced stresses" (climate change, species kill-offs, air and water pollution) threaten earth with an accelerating but still seemingly slow-motion apocalypse. But there is hope. Humans can avoid being "a major [ruinous] geological force for . . . millions of years . . . to come" (18), if there is a fortuitous "major catastrophe . . . like an enormous volcanic eruption, an unexpected epidemic, a large-scale nuclear war, an asteroid impact, a new ice age, or continued plundering of Earth's resources by partially still primitive technology" (18). The irony is subdued but terrifying: people are bound to kill the planet slowly but will not if they manage instead to do the job fast, or if the planet rids itself of its human malignancy. (Crutzen and Stoemer also suggest, less eschatologically, that human beings "develop a world-wide accepted strategy leading to sustainability" [18].)

One recent, and well-known, dystopian novel suggests that the planet's desire to return to wildness will require more than the extinction of its most pernicious species: in writing its signature on nature, humanity has left markers that will remain long after the last person is gone. Something happens in Cormac McCarthy's *The Road* (2006). Readers do not learn exactly what, other than that "The clocks stopped at 1:17. A long shear of light and then a series of low concussions" (52). Perhaps a nuclear event, or an asteroid strike, or a natural explosion in Yellowstone—in any event, the Anthropocene shuts down and the posthuman epoch awakens. The spread of Western reason, and all that *civilization* signifies, abruptly stops and reverses itself. A man and his son journey through the postapocalyptic landscape of the mountains on their way to the ocean, and yet the man refuses to give up on humanity. His wife is clear-eyed about the situation (and, as a result, kills herself). As the boy's mother tells the man, "You cant protect us. . . . Sooner or later they will catch us and they will kill us. They will rape me. They'll rape him. They are going to rape us and kill us and eat us and you wont face it" (56). The man believes that he and his son can "[c]arry the fire" (278). He is irrational under the current circumstances and travels down the road in hopes of surviving. One scholar tracking the route taken by the man and the boy claims that, early in the book, "the road" is identifiable as US 25E—the Wilderness Road (Morgan). That is, after the apocalypse, they are taking the same route by which Thomas Walker et al. inscribed reason on Appalachia; only McCarthy's road is reversed.

While novels like *The Land Breakers* and Arnow's roads trilogy imply, perhaps even naively, a cautionary master narrative of anthropogenic conquest, McCarthy's novel clarifies and concentrates the brutally apocalyptic concerns of his earlier fiction. About McCarthy's earlier Appalachian novels, K. Wesley Berry writes, "McCarthy's prose implies a vision of ecological holocaust, as if the collapse of the earth as we know it lurks in the near future—a devastation spurred by our fossil-fuel-driven, hurry-up economy of fire" (55). With *The Road*, McCarthy delivers on a vision that complements the eschatological fears of Crutzen and Stoermer, but without even their scant hope. The "fire" carried by man and boy, that is, signifies hope, reason, and humanity's first attempt to chase night and cold away and thus conquer nature. The fire, in other words, suggests that a "fossil-driven, hurry-up economy" was an inevitable result of human rationality and will be once more if the spark again catches. The road leads the man and the boy past taunting reminders of humanity's faith in progress. Technofossils literally litter the landscape "along the blacktop": "Tall clapboard houses. Machinerolled metal roofs. A log barn in a field with an advertisement in faded ten-foot letters across the roofslope. See Rock City" (21). Everywhere are signifiers of the ultimately fruitless human drive to control and exploit. How the man and boy conceptualize their journey—by consulting a "tattered oilcompany roadmap"—miniaturizes the reversal of human fortune. The "black lines on the map" remain, though the oil companies are gone. The "state roads," built of concrete and macadam, will be there for hundreds of postapocalyptic years, but no matter how long the roads last as monuments to human planning, "there wont be any cars or trucks on them" (42–43). The "economy of fire" has hurtled off the road.

The last paragraph of *The Road* appears to suggest nostalgia for Eden, or for nature itself before human reason began manipulating and ultimately harming:

> Once there were brook trout in the streams in the mountains. You could see them standing in the amber current where the white edges of their fins wimpled softly in the flow. They smelled of moss in your hand. Polished and muscular and torsional. On their backs were vermiculate patterns that were maps of the world in its becoming. Maps and mazes. Of a thing which could not be put back. Not be made right again. In the deep glens where they lived all things were older than man and they hummed of mystery. (286–87)

But *The Road* does not end with an escape from the reality of the novel's grim conclusion so much as a reminder of what put humanity on the road to its own destruction. The trout in this paragraph do not exist beyond the realm of destructive humanity but rather as a signifier thereof. The fish appears to a *you* who has, it seems, taken the creature from its mountain stream home. He smells it and feels its muscles and finally compares the marks on its back to maps. With this vision, perhaps a dying man's, nature is restored only to be brought immediately back into the dualistic narrative of Western reason; "maps of the world," a startling and attention-grabbing metaphor, a signal of McCarthy's writerly presence, appear on the fish's back and portend the doom that awaits at the other end of history's road when the "economy of fire" has sputtered out. There is the sense that, having failed to see that they are part of nature themselves, people are getting their just deserts when the anthropogenic world breaks down. In *The Road,* the title phrase appears over two hundred fifty times, or on average of about once a page. By contrast, *nature* does not appear at all. This does not mean that nature itself is absent from the novel, only that it is almost pointless to talk about something that is omnipresent in a multitude of forms. While the word *nature* is not itself uttered, it is implied by every other word McCarthy writes in *The Road*. When he writes that a dam "will be there for a long time. . . . It's made out of concrete. It will probably be there for hundreds of years. Thousands, even" (19–20), he does not indicate even that technofossil will be there forever—but nature, or the environment, will be, even after the concrete crumbles. As the woman says in *The Road*, "We used to talk about death. . . . We don't anymore. Why is that? . . . It's because it's here. There's nothing left to talk about" (56). The ocean is nature, the rivers are nature, and so too are the elements that technology, now in retreat, once kept in check. About ecological apocalypse, the ultimate triumph of people over nature, Bill McKibben writes, "This is . . . the victory we have been pointing to at least since the eviction of Eden—the domination some have always dreamed of" (84). "In McCarthy," Dana Phillips asserts, "the world of nature and the world of men are parts of the same world, and both are equally violent and indifferent to the other" (33). So, terrified of our natural lot, we try to bring reason to the world. We build roads into the wilderness. "The decay in McCarthy's Appalachia can be read," says K. Wesley Berry, "as a healthy natural process rather than an affront to human grandeur" (60). Along with theorists and philosophers like Val Plumwood, McCarthy argues against a dualistic narrative that puts reason here and wildness there, civilization here and nature in some other place. People are not separate and above wildness. People are nature. Roads are nature.

In 1970, Harriette Simpson Arnow wrote about the recently formed Appalachian Regional Commission's ludicrous attempts to "modernize" the Cumberland Plateau. Among the ARC's failures is "the new, limited-access . . . superhighway that has disrupted [this] world" ("Topics: Appalachia"). The problem is not exactly with roads per se; "most back-hill farming communities [need] better local roads," she recognizes. But the ARC paved roads to serve "tourists, truckers, travelers and the country's well-to-do," rather than "the man with only a few worn-out acres." The federal agency tasked with bringing progress to Appalachia spent enormous amounts of money on the wrong kind of roads. Crutzen and Stoermer argue for developing sustainable methods to get us through the Anthropocene without inevitably arriving at the period's apocalyptic denouement. Building the right kind of roads, ones that recognize that human beings' place is *in* nature and not above it, is a start.

WORKS CITED

Arnow, Harriette Simpson. *The Dollmaker.* 1954. Scribner, 2009.

———. *Flowering of the Cumberland.* 1963. Michigan State UP, 2013.

———. *Hunter's Horn.* 1949. Michigan State UP, 1997.

———. "Introduction to *Mountain Path,* First Appalachian Heritage Edition." *Harriette Simpson Arnow: Critical Essays on Her Work,* edited by Haeja K. Chung, Michigan State UP, 1995, pp. 241–48.

———. *Mountain Path.* 1936. UP of Kentucky, 1985.

———. *Old Burnside.* UP of Kentucky, 1977.

———. "Topics: Appalachia Will Not Go Away." *New York Times* (1857–Current file), 28 March 1970. ProQuest Historical Newspapers The New York Times (1851–2006), ProQuest. Web. Accessed 17 March 2017.

Baer, Barbara L. "Harriette Arnow's Chronicles of Destruction." *Harriette Simpson Arnow: Critical Essays on Her Work,* edited by Haeja K. Chung, Michigan State UP, 1995, pp. 53–62.

Berry, K. Wesley. "The Lay of the Land in Cormac McCarthy's Appalachia." *Cormac McCarthy: New Directions,* edited by James D. Lilley, U of New Mexico P, 2002, pp. 47–73.

Bingham, George Caleb. *Daniel Boone Escorting Settlers through the Cumberland Gap.* 1851–1852. Kemper Art Museum, St. Louis. *Kemper Art Museum.* https://www.kemperartmuseum.wustl.edu/collection/explore/artwork/193. Accessed 23 March 2017.

Crutzen, Paul J., and Eugene F. Stoermer. "The 'Anthropocene.'" *IGBP Newsletter,* vol. 41, 2000, pp. 17–18.

Ehle, John. *The Land Breakers.* Harper, 1964.

———. *The Road.* 1967. U of Tennessee P, 1998.

Filson, John. *The Discovery, Settlement and Present State of Kentucke (1784): An Online Electronic Text Edition.* Wilmington: James Adams, 1784. Digital Commons @ University of Nebraska–Lincoln. Accessed 15 March 2017.

Haff, Peter K. "Technology as a Geological Phenomenon: Implications for Human Well-Being." *A Stratigraphical Basis for the Anthropocene,* edited by Colin N. Waters et al., Geological Society, 2013, pp. 301–9.

Lilley, James D., editor. *Cormac McCarthy: New Directions.* U of New Mexico P, 2002.

McCarthy, Cormac. *The Road.* Vintage International, 2006.

McKibben, Bill. *The End of Nature.* Random House, 1989.

Morgan, Wesley G. "The Route and Roots of The Road." *The Cormac McCarthy Journal,* vol. 6, 2008, pp. 39–47.

Phillips, Dana M. "History and the Ugly Facts of *Blood Meridian.*" *Cormac McCarthy: New Directions,* edited by James D. Lilley, U of New Mexico P, 2002, pp.17–46.

Plumwood, Val. "Being Prey." *The New Earth Reader: The Best of Terra Nova,* edited by David Rothenberg and Maria Ulvaeus, MIT Press, 1999, pp. 76–91.

Turner, Frederick Jackson. *The Frontier in American History.* Holt, 1947.

Zalasiewicz, Jan, et al. "The Technofossil Record of Humans." *The Anthropocene Review,* vol. 1, no. 1, 2014, pp. 34–43.

"Home Is Where the Hatred Is"

Gil Scott-Heron's Toxic Domestic Spaces and the Rhizomatic South

JOSEPH M. THOMPSON

In 1971, Gil Scott-Heron's second album, *Pieces of a Man,* featured the song "Home Is Where the Hatred Is." Scott-Heron sings from the point of view of an intravenous drug addict:

> Home is where the needle marks
> Try to heal my broken heart
> And it might not be such a bad idea if I never went home again.

In the wake of Daniel Patrick Moynihan's 1965 report, *The Negro Family,* the idea of the home as a location of black pathology emerged as a widely accepted, albeit always contested, truth in US society, especially among policy experts. The report filled the national imagination with images of black communities consisting of absent fathers, overbearing matriarchs, and untamed youth. Using social science methods to paint a seemingly objective portrait of African American home life, the Moynihan Report informed popular conceptions of black life that helped lead to the devaluing of nonpatriarchal family structures and the gradual gutting of social safety nets over the last thirty years of the twentieth century.[1]

For Scott-Heron, the culpability lay less with the failures of black individuals and more with the systematic destruction of the black home at the hands of the federal government, specifically the military-industrial complex. Songs like "The Revolution Will Not Be Televised," "Whitey on the Moon," and "South Carolina (Barnwell)" all connect the economic and environmental degradation experienced in black homes to defense expenditures that kept the United States prepared for perpetual war. Importantly, the link between defense spending and the oppression of African Americans implicates the US South. This region relied heavily on the Pentagon for its share of federal largesse as it transitioned from an agricultural economy to its midcentury incarnation as a part of the Sunbelt, stretching from the former Confederacy to California along the southern border of the nation.

However, instead of seeing southern politics as the lone or exceptional factor in the degradation of black communities, Scott-Heron's work encourages an ecocritical reading of the South's place within a global history of environmental racism. Rather than a single root source of racist political philosophies and practices, the South functions as a node (and a set of nodes) within a network of people, government institutions, and political economies marked by the support of and fight against systemic white supremacy. This is the rhizomatic South. In botany, a rhizome is a creeping underground stem that creates a network of interconnected roots, shoots, and nodes.[2] Think of crabgrass or ginger and how these plants grow in segments that spread in different directions. The rhizome also suggests a way to think about cultural change over time. Philosophers Gilles Deleuze and Félix Guattari proposed the concept of the rhizome as an alternative to the tap root or tree models that name an easily identifiable beginning point for a cultural phenomenon. For these thinkers, the rhizome model could deal more accurately with the issue of historical causality by recognizing the multiplicity of roots and outcomes. In the rhizome model, there is no binary of cause and effect or beginning and end. The rhizome is always in the process of becoming and growing in seen and unseen directions. It is, in the words of Deleuze and Guattari, an "anti-genealogy." The rhizome is a map that reveals multiple beginnings and endings.[3]

Using the rhizome as a metaphor for understanding the South helps to see the cultural changes that gave the region its particular characteristics at a given historical moment. There is no clear beginning and end to the rhizomatic South, and no South exists in simple binary opposition to another direction or region like the North. The rhizomatic South is always already part of the intersecting lines created by historical actions from within and beyond any geographical borders that might attempt to define it. The South is a shape-shifting construct forever being remade by environmental changes and human actions at different moments in time. It is always in the middle of establishing new roots that trail off in different directions. And in the case of Gil Scott-Heron's view of the South, the rhizomatic lines of historical change he saw crisscrossing the region stemmed from the federal defense spending priorities of the Cold War.

This is the rhizomatic South about which Scott-Heron wrote and sang, a region that was remade in the mid-twentieth century by the politicians, workers, and industries engaged in the proliferation of the military-industrial complex, often at the cost of the planet's ecological health. In calling attention to the brokenness and potential for redemption in black home life, Scott-Heron, a sort of poet laureate of policy analysis, forged a critique of environmental racism. He did so by understanding and mapping the rhizomatic lines that connected the building of Cold War defense strategies, the South's political ties to the Pentagon, and the destruction of African American domestic spaces.

Music critics, biographers, and historians have wrestled with the legacy of Gil Scott-Heron, debating his role as the "godfather of rap," his late-life reputation as a drug addict, and the political energy of his songs.[4] Only historian Claudrena N. Harold has examined Scott-Heron as a southerner. Writing shortly after his death in 2011, Harold cited songs like "95 South" and "South Carolina (Barnwell)" to comment on the poet-musician's "indebtedness to the South and his deep love for its people, its culture, and its political struggles" (Harold). Yet Scott-Heron's posthumously published memoir, *The Last Holiday* (2012), pushed this implicit, textual relationship between his art and the South to the forefront, with an emphasis on how the region influenced his conception of home. When Scott-Heron spoke of home, he meant the South, and he meant, specifically, Jackson, Tennessee. Although born in Chicago in 1949, as a toddler Scott-Heron moved to Jackson, his mother's hometown about ninety miles northeast of Memphis, following his parents' divorce and leaving his maternal grandmother to raise him. As he notes in his memoir, "No matter where I went —to Chicago, New York, Alabama, Memphis, or even Puerto Rico in the summer of 1960—I always knew I'd be coming back home to Jackson. . . . It was where I began to write, learned to play piano, and where I began to write songs" (1).

Scott-Heron acknowledges the seemingly stereotypical arrangement of his upbringing in his poem "Coming from a Broken Home" from the album *I'm New Here* (2010). In the first verse, he describes how "women folk raised me and I was full grown / before I knew I came from a broken home." He also locates his upbringing in Jackson, where he was "Sent to live with my Grandma down south / [wonder why they call it down if the world is round]." The scene he portrays here reflected his self-awareness regarding the alleged pathology of black domesticity,

> where my uncle was leavin'
> and my grandfather had just left for heaven, they said,

and as every ologist would certainly note
I had NO STRONG MALE FIGURE! RIGHT?

Scott-Heron mocks every "ologist" who might echo Moynihan and deem his upbringing insufficient, and he celebrates the strong women who raised him and taught him to challenge racial inequality. After his grandmother died, his mother returned to Jackson, encouraging him to volunteer with two other students to integrate the city's Tigrett High School, which he did in 1962. That same year, Scott-Heron's time in Jackson came to an end when he encountered the environmental destruction of the federal government for the first time. The infrastructure of Cold War armament and consumerism literally destroyed Scott-Heron's home when his grandmother's house, along with much of Jackson's middle-class African American neighborhood, fell in the path of construction for the national highway system.[5] With this construction, the government demolished the one environment of domestic peace and love Scott-Heron had known in his young life to connect a small southern town to the rhizomatic network of asphalt created by Eisenhower's National Interstate and Defense Highways Act. The mother and son then moved to New York City, where the teenaged Scott-Heron began soaking up new sounds and new politics. He finished high school on a scholarship at the exclusive Fieldston Prep School in the Bronx and attended Lincoln University, where he met Brian Jackson, his musical partner during the next decade of astounding artistic output.[6]

The federal highway system that destroyed Scott-Heron's Tennessee home offered only one manifestation of the enormous impact the government had on the South's environment and economics. While the government had made inroads into the southern economy during the Great Depression, the full impact of federal spending in boosting the region and pushing the government into everyday life began in earnest during the mobilization for World War II.[7] After securing wartime deals with the government, defense industry contractors established factories throughout the South, taking advantage of the region's underemployed workforce, its general skepticism of organized labor, and lower wages. This mode of economic development continued after the war and depended heavily on the disproportionate congressional power wielded by southern politicians on the Armed Services Committees. When not channeling defense industry into the South, these politicians encouraged economic development through the expansion of military installations.[8] This strategy of military Keynesianism pumped enormous sums of federal dollars into local economies via defense installations and contractors and established the rhizomatic connections between the South, the Pentagon, private defense contractors, and Cold War militarism. And as Scott-Heron made plain, African American communities paid an exacting ecological toll for much of this progress, while government investment lifted parts of the South out of its prewar economic patterns and transformed the region over the last half of the twentieth century.

Scott-Heron made his recording debut in 1970 with the album *Small Talk at 125th and Lenox,* and he wasted no time in connecting the dots between government defense spending and the divestment of African American communities. The lead track, and perhaps his most well-known composition, "The Revolution Will Not Be Televised," eviscerates the nation's political leadership, including a strategic hit on South Carolina congressman and "patriarch of the armed forces," Mendel Rivers. He warns listeners that,

> The revolution will not show you pictures of
> Nixon blowing a bugle and leading a charge by
> John Mitchell, General Abramson, and Mendel Rivers
> to eat hog maws confiscated from a Harlem sanctuary.

He also uses this track to take on the imaginary South of popular culture with lines like

> *Green Acres, Beverly Hillbillies,* and *Hooterville Junction*
> will no longer be so Goddamned relevant
> and women will not care if Dick finally screwed Jane
> on *Search for Tomorrow*
> because black people will be in the streets looking for
> *A Brighter Day.*
> The revolution will not be televised.

With three quick television references, Scott-Heron takes his verbal wrecking ball to the idyllic southern/midwestern mash-up countryside of Hooterville Junction and the natural resources jackpot experienced by the Clampetts. No more could pure white buffoonery provide a fantasy of bucolic peace, because black revolution in America's streets was imminent.

The same album featured "Whitey on the Moon," one of Scott-Heron's most overt critiques of government economic priorities and their relationship to the degradation of African American homes.

> A rat done bit my sister Nell
> (with Whitey on the moon)
> Her face and arms began to swell
> (and Whitey's on the moon).

Scott-Heron's details of vermin infestation, juxtaposed with the indictment of federal spending priorities represented in the refrain "Whitey on the moon," shocked audiences into considering the sharp disparities between Cold War research and development budgets and the poverty experienced in the ghettoes of US cities. A home in the poorest spaces of black America could not match the happy-go-lucky white fantasy of Hooterville Junction, not as long as the government spent so much of the nation's money getting to the moon.

The title of Scott-Heron's record, *Small Talk at 125th and Lenox,* placed him at the heart of the city's most famous black community, smack in the middle of Harlem, itself a node in the rhizomatic extensions between the North, the South, and the Global South. Harlem had served as a destination for generations of black southerners fleeing southern states and the Caribbean since the 1910s (Field 693–718). But despite generations of political and cultural flourishing, abject poverty and environmental degradation persisted and gave Harlem a reputation as the quintessential scene of black ghetto life. Scott-Heron's details of rat bites echoed the pervasive news stories of vermin infestation and slumlords that emerged in the black press and that motivated activists of the 1950s and 1960s. As early as 1959, black community leaders like Jesse Gray organized Harlem's impoverished tenants in rent strikes and rallies for sanitation and building code enforcements against the exploitative practices of absentee slumlords. These tenants' protests also focused on rat abatement as a central concern regarding the health and safety of their neighborhoods.[9] Years of negligent garbage collection services led to the piling of refuse on sidewalks and in the alleys and abandoned buildings throughout New York City's poorest sections. This garbage acted as feeding and breeding sites for the city's vermin population, and rat infestations continued into the 1970s.[10]

New York City logged over four hundred *reported* rat bites in 1969, the year before Scott-Heron released "Whitey on the Moon." To address the twin problems of refuse and vermin, the Health Department's Bureau of Pest Control

JOSEPH M. THOMPSON

embarked on a "Starve a Rat Today" public relations campaign to raise awareness about the correlation between proper waste disposal and rat abatement. With a yearly budget of $4.5 million and a staff of 420 workers for the entire city in 1970, the bureau could only accomplish so much.[11] That same year, the combination of garbage-filled streets, predatory landlords, abandoned buildings, muggings, a blatant heroin trade, and a lack of police patrols led Glester Hinds of the Peoples Civil League to describe Harlem as "the modern 'Tobacco Road' and the stepchild of the city" (Matthews 1). As this reference to Erskine Caldwell's novel of Depression-era southern poverty indicates, the black inner city had joined or perhaps replaced the prewar South as the measuring stick of economic and environmental depravity. Scott-Heron's piercing, poetic analysis mapped the networks that connected these spaces, tracing the rhizomatic lines that linked the North and the South, the rural and the urban, the terrestrial and the lunar, and the scientific expertise of the National Aeronautics and Space Administration (NASA) with the lowest ranks of the US political-economic system.

In the second verse of "Whitey on the Moon," Scott-Heron depicts how landlords held the poorest residents captive while raising their rental fees in spite of the filthy conditions.

> The man just upped my rent last night
> (because Whitey's on the moon)
> No hot water, no toilets, no lights
> (but Whitey's on the moon)
> I wonder why he's upping me?
> (because Whitey's on the moon?)
> I was already giving him fifty a week
> (with Whitey on the moon).

For Scott-Heron, there remained an undeniable hypocrisy in the fact that the nation's impoverished citizens struggled to maintain the most basic living conditions, and yet NASA could spend $20 billion on Project Apollo alone in an unprecedented and myopic spending frenzy to place a man on the moon. Moreover, these funds not only built the machinery to take Americans to the moon, they also paid for the expertise to build the machinery, including over $130 million on graduate training and laboratory construction in their Sustaining University Program.[12]

Importantly, this educational training also mirrored the systemic racism embedded within so much of federal spending. The need for a local, educated workforce at the Marshall Spaceflight Center led to the construction of the University of Alabama at Huntsville, which was essentially built with NASA money. Likewise, NASA constructed the $60 million Manned Spacecraft Center in Houston, Texas, beginning in 1961. Twenty-nine contractors followed NASA to Houston, and by 1965, the city led the Southwest in population and manufacturing payroll.[13] These jobs disproportionately benefited white engineers. Of the 11,447 science and engineering jobs in Houston in 1970, only 427 went to black workers. Furthermore, NASA destroyed the African American town of Allenhurst, Florida, founded in 1872 by former slaves, to build the Vehicle Assembly Building near the launch pad at Cape Canaveral (Paul and Moss 245, 32–41).

When Scott-Heron called out the spending disparities between the maintenance of black communities and the space race, he did not direct his rhetorical aim at Neil Armstrong and Buzz Aldrin as individuals. He directed listeners' attention to the injustices revealed by a government that invested in a space program that spurred the economic growth of Sunbelt cities and paid for the educations of predominantly white engineers. Meanwhile, the nation's poor, black urban tenants felt the pinch of $50 a week rent and battled the living conditions that belied the national narrative of technological triumph over the Soviets in the race to the moon. In this way, Scott-Heron's piece had less to do with who was winning the space race and more to do with who was winning the race to leave US cities for the clean, segregated spaces of the government-subsidized, suburbanizing Sunbelt.

This focus on government spending continued on Scott-Heron and Jackson's 1975 release *From South Africa to South Carolina*. As the title suggests, Scott-Heron made pan-African connections between the struggle against apartheid in Johannesburg and the ongoing fight for racial equality in the United States, adding a transnational node connected to the rhizomatic South. And once again, he linked environmental racism and the military-industrial complex, this time on the track "South Carolina (Barnwell)." Finger snaps and a djembe introduce the tune, followed by piano, bass, drums, and guitar. Scott-Heron's voice, a weathered, subtle baritone, delivers the first lines as though he is confiding a secret.

> I heard they're building a factory down in South Carolina
> With a death potential that's uncontrolled by government designers

That would house atomic waste and be a constant reminder
That they got a great big time bomb tickin' in South Carolina.

He then launches into a series of four rhetorical questions in the chorus
that criticize the apparent apathy of New Left activists after the end of the
Vietnam War. The New Left's coalition of civil rights and antiwar activists had
helped gain major victories for the black freedom struggle and the student
movement during the 1960s and early 1970s. However, Scott-Heron called
out this generation of activists, as many of them slipped into the comfort of
middle-age stability in a post-Vietnam America. "Said whatever happened to
the protests and the rage?" he asks, joined by a backing vocalist.

Whatever happened to the voices of the sane?
Whatever happened to the people who gave a damn?
Did that just apply to dyin' in the jungles of Vietnam?

With this song, Scott-Heron sounded an alarm regarding the threatening
presence of nuclear waste in South Carolina and offered a chance to consider
another way the rhizomatic South connected to Cold War defense spending.
South Carolina held a long history with atomic energy that dated back nearly
twenty-five years by the time the poet released this track. In the early 1950s,
the Atomic Energy Commission (AEC) began construction near Aiken, South
Carolina, on the Savannah River Plant (SRP), a three-hundred-square-mile facility that housed five nuclear reactors, making it the largest federal construction project in history. Although it was technically owned by the AEC, the Du
Pont Corporation conducted the day-to-day operations at the SRP, which initiated production in 1955, manufacturing materials like plutonium and tritium
for the hydrogen bomb.[14] The construction of the "bomb plant," as locals called
the SRP, made an enormous impact on the region's environment even before
it began its weapons production, as the AEC appropriated farmland, displaced
6,000 citizens, and literally destroyed entire towns like Dunbarton and Ellen-
ton. In exchange, this corner of South Carolina received an influx of high-tech
workers, a boost in infrastructure investment, and, at the peak of Cold War
militarism, 25,000 jobs for the region's men and women.[15]

Scott-Heron's song could do little to stymie the militarization represented
by the SRP, but he did alert listeners to the threat of nuclear industries trying
to expand in South Carolina in the mid-1970s. The "factory" to which he re-

ferred was a $360 million (1977 dollars) facility called the Barnwell Nuclear Fuels Plant (BNFP), which broke ground in 1971 to extract reusable uranium from high-level nuclear waste.[16] Allied-General Nuclear Services (AGNS), a joint venture of Allied Chemical Corporation and General Atomic Corporation, owned the plant and planned to join the SRP in nuclear production. But before the BNFP could gain government approval to begin operations, President Jimmy Carter issued a halt to all commercial nuclear waste reprocessing operations on April 7, 1977, in the face of concerns regarding nuclear weapons proliferation. Carter's decision sidelined the BNFP and left AGNS with an idle plant.[17]

AGNS received seemingly good news with the election of Ronald Reagan, whose promises of rejuvenated defense spending boded well for nuclear industries, but the company faced stiff opposition on the ground. While the new president declined to grant government funding to the BNFP, AGNS remained hopeful that the new administration's vows of deregulation would kick-start its business in South Carolina. In 1981, Reagan stated how the Department of Energy "should consult with industry to determine which regulatory barriers are of greatest concern to it and . . . should develop recommendations for my further review on how to create a more favorable climate for private reprocessing efforts." Still, activists in the antinuclear group Palmetto Alliance, along with the Southeastern Natural Guard Coalition, the Sierra Club, and the South Carolina League of Women Voters effectively pushed back against private nuclear waste reprocessing in the state. The Palmetto Alliance, for instance, had staged two protests of civil disobedience in 1978 and 1979 that each drew crowds of about 2,000 people. The 1979 rally included civil rights veteran Modjeska Simkins and a brief concert in a soybean field by Graham Nash,[18] fresh off the "No Nukes" concert at Madison Square Garden, where Scott-Heron had also performed.[19] On a superficial level, a soybean field in South Carolina was a long way from Madison Square Garden. Yet the rhizomatic connections among local protests, celebrity activism, Cold War militarism, and popular music shrunk that distance, and Scott-Heron's music created a way to see all of these pieces as nodes in the same network.

The nuclear armament and waste disposal protested by Scott-Heron also met with legislative resistance. Harriet Keyserling, a representative in South Carolina's State House, fought against the BNFP during her entire sixteen-year political career. In 1982, she stood up to both AGNS and the Reagan administration when the president floated the idea of accepting nuclear waste from West Germany and Japan for commercial reprocessing in Barnwell.[20] In the mid-1990s, Keyserling fought the nuclear industries by joining with the League of Women Voters, the Sierra Club, the South Carolina Wildlife Federation, and the Energy Research Foundation to maintain environmental regulations at the SRP, which had changed its name to the Savannah River Site when Westinghouse took over operations in 1989.[21] She also joined with these watchdog groups to sue South Carolina governor David Beasley in an attempt to stop the use of an unlined, 235-acre underground nuclear dump in Barnwell County, which housed and continues to hold nearly 90 percent of the nation's low-level nuclear waste (Brook).

The Chem-Nuclear Corporation had operated the Barnwell dump since it had opened in 1971, and residents of the nearby town of Snelling, South Carolina, expressed differing views on the presence of the facility. By the late 1990s, Tim Moore, who had served as Snelling's mayor since 1969 and whose cousin had sold the land to Chem-Nuclear, was bragging that the town earned $44,000 a year in taxes from the company. He did not fear the long-term storage of nuclear waste on the property but welcomed it, suggesting that, at least for some local residents, the Barnwell facility represented the opposite of the Not In My Backyard movement that characterized local environmental activism in the 1980s and 1990s. But not everyone shared his optimistic vision. Rev. John Young, pastor of the African American congregation at St. Paul Missionary Baptist Church, located just outside the gates of the dump, expressed a different opinion. He worried about his church's proximity to the facility. At one Wednesday night Bible study in October 1999, Reverend Young led his congregation in prayer: "We pray that you would take this situation and make something good come out of it." With the entire community on well water, prayers were certainly in order (Graves 1-A, 8-A). Environmental scientists first detected leakage from this dump in 1978, a problem that has continued ever since as measured by the constant presence of tritium in the Savannah River, a source of drinking water for communities all the way from Augusta, Georgia, to Hilton Head, South Carolina.[22] When Scott-Heron noted that there was a "time bomb tickin' in South Carolina" back in 1975, he likely imagined a single explosion or meltdown. However, the threat appears to be less in the form of one catastrophic blast and more of long-term, insidious pollution whose effects may take generations to assess.[23] Regardless of when or how quickly this poison travels, Scott-Heron's work reminded listeners of an essential point: the fight against such toxicity implicated the South's and indeed the nation's political and economic power structures in the environmental degradation of its communities.

Juxtaposing the achievements of the space program, defense contractor profitability, and nuclear energy with the poverty and pollution experienced by African Americans, Scott-Heron implicitly and explicitly linked the military-industrial complex to the environmental racism experienced in the geographic and rhizomatic Souths. On his last album from 2010, released just a few months before his death, Scott-Heron recorded a tune called "New York City Is Killing Me." He sings,

> The doctor don't know that New York is killing me
> Bunch of doctors come around, they don't know that New York is killing me
> Yeah, well, I need to go home and take it slow in Jackson, Tennessee.

Nostalgia and regret color Scott-Heron's voice as he sings, "Let me tell you that city livin' ain't all it's cracked up to be / Yeah see I need to go and slow down in Jackson, Tennessee." Scott-Heron would never make it back to Jackson. That place and that time were gone, paved over to connect Jackson with the interstate highway. What is clear is that wherever he went in body or in song—to Jackson, Tennessee; New York City; or Barnwell County, South Carolina—the warfare state was already there, delivering toxicity of all kinds to black homes around the nation with the full, legal authority of the federal government.

NOTES

1. See Moynihan; Rainwater and Yancey; Greenbaum.

2. See *A Dictionary of Plant Sciences* on the definition of rhizomes.

3. Deleuze and Guattari 3–25.

4. On the legacy of Scott-Heron, see Tate 149–52; Baram 234–75; Hamilton 113–26; Werner 158–60; Ramsey 165; Wilkinson; Litwack 3–28.

5. In his autobiography, Scott-Heron refers to "a four-lane highway coming through from the south that would connect to Interstate 70," which destroyed his neighborhood. While I-70 does not go through Jackson, US Highway 70 does, as does I-40. It appears that he meant US 70 connecting to I-40, although my point and his remain the same. See Scott-Heron 53.

6. Baram 30–38, 62–68.

7. See Sparrow, especially 19–47.

8. Schulman 89–90, 97; Cook.

9. Sugrue 404–5.

10. McLaughlin 541–61; Biehler 168–69.

11. "'Starve A Rat Today'" 4.

12. Lanius 68–69.

13. Schulman 148, 149.

14. Frederickson 1.

15. Ibid., 50–74, 6; "Bad News, Big Worries."

16. Kearney.

17. "Barnwell Nuclear Fuel Plant—Its Role in the Nuclear Fuel Cycle"; "Bad News, Big Worries."

18. "Barnwell: It's Your Backyard"; "Come to Barnwell."

19. Grein 4, 78.

20. Keyserling Press Release.

21. Keyserling 174–93.

22. Fretwell.

23. See Nixon, particularly 150–74.

WORKS CITED

"Bad News, Big Worries." *The Columbia Record* and *The State,* 30 April 1980, 18, Box 18, Mary Kelly Papers, South Carolina Political Collections, University of South Carolina.

Baram, Marcus. *Gil Scott-Heron: Pieces of a Man.* St. Martin's Press, 2014.

"Barnwell: It's Your Backyard," Palmetto Alliance booklet, Box 6, Mary Kelly Papers, South Carolina Political Collections, University of South Carolina.

"Barnwell Nuclear Fuel Plant—Its Role in the Nuclear Fuel Cycle," Allied-General memorandum, Box 6, Mary Kelly Papers, South Carolina Political Collections, University of South Carolina.

Biehler, Dawn Day. *Pest in the City: Flies, Bedbugs, Cockroaches, and Rats.* U of Washington P, 2013.

Brook, Nina. "Barnwell 'bobtailing' suit planned." *The State,* 6 Sept. 1995, Box 14, The Harriet Keyserling Papers, South Carolina Political Collections, University of South Carolina.

"Come to Barnwell" flyer, Box 24, Records of the Palmetto Alliance, Inc. (Columbia, SC), South Caroliniana Library, University of South Carolina.

Cook, James F. *Carl Vinson: Patriarch of the Armed Forces.* Mercer UP, 2004.

Deleuze, Gilles, and Félix Guattari. *A Thousand Plateaus: Capitalism and Schizophrenia.* Translated with a foreword by Brian Massumi, U of Minnesota P, 1987.

Field, Kendra T. "'No Such Thing as Stand Still': Migration and Geopolitics in African-American History." *Journal of American History,* vol. 102, no. 3, 2015, pp. 693–718.

Frederickson, Kari. *Cold War Dixie: Militarization and Modernization in the American South.* U of Georgia P, 2013.

Fretwell, Sammy. "SC Gov. Haley opposes reopening Barnwell nuclear waste site to more states." *The State,* 19 March 2015, http://www.thestate.com/news/local/article15509438.html. Accessed 22 Oct. 2016.

Graves, Rachel. "Company Town: Most unafraid of Barnwell County dump site." *The Post and Courier,* 31 Oct. 1999, pp. 1-A, 8-A, Box 6, Mary Kelly Papers, South Carolina Political Collections, University of South Carolina.

Grein, Paul. "Risky Album, Elektra/Asylum Put On Spot With 'No Nukes' LP Advance." *Billboard,* 24 Nov. 1979, pp. 4, 78.

Greenbaum, Susan D. *Blaming the Poor: The Long Shadow of the Moynihan Report on Cruel Images About Poverty.* Rutgers UP, 2014.

Hamilton, Jack. "Pieces of a Man." *Transition,* no. 106, 2011, pp. 113–26.

Harold, Claudrena N. "Deep in the Cane: The Southern Soul of Gil Scott-Heron." *Southern Spaces,* 12 July 2011, https://southernspaces.org/2011/deep-cane-southern-soul-gil-scott-heron. Accessed 28 Sept. 2016.

Kearney, Richard C. "Nuclear Fuel Reprocessing and the Barnwell Nuclear Fuels Plant." *Public Affairs Bulletin,* April 1981, Box 6, Mary Kelly Papers, South Carolina Political Collections, University of South Carolina.

Keyserling, Harriet. *Against the Tide: One Woman's Political Struggle.* U of South Carolina P, 1998.

———. Press Release, 12 Aug. 1982, Box 14, The Harriet Keyserling Papers, South Carolina Political Collections, University of South Carolina.

Lanius, Roger. *NASA: A History of the U.S. Civil Space Program.* Krieger Publishing Co., 1994.

Litwack, Leon. "'Fight the Power!': The Legacy of the Civil Rights Movement." *The Journal of Southern History,* vol. 75, no. 1, 2009, pp. 3–28.

Matthews, Leslie. "Crime In Harlem Gives 'Tobacco Road' Image." *New York Amsterdam News,* 29 Aug. 1970, p. 1.

McLaughlin, Malcolm. "The Pied Piper of the Ghetto: Lyndon Johnson, Environmental Justice, and the Politics of Rat Control." *Journal of Urban History,* vol. 37, no. 4, 2011, pp. 541–61.

Moynihan, Daniel Patrick. *The Negro Family: The Case for National Action.* Office of Policy Planning and Research, United States Department of Labor, 1965.

Nixon, Rob. *Slow Violence and the Environmentalism of the Poor.* Harvard UP, 2011.

Paul, Richard, and Steven Moss. *We Could Not Fail: The First African Americans in the Space Program.* U of Texas P, 2015.

Rainwater, Lee, and William L. Yancey. *The Moynihan Report and the Politics of Controversy.* MIT Press, 1967.

Ramsey, Guthrie P., Jr. *Race Music: Black Cultures from Bebop to Hip-Hop.* U of California P, 2003.

Reagan, Ronald. "Memorandum for the Secretary of Energy: Decisions on Department of Energy Budget Appeal," 20 March 1981, Box 14, The Harriet Keyserling Papers, South Carolina Political Collections, University of South Carolina.

"Rhizome." *A Dictionary of Plant Sciences,* 3rd ed., 2012.

Schulman, Bruce J. *From Cotton Belt to Sunbelt: Federal Policy, Economic Development, and the Transformation of the South, 1938–1910*. Oxford UP, 1991.

Scott-Heron, Gil. "Coming from a Broken Home." *Now and Then: The Poems of Gil Scott-Heron*. Payback Press, 2000, p. 1.

———. "Home is Where the Hatred Is." *Pieces of a Man*, Flying Dutchman Records, 1971.

———. *The Last Holiday: A Memoir*. Grove Press, 2012.

———. "The Revolution Will Not Be Televised." *Small Talk at 125th and Lenox*, Flying Dutchman Records, 1970.

———. "Whitey's on the Moon." *Small Talk at 125th and Lenox*, Flying Dutchman Records, 1970.

Scott-Heron, Gil, and Brian Jackson. "South Carolina (Barnwell)." *From South Africa to South Carolina*, Arista Records, 1975.

Sparrow, James T. *Warfare State: World War II and the Age of Big Government*. Oxford UP, 2011.

Sugrue, Thomas J. *Sweet Land of Liberty: The Forgotten Struggle for Civil Rights in the North*. Random House, 2008.

Tate, Greg. "Gil Scott-Heron." *Flyboy 2: The Greg Tate Reader*. Duke University Press, 2016.

Werner, Craig. *A Change is Gonna Come: Music, Race, and the Soul of America*, revised and updated. U of Michigan P, 2006.

Wilkinson, Alec. "New York is Killing Me: The unlikely survival of Gil Scott-Heron." *The New Yorker*, 9 July 2010, http://www.newyorker.com/magazine/2010/08/09/new-york-is-killing-me. Accessed 10 Oct. 2016.

III

FARMING
& FOODWAYS

Faulkner's Ecologies and the Legacy of the Nashville Agrarians

SAM HORROCKS

Though J. Hector St. Jean de Crèvecoeur's celebration of the "Situation, Feelings, and Pleasures" of an American farmer marks the genesis of the robust and enduring literary tradition of agrarian sociopolitical thought in the United States, his *Letters from an American Farmer* (1782) is, like the tradition itself, haunted by the specter of slavery and racism. The problem was canonized within the literary establishment with the 1930 publication of *I'll Take My Stand,* an agrarian manifesto collecting essays by "Twelve Southerners" known as the Southern, or Nashville, Agrarians.[1] The collection provides a biting critique of the effects of industrialization on rural communities, but largely elides the complex history of racial subjugation entwined with southern agriculture and often reveals a simplistic nostalgia for Confederate values imbued with racial injustice. Thus, while the American agrarian tradition today thrives both economically and intellectually as expressed in recent movements toward local, sustainable food networks, agrarianism is still regarded with a measure of skepticism within the literary-critical establishment despite its apparent relevance to the recent turn to environmental criticism. Indeed, the ecocritical response to the Nashville group—who performed extensive and explicit literary-critical plumbing of the nexus of nature and culture decades before the term *ecocriticism* was coined—has largely been to ignore them.[2] This is limiting, because the full breadth of the agrarian tradition offers animated and apposite critique of the ways globalizing industrial processes entail negative relationships between humans and their environments. And, perhaps more importantly, the agrarian tradition provides a radically responsive economic program for extricating ourselves from those damaging relationships, which is sorely lacking in mainstream ecocriticism. Unfortunately, Wendell Berry's decades-old refrain that environmentalism "has no economic program, and [thus] has the status of something exterior to daily life," still rings true: ecocriticism's activist intent and promise continue to be stymied by a reluctance to theorize the economic changes necessary to foster ecological health (77).

This essay will reexamine the legacy of race in the agrarian tradition by turning to a contemporary of the Nashville Agrarians whose treatment of race, rurality, agriculture, and modernity has occasioned overwhelming critical praise rather than reproof: William Faulkner. By transcending the Nashville Agrarians' narrow polemics in expansive narrative surveys of an entire southern landscape, Faulkner reveals that the difference between agrarianism and industrialism is more than merely ideological, but also at its core *ecological*. Through the dramatization of settings spanning the continuum between industrial and agrarian ecologies, Faulkner's fiction exposes the fundamental flaw in the nostalgic Nashville argument: plantation (agri)culture in the South, and its racist social legacy, is the antithesis of agrarian ecological interaction, rather than its fullest expression. Agrarian ecologies feature flows of energy that build and conserve the health of all beings comprising the land, whereas the plantation ecologies lauded by many of the Nashville group entail the extraction of energy at the expense of human and environmental health for the sake of profit. As such, plantation landscapes more accurately feature characteristics of industrial ecologies, such as racist ideologies rationalizing the exploitation of people and land. Faulkner's novels both demonstrate this connection between racism and industrial plantation ecologies and display the disruption of racist interactions in the more truly agrarian ecologies he narrativizes. After highlighting this dynamic in readings of *Absalom, Absalom!* (1936) and *Flags in the Dust* (1927), I will turn to *Go Down, Moses* (1942) to explore how a renewed agrarian vision can effect positive change within both ecocritical scholarship and today's global landscape of environmental racism and injustice.

It is remarkable how little the early twentieth-century South's premier novelist had to do with the literary renaissance occurring just a few hours north of Oxford in Nashville. While the Nashville group viewed themselves as a literary cohort solidifying a distinct southern response to the global modernist landscape, Faulkner was, so he would say, "not really a literary man" but more "a farmer, a country man [who] like[s] to write" (qtd. in Meriwether 191). Allen Tate, annoyed by these georgic pretensions and Faulkner's social standoffishness, said plainly that Faulkner was "a man I did not like," though he, with the vast majority of the Nashville group, greatly admired Faulkner's writings; Cleanth Brooks stated that the group, "from a very early date, were aware of, and on record about, Faulkner's promise and his genius" (Watkins 106, Brooks 26). Faulkner, on the other hand, preferred to live and work in his native Oxford community rather than the cosmopolitan university circles of the Nashville Agrarians, and he showed little interest in either their literary or critical output. But despite these personal differences, Faulkner and the Nashville Agrarians shared much the same agrarian philosophical foundations: namely, a belief in the moral worth of a life spent farming the land.

The central thrust of *I'll Take My Stand* posits the dominant American ideology of capitalist industrialism as a distortion of the "right" relationship between humanity and nature.[3] This occurs as property and the means of production are amassed into fewer hands, changing former proprietors into modern employees. This shift generates an alienating layer of corporate bureaucracy between the individual and the land that sustains it and creates concentrated profit by spreading general poverty under the guise of a "progress" that is in fact merely increased consumption. Centrally, this poverty is not only economic but psychological and spiritual, too, as "nature industrialized, transformed into cities and artificial habitations, manufactured into commodities, is no longer nature but a highly simplified picture of nature. We receive the illusion of having power over nature, and lose the sense of nature as something mysterious and contingent" (xlii). Thus, industrialism is not only "the economic organization of the collective American society" but also its modern "gospel": a hegemonic, self-fulfilling paradigm that permits recognition only of further industrialization as a cure for the ills it creates. Against this industrial ideology, *I'll Take My Stand* advocates an "agrarian" one, which posits "the culture of the soil" to be the "best and most sensitive of vocations, and [suggests] that therefore it should have the economic preference and enlist the maximum number of workers" (xlvii).

Most would agree that Faulkner, in statements both in his fiction and without, appears to largely agree with the basic tenets of this resistance to modernity, though his mode of expression is never so didactic. In the words of Floyd Watkins, Faulkner and the Nashville Agrarians tend to "philosophically like the same things: a close relationship to the land and nature, the historical and the traditional, farming, the rural, the South, individualism and small communities, labor . . . and a simple religion" (53). Brooks goes a step further, arguing that "for all their differences in forms, tonalities, and specific subject matters, [Faulkner and the Nashville Agrarians] differed very little in their devotion to their native region and what they have to say about it in praise and in reproof" (39). Though the remainder of this essay will assert a major difference of "praise and reproof," I concur that the core of Faulkner's agreement with the Nashville Agrarians is that "devotion" to his "native region": the deep and abiding love for the ecology—animal, plant, human, soil, water, and wind—of northern Mississippi that remains among the most commented-upon characteristics of his writing and his worldview. Faulkner refers to the South as "the only really authentic region in the United States, because a deep indestructible bond still exists between man and his environment"; for Faulkner, as for the Nashville group and indeed all agrarian thinkers, the essence, the shape of this inevitable bond reflects all other ties within the total ecology of a given landscape (qtd in Meriwether 72).

The source of the apologies for slavery and other racist positions found in many of the essays comprising *I'll Take My Stand* is a failure to discern key differences between the ecological characteristics of plantation and yeoman agriculture. Indeed, the Nashville Agrarians often conflate the two systems. Frank Lawrence Owsley displays this assumption most succinctly in his presentation of the southern historical narrative that Paul Conkin asserts to be "accepted by all the contributors" of *I'll Take My Stand* (81). Owsley writes,

> the system of society which developed in the South, then, was close to the soil. It might be organized about the plantation with its wide fields and its slaves and self-sufficiency, or it might center around a small farm . . . tilled by the owner, undriven by competition, supplied with corn by its own toil and with meat from his own pen. . . . It might be crude or genteel, but it everywhere was fundamentally alike and natural. (72–73)

But plantations and agrarian farms are *not* fundamentally alike, differing in their economics, social relations, politics, environmental engagement, and even logics.[4] In short, their entire ecology, the broader network of all these systemic relations, is different. The Nashville Agrarian who grasps this most firmly is Andrew Lytle, whose "The Hind Tit" describes the traditional agrarian ideal of an economic ecology organized around the workings of various small, owner-operated, agriculturally diversified farmsteads that rely on a family-based workforce and a simple local market for small trade. A preponderance of such small farmsteads is the key to the American agrarian ideal, because the personal responsibility and management of a farm provides a constant reminder of the entwined fates of humanity and land that facilitates an active respect for both. This is recognized from Crèvecoeur and Thomas Jefferson (whose own troubled legacy of agrarianism and race looms large in Faulkner's Yoknapatawpha County) to modern agrarian thinkers. In the introduction to his essay collection *The New Agrarianism: Land, Culture, and the Community of Life* (2001), editor Eric Freyfogle writes that agrarianism "is moral orientation as well as a suite of economic practices, all arising out of the insistent truth that people everywhere are part of the land community, just as dependent as other life on the land's fertility. . . . From this recognition of interconnected life comes an overriding attentiveness to the health of the land" (xiii, xix). This entwined ethical and economic "attentiveness" generates the sustainable and just biological relationships that comprise an agrarian ecology. To an agrarian mind—as defined, for instance, by Freyfogle—the exploitation of chattel slavery would be as ethically reprehensible as abusing the land to which one's own well-being is concomitant.

By contrast, the plantation society celebrated by Nashville Agrarians like Owsley relies on precisely such abuse and requires not an agrarian but an industrial ecology, or an ecosystem in which the network of actant relations has been reordered to suit the logic and goals of industrialism. Like the farms comprising most of our agricultural system today, southern plantations were monocultural and profit-driven, depending entirely on both an industrialized global market for processing and sale of goods and a vast exploited workforce for labor. Ironically, plantation agriculture is the foundation upon which rests the entire industrial program that the Nashville "Agrarians" disdain. It is only by appropriating the virtues of slaveless, small-scale agrarian ecologies that Owsley can arrive at the troublesome conclusion that "slavery . . . was part of the agrarian system, but only one element and not an essential one," and other contributors can continually invoke his claim that "the irrepressible conflict" leading to the Civil War "was not between slavery and freedom, but between the industrial and commercial civilization of the North and the agrarian civilization of the South" (73–74). But small, agrarian family farms abounded on both sides of the antebellum Mason-Dixon, as did industry: mechanical in the North and agricultural in the South. Thus, the Nashville Agrarians mistake the South's embedded racial subjugation as an aspect of its agrarian tradition, rather than as a symptom of the South's societal aberration from the agrarian ideal, which was ironically more widely realized in the less-Confederate upland South and rural North before the war.

Faulkner, however, harbors no such illusions, and rather than eliding or apologizing for the South's racial injustices, he delves directly into their horrors and causes. Robert Penn Warren, the Nashville Agrarian who most redeemed his earlier segregationist views, writes that Faulkner's work "undercuts the official history and mythology" of the South that the Nashville Agrarians perpetuate by demonstrating that an individual's status as "Negro . . . is such by social definition and not by blood" (259). Warren argues that this truth arises within Faulkner's work from his very agrarian presumptions. For Faulkner, racist cultural structures derive from the same basic flaw of industrial use of land as do many other modern ills. As Warren explains, "the rejection of the brother, the kinsman, [is] a symbolic representation of the crime that is the final crime against both nature and the human community": "the sin against reality, the sin of abstraction, the lack of reverence for nature that permits one to manipulate and violate it" (262, 253). In Warren's words, Faulkner's work reveals that "the right attitude toward nature and man is love. And love is the opposite of the lust for power over nature or over other men" (51). The remainder of this essay will explore, first in Faulkner's fiction and then in our present world, where we can locate that "right attitude toward nature."

Thomas Sutpen is one of Yoknapatawpha County's most villainous inhabitants, the man whose sins against humanity, nature, and God curse the land and all relationships springing from it for generations. Though not the only cruel slave owner in Faulkner's fiction, Sutpen casts the longest shadow, his actions assuming near-biblical proportions as traced in *Absalom, Absalom!* Sutpen's chronicle thus presents the closest Faulkner comes to a defined spiritual and economic indictment of the character of southern agricultural society itself, one which depicts the sins of slavery as originating in the improper industrial relationship to land.

Sutpen is born in what is now West Virginia in 1807, the upland frontier of Jefferson's commonwealth geographically ill-suited to plantation agriculture. Sutpen's early experiences are of hunting and gardening within an agrarian social ecology in which "the land belonged to anybody and everybody and so the man who would go to the trouble and work to fence off a piece of it and say 'This is mine' was crazy" (220). Sutpen's economic lifestyle accords to an agrarian logic in which human and nonhuman communities exist equally in the same ecological mesh, with each individual being vying for survival through energy, violence, and luck. The concept of ownership is foreign to Sutpen; his family cannot comprehend "the vague and cloudy tales of Tidewater splendor that penetrated even his mountains," because "only a crazy man would go through the trouble to take or even want more than he could eat or swap for powder and whiskey" (221). Though Quentin's prelapsarian description of Sutpen's West Virginia is less historical reality than a conjured agrarian ideal—Sutpen's West Virginia is as foreign to Quentin as the Tidewater was to Sutpen—its emphasis on the issue of ownership highlights the way social mores accord to ecological-economic relationships. Just as the description of Eden in Genesis lasts only a few short verses, so the family quickly "tumbled head over heels back to Tidewater by sheer altitude, elevation and gravity, as if whatever slight hold the family had had on the mountain had broken" (222). Entering the Tidewater, Sutpen's family relinquishes "whatever slight hold" they had on the land, opening up the possibility of new social relationships unmoored from firm ecological attachment.

Sutpen's "fall" into Virginia's industrial Tidewater emphasizes the total difference between that place and his mountain home, a difference not only of geography and economy but of ecological logic itself. The classless ideology into which he was born precludes an understanding of a society in which the class and racial distinctions required by plantation agriculture shape the entire ecology of a "country flattened out now with good roads and fields and niggers working in the fields while white men sat fine horses and watched them" perform drudging labor "brutish and stupidly out of all proportion to its reward: the very primary essence of labor, toil, reduced to its crude absolute" (225, 236). Labor has no purpose within the Tidewater for those who perform it. This separation of the act of labor from its results is the essence of the industrial relationship, and sustaining that separation requires a division between classes and races. "You knew that you could hit [black individuals, Sutpen] told Grandfather, and they would not hit back or even resist. But you did not want to, because they (the niggers) were not it, not what you wanted to hit" (230). What Sutpen wanted to hit were the attitudes of hate and resentment toward land, nonhumans, and humans that sustained the industrial Tidewater ecology. But the very logic of that system prevents that recognition, and Sutpen's Tidewater experience instead culminates in an ontological "explosion" (238). "To combat them," Sutpen discovers within the industrial idea, "you have got to have what they have that made them do what the man did. You got to have land and niggers and a fine house to combat them with" (238). As the Nashville Agrarians articulate, industrial ecology is enmeshed with a modern system of logic that engenders and sustains it, and permits no alternative. Sutpen's explosive realization is a total ontological revision, a loss of the logic of his agrarian origins and an acceptance, instead, of the industrial ideology. Within that logic, there is only one path to success: material accumulation in the capitalist model, a path that requires the subjugation of land and people.

The only thing that can break the strong historical cords of industrial ecology is fostering new relationships not merely with other humans, but to the land as well. *Absalom, Absalom!* is full of characters who attempt to break the cycle of resentment through empathetic appeals to their human compatriots—Miss Coldfield being the clearest example—yet the entrenched industrial logic of strict classist and racist divisions blocks their efforts. This situation can only be altered through a fundamental change to the underlying ecological operations of the Sutpen plantation, and the only force large enough to effect such a disruption in the novel is the Civil War. Sutpen and his slaves are then absent, and the financial ties that enable the plantation's normal industrial operations are interrupted. This leaves "Judith and Clytie making and keeping a kitchen garden of sorts to keep them alive" (124). All members of the household must now participate in ecological interactions such as "plowing corn and cutting winter wood" that the antebellum plantation economy relegated along class and racial lines (125). And social changes accompany these shifts in ecological-economic relations. Wash Jones, "who until Sutpen went away, had never approached nearer than the scuppernong arbor behind the kitchen," is permitted to "even enter the house now" (125). Judith, Clytie, Rosa, and Wash

> grew and tended and harvested with [their] own hands the food [they] ate, made and worked that garden just as [they] cooked and ate the food which came out of it: with no distinction among the three of [them] of age or color but just as to who could build this fire or stir this pot or weed this bed or carry this apron full of corn to the mill for meal with least cost to the general good in time or expense of other duties. It was as though [they] were one being, interchangeable and indiscriminate, which kept that garden growing, spun thread and wove the cloth [they] wore. (155)

Since in the course of the shared labor of this wartime existence "flesh [must] touch with flesh," so it requires "the fall of all the eggshell shibboleth of caste and color too" (139). This new agrarian ecology engenders, in reverse order to Sutpen's fall, a reapprehension of the nonindustrial ontology he left in the mountains. Georgic labor reveals the essential connection between human and land, between Judith and Clytie and the plants that make them and the soil that builds the plants and the sun that warms the soil. Direct activity in this entire process—rather than the compartmentalization required by industrialism, with some merely consuming while others live merely to perform the most drudging tasks of production—inculcates apprehension of the "one being, interchangeable and indiscriminate" of race, class, human, or nonhuman status, that comprises the energetic pulse of the earth. The war years are no Edenic paradise, just as Sutpen's life in West Virginia was not—agrarian ecologies do not allow much time for human indolence or luxury—yet it is relatively lacking in the racist and classist resentment fostered by the plantation system. But when Sutpen returns, he does "not even pause for breath before undertaking to restore his house and plantation as near as possible to what it had been," and thus industrial ecology reemerges, rendered only slightly less extreme by the shift from slavery to sharecropping, and, as a result, the cycle of racial and class-based resentment continues (160).

However, elsewhere in his fiction, Faulkner depicts characters able to sustain agrarian ecologies over longer periods of time. M. E. Bradford, a student of the Nashville Agrarian Donald Davidson, recenters Faulkner's world on the yeoman farmer rather than the planter, claiming that "no group of characters in the Yoknapatawpha Cycle offers more insight into the human qualities which Faulkner most admires than do his yeoman farmers" (29). The most notable of these is the MacCallum clan, who feature prominently in Faulkner's first foray into Yoknapatawpha County, *Flags in the Dust*. The novel surveys the region's ecology across a continuum of industrial to agrarian landscapes: from plantation to town, sharecropping farm to independent homestead. Representing the latter setting, the MacCallums inhabit the land of "smaller croppers with their tilted fields among the hills" northeast of Jefferson (288). They own their own land, raise crops, hunt for their own consumption and small trade, and measure value less in transferability and more in use, because their daily economy resides more directly with the processes that sustain it. Whereas the Sartorises of *Flags in the Dust* exist in a "cage" of "civilized" customs, the economic lifestyle of the MacCallums appears to be little separated from their environment (71). And this agrarian ecology, entailing as it does continual and substantive interaction and interdependency, extends to respect for fellow humans. Though Bradford's focus on the yeoman allows him to elide issues of race in the South, it is important to note that the MacCallums and other yeomen farmers of Yoknapatawpha do not own slaves before the war and employ no exploited tenants afterward precisely because those exploitative relationships are not consistent with their agrarian economic ecology.[5]

That Faulkner chose the hilly upland to the northeast of Oxford as the site of his own Greenfield Farm, which he bought in 1938, suggests perhaps best his approval of the area's economic ecology. Managed primarily by his brother and worked by African American tenant laborers, the farm was relatively diversified, raising corn, cotton, hogs, horses, and, most importantly to Faulkner, mules, which at the time represented resistance to encroaching agricultural mechanization (Fargnoli 399). Mules, he writes in *Flags in the Dust*, remain "more than any other one creature or thing . . . steadfast to the land when all else falter[s]," a statement perhaps that reveals Faulkner's own (agri) cultural goals, given that his farm rarely turned a profit and yet was noted for its good treatment of tenants and the land (*Flags* 289, Fargnoli 399).

Though the legacy of the Sutpens and the example of the MacCallums suggest that nonindustrial, agrarian ecologies actively resist racist attitudes and violence, they do not address whether there is any conceivable way to enact the more egalitarian ecological ontologies of agrarian life within the confines of a space laden with the legacy of racial hatred perpetuated by industrialism. This reflects one of ecocriticism's most pressing questions: How can an individual or community economically practice a biocentric ethic? What would such an economy look like? Unfortunately, this question has been largely neglected by ecocriticism, first in a reverence for a wilderness divorced from economic concerns, and more recently in calls for environmental justice that privilege the representation of problems over envisioning solutions, which it is too often assumed will come through the reforms of intrinsically industrial institutions.[6] Ecocritical treatments of Faulkner reflect this problem, in that they tend to focus narrowly on the wilderness retreats of *Go Down, Moses,* at the expense of the plantation and town ecologies much more prevalent in and economically important to both that novel and to the rest of Faulkner's world.[7] A large part of this problem is due to the literary-critical skepticism of the very term *agrarianism* in the wake of the Nashville group. The MacCallums are as neglected in ecocritical treatments of Faulkner as agriculture is in ecocriticism more broadly, despite the profound influence of agrarian thinking both in Faulkner's South and in our current environmentalist movement.

Yet ecocriticism cannot merely pivot to the wholesale endorsement of some agrarian ideal. While the MacCallums succeed in living a good life relatively free of racist social structures and actions, they are able to do so only by isolating themselves from broader human society. Regardless, the majority of us today cannot simply become yeoman farmers, for, as in the days of Faulkner and the Nashville Agrarians, the very structure of industrial economics resists such a possibility. Faulkner's fiction does not linger in the agrarian MacCallum place, because even at the beginning of his writing career that way of life was already disappearing. More relevant to the American experience then and now are Faulkner's industrial settings of town and plantation, where residents are forced to grapple with the legacy of slavery in the face of a new hyperindustrial age. Faulkner's greatest artistic interrogation of the racial legacy of southern agriculture, *Go Down, Moses,* deals directly with this problem, depicting multiple generations of the McCaslin family attempting ethical action, while—like the vast majority of Americans today—already being implicated in slavery or its ongoing legacy.

As Granville Hicks puts it, Buck and Buddy McCaslin "seem to be introduced for the express purpose of permitting Faulkner to say something about not only slavery and the Negro but economics in general" (278). For Faulkner writes that Buck and Buddy

> not only possessed, but put into practice, ideas about social relationships [and] about land. They believed that land did not belong to people but that people belonged to land and that the earth would permit them to live on and out of it and use it only so long as they behaved and that if they did not behave right, it would shake them off just like a dog getting rid of fleas. (*Unvanquished* 43)

This statement, and similar ones made later in *Go Down, Moses,* are the essence of Faulkner's agrarian belief and would likely meet with agreement from most of the Nashville group. Yet Faulkner surpasses their understanding in the extent to which he makes Buck, Buddy, and later Isaac recognize plantation agriculture in the South as not an agrarian, but an industrial ecology which must be not lamented but challenged. Thus, Buck and Buddy turn their father's mansion into slave quarters, live themselves in a two-room cabin, and develop a complex "system of bookkeeping" by which slaves may purchase their freedom through work (*Unvanquished* 43). This system succeeds in rendering the ecology of the McCaslin plantation less industrial, but because it still relies economically on the large-scale monocultural production of a cash crop, it must retain some industrial elements, including the racist attitudes that permit slavery and exploitation. Later, Isaac recognizes that Buck and Buddy's adjustment of human relationships is not sufficient to eradicate the specter of racism, and he extends their actions into the ecological realm. The problem, Isaac realizes, is the industrialized agricultural ecology their plantation requires: so long as the land is treated as a disposable site for profit extraction, so will be humans. Hence, he famously repudiates his inheritance of the McCaslin plantation and foregoes all acts of ownership and industrial interaction. Many recent readers, such as ecocritic Robert Myers, suggest that Isaac "retreats into escapism, rejecting his ethical obligation to manage the land and the people on it" (660).[8] Yet such responses frequently argue from industrialist logic. Myers, for instance, cites a conflated land and people (implicitly, black people) as something that must be hierarchically managed either by Isaac, his relatives, or some other powerful human actor. An agrarian mind instead views land as an ecology of equally active and respectable human, plant, animal, and mineral beings with whom an ethical individual must civilly negotiate. By recognizing that the industrial structure of the plantation system precludes such negotiation and by seeking to construct alternate economic relationships beyond it, Buck, Buddy, and Isaac are to varying degrees able to represent agrarian belief and action in more just and effective ways than do the Nashville Agrarians.

But I do not intend to sanctify these characters as ideal ethical actors. Indeed, precisely what allows Faulkner's agrarian vision to surpass that of the Nashville group is his fictive wallowing in the depths of human moral ambiguity. No action can be entirely good, but where Buck, Buddy, and Isaac do succeed is in recognizing their complicity in unethical arrangements and seeking to ameliorate the effects of their own actions and lifestyle within the confines of the industrial ecology in which they are inevitably enmeshed. It is in advocating this response to modernity that the Nashville Agrarians are at their best. As Andrew Lytle writes, "until [the small farmer] and the agrarian West and all the conservative communities across the United States can unite on some common political action"—which seems even more unlikely today than in 1930—"he must deny himself the articles the industrialists offer for sale" (244). Rejection or reduction of industrial consumption in favor of local or home production is effective agrarian activism because it adjusts an individual's ecological-economic connection to the land itself. This strategy can be extended to viewing one's financial interactions as ethical ones, and thus divesting personal and community capital from interests engaged in industrial exploitation of any beings.

Too often does environmentalist activism rest on the premise that widespread adoption of the sort of biocentric, ecological paradigm it advocates will lead to positive economic change. This political strategy of consciousness raising elides the extent to which all consumers in an industrialized society remain the beneficiaries of continuing industrial exploitation of marginalized beings by suggesting that merely denouncing the idea of exploitation, or the racism that serves so often as its social arm, is activism enough. Finding fault first in others—for instance, in Nashville Agrarianism for the racism of some of its speakers—may distract from confronting one's own implication in racist social structures as a twenty-first-century economic citizen of the "developed" world. Buck and Buddy do own slaves, and that is undoubtedly wrong, but today's readers of this essay are also likely wearing some item of cotton clothing purchased at an artificially low price subsidized by foreign exploitation of people and place, and that is wrong, too. An agrarian ecological vision finds fault first within one's own enmeshment within the industrial order and acts first to adjust one's home and local economy to resist social and environmental injustice. A failure to do this is ironically the Nashville Agrarians' largest problem: they do not recognize that the plantation ecology they idealize is implicated in the very industrial systems they critique. Ecocriticism can learn from this mistake by turning attention to the economic implications of its cultural critique and by heeding the agrarian imperative to live out economically one's ecological vision.

NOTES

1. The group is known variously as the Nashville, Vanderbilt, Fugitive, or Southern Agrarians, and often simply as "the Agrarians." To avoid conflating the group with all agrarian writers, economists, and farmers of the South, I will refer to them throughout as the "Nashville Agrarians."

2. See Major or Vernon's "Problematic" for reviews of the ecocritical response to Nashville Agrarianism.

3. Freyfogle notes in the introduction to his collection *The New Agrarianism* that throughout the agrarian tradition "industrialism" is often substituted with terms such as "capitalism," "materialism," "technification," "possessiveness," "consumption," and, I might add, consumerism (xl). Following Freyfogle, I will, in this essay, employ "industrialism" "in the same suggestive, encompassing way as did the Twelve Southerners" (Freyfogle xl).

4. See Kirby for a thorough exploration of the South's various agricultural regions and phases that emphasizes "the diversity of the South in terms . . . of topography and crop types, which fundamentally relate to farming systems and to what is broadly called culture" (xv).

5. See Fox-Genovese and Genovese for a study of Bradford's "excision" of "the memory of slavery" from Faulkner's work (91).

6. See Horrocks for an elaboration of this argument.

7. See Vernon, "Being Myriad," Buell, Myers, Harrington, and Welling.

8. See Peters for an overview of the critical response to Isaac.

WORKS CITED

Berry, Wendell. "The Whole Horse." *The New Agrarianism,* edited by Eric Freyfogle, Island Press, 2001, pp. 63–79.

Bradford, M. E. "Faulkner's 'Tall Men.'" *South Atlantic Quarterly,* vol. 61, 1962, pp. 29–39.

Brooks, Cleanth. "Faulkner and the Fugitive-Agrarians." *Faulkner and the Southern Renaissance,* edited by Doreen Fowler and Ann J. Abadie, UP of Mississippi, 1982, pp. 22–40.

Buell, Lawrence. "Faulkner and the Claims of the Natural World." *Faulkner and the Natural World,* UP of Mississippi, 1999, pp. 1–18.

Conkin, Paul. *The Southern Agrarians.* University of Tennessee P, 1988.

Crèvecoeur, J. Hector St. Jean de. *Letters from an American Farmer.* Oxford UP, 1998.

Fargnoli, Nicholas, Michael Goley, and Robert Hamblin. *A Critical Companion to William Faulkner.* Facts on File, 2008.

Faulkner, William. *Absalom, Absalom!* Vintage Books, 1972.

———. *Flags in the Dust.* Vintage International, 2006.

———. *Go Down, Moses.* Modern Library, 1970.

———. *The Unvanquished.* Vintage International, 1990.

Fox-Genovese, Elizabeth, and Eugene D. Genovese. "M. E. Bradford's Historical Vision." *A Defender of Southern Conservatism,* edited by Clyde N. Wilson, U of Missouri P, 1999, pp. 78–91.

Freyfogle, Eric T. "Introduction: A Durable Scale." *The New Agrarianism: Land, Culture, and the Community of Life,* edited by Eric T. Freyfogle, Island Press, 2001, pp. xiii–xli.

Harrington, Gary. "The Destroyers in *Go Down, Moses.*" *ISLE,* vol. 16, no. 3, 2009, pp. 517–24.

Hicks, Granville. "Faulkner's South: A Northern Interpretation." *Georgia Review,* vol. 5, no. 3, 1951, pp. 269–84.

Horrocks, Sam. "Planting-out after *Blithedale:* Transcendental Agrarianism and Ecocritical Economy." *Resilience,* vol. 4, no. 1, 2017, pp. 44–59.

Kirby, Jack Temple. *Rural Worlds Lost.* Louisiana State UP, 1987.

Major, William. *Grounded Vision.* U of Alabama P, 2011.

Meriwether, James, and Michael Millgate. *Lion in the Garden: Interviews with William Faulkner.* Random House, 1968.

Myers, Robert. "Voluntary Measures: Environmental Stewardship in Faulkner's *Go Down, Moses.*" *Mississippi Quarterly,* vol. 66, no. 4, 2013, pp. 645–68.

Peters, John. "Repudiation, Wilderness, Birthright: Reconciling Conflicting Views of Faulkner's Ike McCaslin." *English Language Notes,* vol. 33, no. 3, 1996, pp. 39–46.

Twelve Southerners. *I'll Take My Stand: The South and the Agrarian Tradition.* Baton Rouge: Louisiana State UP, 1977.

Urgo, Joseph, and Ann Abadie, editors. *Faulkner and the Ecology of the South.* UP of Mississippi, 2007.

Vernon, Zackary. "'Being Myriad, One': Melville and the Ecological Sublime in Faulkner's *Go Down, Moses.*" *Studies in the Novel,* vol. 46, no. 1, 2014, pp. 63–82.

———. "The Problematic History and Recent Cultural Reappropriation of Southern Agrarianism." *ISLE,* vol. 21, no. 2, 2014, pp. 337–52.

Warren, Robert Penn. *Faulkner: A Collection of Critical Essays.* Prentice-Hall, 1966.

Watkins, Floyd. "What Stand Did Faulkner Take?" *Faulkner and the Southern Renaissance,* edited by Doreen Fowler and Ann J. Abadie, UP of Mississippi, 1982, pp. 40–63.

Welling, Bart. "A Meeting with Old Ben: Seeing and Writing Nature in Faulkner's *Go Down, Moses.*" *Mississippi Quarterly,* vol. 55, no. 4, 2002, pp. 461–96.

Southern Foodways and Visceral Environmentalism

DANIEL SPOTH

I would like to begin by posing the question, without irony, of whether southern environmentalism exists. In asking this, I do not mean to attempt to address the much thornier issue of whether southern environmental *policy* exists, or whether said policy carries the same influence as northern or western
environmental conservation and preservation efforts. Instead, I am interested
in whether we can, with some degree of certainty, delineate an environmental
philosophy that incorporates distinctively southern elements.[1] When we consider the history of American environmental thought and action, we tend to
gravitate toward certain regions and the major figures that represent them:
Emerson and Thoreau in the Northeast and Muir and Abbey in the West, for
instance. There is no clearly equivalent figure in the South, a distinction that
Albert E. Cowdrey has made in *This Land, This South* (1996). "The South has yet
to produce its Thoreau," Cowdrey writes, "but it has not lacked for a diffuse
and oracular poetry of the wild . . . southern writers have apprehended the
landscape as country people do to whom animals, trees, and landforms are
not to be named only but to be encountered" (198). By juxtaposing the intellectual, philosophical pretensions of northeastern Transcendentalist writers
with the less formal and more instinctual tendencies of southern writers, Cowdrey implies that, though the South never produced a Thoreau, it might not
necessarily *need* one—at least, not from the mold into which the northeastern
Thoreau was poured. Though this claim is by no means unassailable, both in
terms of potential southern Thoreaus (Wendell Berry, Annie Dillard, and Marjorie Kinnan Rawlings come to mind) and in terms of the notion that southern
environmentalists are inherently more connected to their country than others,
Cowdrey's position is valuable primarily as a statement of the South's osten-
sible need, or *desire,* for environmental writers who can apprehend the land
without the intervening membrane of the Thoreauvian intellect.[2]

The idea (or fantasy) of an environmental ethos stemming from sensation
and other ephemera that do not necessitate a fully formed aesthetic, philosophical, or intellectual armature is a principle underlying many, if not most,

major works of southern environmental writing. Repeatedly and despite the suspicion toward static notions of place and rootedness in latter-day southern studies, we find the dominance of feeling, belonging, and the concept of "home," all notions impossible to quantify or verify, over more ideated approaches to environmental health. For the purposes of this essay, I term this move toward an essentialized relationship between southerners and landscape "visceral environmentalism," a concern with the natural world stemming from affect rather than intellect, the guts rather than the brain. Scott Slovic has used the term *visceral* in reference to the work of William Faulkner and other southern writers to indicate a "gut-level sense of connectedness to the world," in essence a variety of sensory imagism that sharpens the reader's awareness of the environment both within and outside the text (120). Yet Slovic's visceralism involves "a moral and political valence—a purpose inclusive of and exceeding luxuriation," cultivating place-based awareness and, ultimately, ecological sensitivity (120). However, I am more interested in the means by which, in southern literature in particular, visceral description tends to override (if not simply circumvent) issues of moral or intellectual significance. I see the visceral turn as essentially a reaction to both the problematics of southern history and the notion of postmodern fluidity of identities—an attempt to reify southernness while paradoxically eliding the very elements that have historically defined it. Abundant use of this tactic can be found in the literature and rhetoric surrounding southern foodways.

Though traditional southern dietary habits draw upon a vast network of intersecting culinary traditions dating back centuries, widespread academic interest in southern food as a distinctly regional cuisine may only be as old as John Egerton's *Southern Food* (1993), a collage of snippets of history, encounters with prominent southern dishes, and descriptions of significant restaurants in the region. Egerton opens with the assertion that "the South, for better or worse, has all but lost its identity as a separate place, and its checkered past now belongs to myth and memory, but its food survives" and that "a meal in the South can still be an esthetic wonder, a sensory delight, even a mystical experience" (3). Egerton's linkage of traditional southern cooking to mysticism is twinned by his fetishization of the origins of these same foodstuffs: "the South's food heritage is filled with clues to the character and personality of the region itself. The heritage originated in nature, in sun and earth and water . . . from the beginning, Southerners, like most Americans, were close to the soil. Their lives revolved around the seasons" (35). In tasting southern food, Egerton claims, we experience a veritable transubstantiation of that food into the elements of its composition—a "closeness" to the soil and seasons that we (implicitly) associate with the South as a region. Southern food, Egerton suggests, can invoke a more authentic and complete portrait of southern history and identity than narrative accounts could ever hope to.

In light of the contemporary popularity of local, organic foods and an emphasis on small rather than large-scale production, culinary trends in southern foodways have moved toward heirloom varietals, artisanal growers, and sustainable methods. In *Southern Provisions* (2015), David Shields chronicles and comments upon the drive to discover and revive traditional ingredients of southern cuisine, freeing them from the stranglehold of pesticides and pollution. Suspicious of the tendency toward fetishizing and romanticizing southern foods, Shields nonetheless takes the opportunity to promote the virtues of indigenous, rare varieties of South Carolina rice. "We could all savor the faint hazelnut delicacy, the luxuriant melting wholesomeness of Carolina Gold," he writes, "and we all wondered at those tales of Charleston hotel chefs of the Reconstruction era who could identify which stretch of which river where a plate of gold rice had been nourished. They could, they claimed, *taste* the water and the soil in the rice" (16–17). Through sensory and affective description, Shields both invokes and collapses history—the Carolina Gold becomes simultaneously an artifact and a contemporary visceral experience.

Academia has, over the last decade, begun to regard southern foodways as a sort of universal key to the complex set of environmental, social, sexual, and racial histories that define the region; interpreting southern food, these studies suggest, gives us access to a wide spectrum of regional identity. Marcie Cohen Ferris, in *The Edible South* (2014), reads southern food as a multifaceted, though distinctly bifurcated, signifier: "in food lies the harsh dynamics of racism, sexism, class struggle, and ecological exploitation that have long defined the South; yet there, too, resides family, a strong connection to place, conviviality, creativity, and flavor" (1). What these studies seem to share is the insistence upon food being the key to understanding a set of (all too often positive) affiliations between humans and nature. One of the most direct routes to understanding how southerners occupied, managed, and ultimately *used* their landscapes would seem to be to study, know, and consume traditionally southern foods.[3] However, I believe that these accounts should be taken less as indicators of any authentic character inherent in southern environmentalism than as statements of what the authors—and, potentially, their readers—*want* southern foodways to represent: a fondly recalled, unproblematic communion with the landscape.[4]

Thus, the question in regard to the visceral turn toward southern foodways may not be how authentic a vision of southern environmental philosophy it represents, but the extent to which scholars *create* that authenticity. Lily Kelting, for instance, compellingly asks whether the fetishization of agricultural and labor history that accompanies paeans to southern foodways can potentially coexist with the inclusive, progressive ideals of the region today: "can Southern food have it both ways—renewal and return? Does looking backwards toward an idealized agrarian past as a model for a new Southern multicultural utopia render the labor of food production stylized and therefore erased?" (365–66). Similarly, Ashli Quesinberry Stokes and Wendy Atkins-Sayre caution that celebratory accounts of southern foodways risk "proposing a postracial take on the South, blending all experiences into one" (74). While "historical," "traditional," or "heirloom" ingredients and recipes frequently bear the aura of authenticity, such descriptors frequently elide the oppressive conditions of race, class, and gender that produced those foodstuffs. The same might be said of southern environmental policy vis-à-vis foodways: modern-day valedictions of inventive, forward-thinking ingredients, producers, and chefs can obscure the centuries of poor environmental stewardship that preceded them. It may be more valuable, as Scott Romine suggests in "Where is Southern Literature?" (2002), to regard "authentic" southern culture as "a condition of pure textuality impervious to material, ideological, or even cultural content," a postmodern construction rather than a definite set of criteria. "This, I take it, is the way certain persons eat grits," Romine writes (37). Romine focuses on southern food as a means of producing, rather than reinforcing, southern affiliation, deflating the appeals to authenticity invoked above.

When we discuss visceral appeals to southern foodways, then, we are in truth dealing with how literature and other media construe affective connections to landscape as distinctively southern, independent of any actual historical evidence or circumstance. In contemplating such questions, we frequently turn to literature as a record and articulation of affective connections between humans and landscape, and, in southern literature, such bonds appear only relatively recently. Definite origin points for visceral environmentalism are difficult to locate, but by the turn of the twentieth century the South's agricultural origins, legacy of slavery, and subsequent struggle to reinvent itself had begun to produce narratives of southerners' ostensibly mystical bond with their environment. Charles Chesnutt's well-known short story "The Goophered Grapevine," from *The Conjure Woman* (1899), in many ways deals with the fundamental question of how the postbellum South wished to define and represent its environmental concerns, particularly as compared to other regions. In "The Goophered Grapevine," northern entrepreneurs John and Annie consider purchasing a vineyard in North Carolina because they are told that the "climate and soil were all that could be asked for, and land could be bought for a mere song" (1). The vineyard turns out to be inhabited by the avuncular former slave Julius, who relates a tall tale of the previous owner's attempts to curb the theft of his grapes by first magically poisoning the vintage, then turning an unfortunate slave into a human grapevine.

In Uncle Julius's (admittedly unreliable) account, the relationships between humans and landscape are *literally* mystical, arising from a variety of West African spiritualism enabled by Aunt Peggy, the obeah-woman. They are also distinctly racialized: the slaves on Master Dugal's plantation not only suffer the effects of Aunt Peggy's incantations, but look on in horror as Dugal, on the advice of a northern horticulturalist, uproots the grapevines and douses them in toxic chemicals. By contrast, Dugal's poor environmental practices bring about the ruin of the plantation, and when John and Annie arrive they find that his "shiftless cultivation" has "well-nigh exhausted the soil" (2). Yet even the transplanted couple, who seem on the whole to be better-attuned to the needs of the land, see the plantation only in terms of potential profit; they shrug off Julius's tale as an idle fantasy and restore the farm's yield in short order. While Julius manufactures and distributes local-color scenes for the delectation of the northerners, John and Annie manufacture and distribute grapes destined for the same market: "the vineyard . . . is referred to by the local press as a striking illustration of the opportunities open to Northern capital in the development of Southern industries. The luscious scuppernong holds first rank among our grapes," John proclaims near the end of the piece, "and our income from grapes packed and shipped to the Northern markets is quite considerable" (13). Foods that carry complex racial, geographical, spiritual, and narrative codes in Julius's story become, at the close of John's story, simple commercial window-dressing. Though Chesnutt certainly postulates a visceral connection between humans and their environment, that connection is racially and regionally insoluble; when exported across such boundaries, it loses its significance and power.

Chesnutt's methodology in "The Goophered Grapevine" is proto-environmentalist insofar as it does not necessarily issue a call for awareness of southern environmental issues, though it does denote a variety of means—traditional and affective, modern and impersonal—by which people of differing races and origins apprehend the southern landscape. "The Goophered Grapevine" is also remarkable in an ecocritical sense in that food (the muscadine) acts as catalyst for *both* of these means of interacting with nature. Chesnutt's linkage of food, place, and identity marks something of a change from earlier accounts of southern cuisine in travel writing, which tended to associate said food with lower-class, uncivilized life. As a rule, however, the association that we now hold between the cultivation of unique local foodways and distinctive regional identities in the United States only attains prominence coincidentally with modernity and the cosmopolitanism it encourages. Chesnutt's early account adumbrates both the rise of visceral environmentalism in the modern South and its fracture along racial lines.

When discussing the affective significance of southern foodways, no individual cuisine carries greater cultural currency than soul food, which overtly links categories of racial and emotional belonging and spirituality to diet. Adrian Miller, in *Soul Food* (2013), traces usage of the term to the late 1950s and early 1960s in the United States, concurrent with the rise of soul music. In invoking the soul, Miller contends, black cooks and artists sought to connote something unique and indivisible about racial history and lifestyle. Coincidentally, what came to be known as "soul food" was commonly eaten both within the home and at large Sunday church picnics, a tradition that Frederick Douglass Opie traces back to the antebellum era in *Hog and Hominy* (2008). The continuation of this tradition, especially during the Great Migration, permitted the preservation of a sense of community and belonging in many black populations. In addition, consuming certain foods—Miller takes note of fried chicken and fish, cake, sweet potato pie, red drinks, and watermelon—in a setting that was simultaneously religious and public caused those foods to become associated with black spirituality, frequently in negative ways.[5]

Such is the brief history and etymology of soul food, but what visceral significances does it carry for southern literature and culture? Laretta Henderson attempts a formal definition in "*Ebonyjr!* and 'Soul Food'" (2007): "scholars define soul food in terms of three attributes: a connection to Africa and the diet of enslaved blacks, something inherent in the black body, and a tool to define a black identity" (82). From Henderson's standpoint, soul food both helps to constitute and is itself constituted by African American identity, and as such, like Chesnutt's muscadines, is racially indivisible. Opie arrives at "multiple definitions" of what "soul" might signify: "soul is the product of a cultural mixture of various African tribes and kingdoms. Soul is the style of rural folk culture. Soul is black spirituality and experiential wisdom. And soul is putting a premium on suffering, endurance, and surviving with dignity . . ." (xi). Elsewhere in *Hog and Hominy*, Opie refines these definitions to some extent: "Soul is a hunch about what is good in a racist society that defines most cultural productions associated with black folk as inferior. . . . It served black people as a necessary collective consciousness" (129). Opie accounts for the wealth of connotations accompanying the term by noting that "soul" is, ultimately, "all wrapped up in feelings . . . an art form that comes from immersion in a black community and an intimate relationship with the southern experience" (136–37). In soul food, as I have noted earlier, we have clear and legible patterns of affect between southerners and their traditional foodways, but the link between those subjects and their landscape is conspicuously absent; none of these definitions attempt to make the case for soul food invoking the southern environment in a positive sense. Certainly such a realization problematizes the utopianism that seems to frequently inform accounts of southern foodways.

Is there a means of promoting visceral connections between southerners and their environment that contains the hope for positive change without effacing the troublesome realities of southern environmental history? One potential answer comes in the work of Wendell Berry, the Kentuckian farmer-poet, revered in environmentalist circles for his powerful focus on restoring basic, uncomplicated human/nature relationships. In *Farming: A Hand Book* (1971), Berry (evidently speaking from his own experience) is straightforward in his argument that long agricultural experience leads to visceral affiliations. He writes, in the poem "The Man Born to Farming," that to the titular subject "the soil is a divine drug"; and, in "Prayers and Sayings of the Mad Farmer," he portrays the process of cultivation as evincing a Zen-like unity between the self and the environment: "Having cared for the plants / my mind is one with the air. / Hungry and trusting, / my mind is one with the earth. / Eating the fruit, / my body is one with the earth" (31, 68). Where Berry diverges from some of the more expansive accounts of visceral environmentalism, however, is in his insistence that the attachment of humans to landscape always happens on an individual rather than a collective basis; there is no assertion here that southerners in particular encounter the environment more simply and directly, or even that agricultural laborers do. Rather, the sort of visceral affection that Berry details is reserved for individuals for whom said labor is itself transformative. He writes, "The *real* products of any year's work are the farmer's mind and the cropland itself," implying that personal revelation is more important than actual agricultural production (69). Moreover, Berry implies elsewhere in *Farming* that historical concerns are ultimately subordinate to personal and subjective realizations.

Berry's contention holds relevance for the current status of southern foodways, which today is in the paradoxical—though not necessarily untenable and certainly not unprofitable—position of desiring both visceral authenticity and modern trends as contemporary locavore chefs and critics seek to push against both southern ecological and culinary history. Jane Black, writing for the *Washington Post*, speaks in rapturous terms of Travis Milton, a rising star in the Virginia food scene. After describing his armful of tattoos—many of them depicting heirloom vegetables—she relates the ink to Milton's philosophy as a whole: "Behind the Technicolor vegetables is a cloud of black. 'It shows all the beautiful things coming out of coal country,' Milton says. 'It's not me wearing my heart on my sleeve. It's my plan for Appalachia.'" From a visceral standpoint, the connections articulated by Milton and other localist chefs seek to provide a counternarrative to the stories of poverty, monotony, and malnutrition familiar to southern culture and history, to suggest that there are aesthetically and culinarily pleasing elements buried underneath the veneer of environmental depletion and the dominance of fast food. Similarly, Marcie Cohen Ferris finds in the story of Ben and Vivian Howard's efforts to open a farm-to-table restaurant in rural eastern North Carolina the inspiring message of how "the power of place, personal relationships, hard work, and locally produced and procured seasonal foods tell a southern story," and that "with education, experience, and exposure to artisanship, seasonality, and flavor, hope persists that southerners will reject processed commodity food in favor of their true culinary inheritance" (329). The "true heritage" of the South, Ferris implies, is not necessarily contained in the region's historical record of poverty and convenience foods, but in "the power of place," among other things. Here we see a turn toward visceralism in the linkage of southern subjects to southern landscapes through the medium of food, oftentimes in a manner that either elides or challenges historical, economical, and racial narratives.

However, other critics have tended toward either debunking or openly decrying the tendency to fetishize southern foodways. David Shields makes it clear in *Southern Provisions* that his intent is not to romanticize, or even argue for the distinctiveness of, local cuisines or ingredients: "in no way can southern food claim a distinct and organic character on the basis of [nineteenth-century agricultural] developments. Growers, marketers, and food preparers in the southern states embraced all of the innovations of plant breeding, selling, baking, and cooking that transformed practice throughout the United States and Europe" (28). Similarly, Elizabeth Engelhardt seeks to demystify southern foodways in "Appalachian Chicken and Waffles: Countering Southern Food Fetishism" (2015), claiming that any holistic conception of southern cuisine needs to take account of both historical circumstances and modern developments, both heirloom vegetables and industrial foodways. "Local and processed food may be difficult to study simultaneously," Engelhardt writes, "but this is how people actually eat, historically and into the present. From this perspective, the Appalachian chicken might come from a grandmother's cast iron, or it might be a frozen chicken finger dinner. . . . We should look to the combinations actual eaters make in their daily lives, recounting all of it: the foods from home, factories, and afar" (79). Engelhardt advocates a synthetic view of southern foodways—a fusion of traditional ingredients and means of preparation with mass-produced, heavily processed convenience foods.

Engelhardt's contention, stripped to its core, could be said to be a pronouncement regarding southern environmentalism writ large. On one hand, attempts to portray the South as an untouched or forgotten Edenic landscape seem at least as shortsighted today as when Faulkner populated the denuded Big Woods of "The Bear" with a biblical serpent in 1942. On the other, to claim the region as fundamentally and irrevocably fallen ignores centuries of southerners enacting the (frequently damaging and frequently painful) process of coming to terms with their environment. Any modern conception of southern environmentalism needs to be synthetic in the manner that Engelhardt evokes. We, therefore, must take the appeal to visceral environmentalism for what it is—not a return to the primitive affective roots of humans' relationship with their environments, but a movement that reacts to and depends upon modern development. The fantasized connection between southerners and their landscapes, like the fetishization of the southern diet into a contemporary cuisine, depends upon our existence in a world mediated by industry and technology—the very forces that so frequently inspire a hunger for tradition.[6]

As the world pushes on into the Anthropocene, it has become increasingly impossible to separate concern for human welfare from environmental issues.

The locus of environmental thought and action is shifting ever further from the images of untouched wildernesses empty of any human presence that energized second-wave environmentalism and toward what Rob Nixon calls, in *Slow Violence and the Environmentalism of the Poor* (2011), "vernacular landscapes," regions "shaped by the affective, historically textured maps that communities have devised over generations, maps replete with names and routes, maps alive to significant ecological and surface geological features" (17). These are the landscapes, both historical and contemporary, that have defined the South, and southern writers have long realized, as Christopher Rieger says of Marjorie Kinnan Rawlings's work, that "nature as a network of relations in which humans participate [is] more accurate than a Newtonian, mechanistic view that deepens the divide between nature and humans by assuming an ideal of scientific detachment" (56). What visceral environmentalism can contribute to contemporary environmental thought is not the hoary and romantic notion that southerners are deeply, elementally connected to their landscapes, but that centuries of human inhabitation, use, and abuse of those landscapes produce concepts of environmental stewardship that are inextricable from messy histories, economies, and racial divisions. It is this fundamental messiness, the acknowledgment that environmental history demands a synthetic approach to humans and their landscapes, that visceral environmentalism brings to the table.

NOTES

1. From the perspective of environmental history, the results are not encouraging. Thomas D. Clark, in *The Greening of the South* (1984), claims that the South lacks the record and heritage of wise environmental planning (such as it is) enjoyed by other US regions. Clark's survey of early frontier literature emanating from the South concludes that "there is scarcely a hint of conservative management of resources, not even of the land itself. Southern border heroes were wasteful exploiters of the eden they so joyfully invaded" (4–5). To make a long and dolorous story very short, the deforestation, destruction of native species, mining, and other extractive industries instituted in the antebellum South and intensified during Reconstruction show few signs of abating today; the bulk of evidence seems to fall in line with Jack Kirby's blunt assertion, in *Mockingbird Song* (2006), that "Southerners . . . have infested a lush country and imperiled, if not ruined it" (34).

2. For more on the idea (however illusory) that southerners relate to their environments in a more ephemeral, less mediated manner than people from other regions, see Dorinda Dallmeyer's *Elemental South,* a 2004 anthology of southern nature writing. The significance

of the title is twofold, introducing the central conceit of the volume (contributions are arranged into sections labeled "earth," "air," "water," and "fire") and hinting at its underlying tone—encounters between humans and their environments phrased in terms of essential natural forces.

3. Southern cookbooks are a contributing factor in the discourse surrounding the linkage between southern food, people, and landscapes. Joseph Dabney's *Smokehouse Ham, Spoon Bread, & Scuppernong Wine* (1998), for instance, pairs one selection of recipes with bits of folk wisdom: "everyone in the hill country knows that you should never attempt to kill a hog on a dark moon, otherwise some of your meat will just vanish. It's always best to slaughter your swine when the moon is shrinking" (60).

4. There is also a tendency to regard southern food and its significance as overriding the frequently complex or painful circumstances underlying its development. Tara Powell, in "Foodways in Contemporary Southern Poetry" (2014), regards southern foodways as "a safe location in which to perform southernness. It is possible to find community at the table across divisions of race, class, and gender" (217).

5. Miller claims that white southerners, desirous of restoring their elite status following the Civil War, "often observed these conspicuous communal and public celebrations from afar and got grist for their mill of endless stereotyping" (31).

6. Thus, a paean to the virtues of elemental living on the order of Barbara Kingsolver's *Animal, Vegetable, Miracle* (2007), an account of the author and her family moving from Tucson to a farm in Virginia and raising their own food and livestock over the course of a year, may well be as much a critique of modernity as it is a visceral appeal to agricultural simplicity. According to Kingsolver, the family leaves the urban hellscape of Arizona "like rats leaping off the burning ship" in search of a place "where rain falls, crops grow, and drinking water bubbles right up out of the ground" (2–3).

WORKS CITED

Berry, Wendell. *Farming: A Hand Book*. Counterpoint, 2011.

Black, Jane. "The next big thing in American regional cooking: Humble Appalachia." *The Washington Post*, 29 June 2016, https://www.washingtonpost.com/lifestyle/food/the-next-big-thing-in-american-regional-cooking-humble-appalachia/2016/03/28/77da176a-f06d-11e5-89c3-a647fcce95e0_story.html?noredirect=on&utm_term=.dd02f97c0ee4. Accessed 25 Apr. 2017.

Chesnutt, Charles. *Conjure Tales and Stories of the Color Line*. Penguin Classics, 2000.

Clark, Thomas D. *The Greening of the South: The Recovery of Land and Forest*. UP of Kentucky, 1984.

Cowdrey, Albert E. *This Land, This South: An Environmental History*. Revised edition. UP of Kentucky, 1996.

Dabney, Joseph E. *Smokehouse Ham, Spoon Bread, & Scuppernong Wine: The Folklore and Art of Southern Appalachian Cooking*. Cumberland House, 1998.

Dallmeyer, Dorinda G. *Elemental South: An Anthology of Southern Nature Writing.* U of Georgia P, 2004.

Davis, David A., and Tara Powell, editors. *Writing in the Kitchen: Essays on Southern Literature and Foodways.* UP of Mississippi, 2014.

Egerton, John. *Southern Food: At Home, On the Road, In History.* U of North Carolina P, 1993.

Engelhardt, Elizabeth S. D. "Appalachian Chicken and Waffles: Countering Southern Food Fetishism." *Southern Cultures,* vol. 21, no. 1, Spring 2015, pp. 73–83.

Ferris, Marcie Cohen. *The Edible South: The Power of Food and the Making of an American Region.* U of North Carolina P, 2014.

Henderson, Laretta. "*Ebonyjr!* and 'Soul Food': The Construction of Middle-Class African American Identity through the Use of Traditional Southern Foodways." *MELUS,* vol. 32, no. 4, Winter 2007, pp. 81–97.

Jones, Suzanne W. *South to a New Place: Region, Literature, Culture.* Louisiana State UP, 2002.

Kelting, Lily. "The Entanglement of Nostalgia and Utopia in Contemporary Southern Food Cookbooks." *Food, Culture & Society,* vol. 19, no. 2, 2016, pp. 361–87.

Kingsolver, Barbara. *Animal, Vegetable, Miracle: A Year of Food Life.* Harper Perennial, 2008.

Kirby, Jack Temple. *Mockingbird Song: Ecological Landscapes of the South.* U of North Carolina P, 2008.

Lefler, Lisa J. *Southern Foodways and Culture: Local Considerations and Beyond.* Newfound Press, 2013.

Miller, Adrian. *Soul Food: The Surprising History of an American Cuisine, One Plate at a Time.* U of North Carolina P, 2013.

Nixon, Rob. *Slow Violence and the Environmentalism of the Poor.* Harvard UP, 2011.

Opie, Frederick Douglass. *Hog and Hominy: Soul Food from Africa to America.* Columbia UP, 2008.

Rieger, Christopher. *Clear-cutting Eden: Ecology and the Pastoral in Southern Literature.* U of Alabama P, 2009.

Romine, Scott. "Where Is Southern Literature? The Practice of Place in a Postsouthern Age." *South to a New Place: Region, Literature, Culture,* edited by Suzanne W. Jones and Sharon Monteith, Louisiana State UP, 2002, pp. 23–43.

Shields, David. *Southern Provisions: The Creation & Revival of a Cuisine.* U of Chicago P, 2015.

Slovic, Scott. "Visceral Faulkner: Fiction and the Tug of the Natural World." *Faulkner and the Ecology of the South,* edited by Joseph R. Urgo and Ann J. Abadie, UP of Mississippi, 2005, pp. 115–32.

Stokes, Ashli Quesinberry, and Wendy Atkins-Sayre. *Consuming Identity: The Role of Food in Redefining the South.* UP of Mississippi, 2016.

IV

FLOODS
& SOUTHERN
WATER STUDIES

Refrigerators, Mosquitoes, and Phosphates

The Environmental Rhetoric of David E. Lilienthal

LUCAS J. SHEAFFER

In order to understand the environmental legacy of the Tennessee Valley Authority (TVA), one must examine the environmental rhetoric of David E. Lilienthal. The TVA's legacy now stretches across more than a quarter of a million acres of reservoir land, and its power production electrifies 80,000 square miles and provides for more than 9 million people ("TVA" 2). The TVA's current quantifiable energy portfolio includes nuclear, fossil, and renewable sources that exist alongside its more philosophical claims for environmental stewardship. Using skillful political rhetoric, Lilienthal crafted the TVA's early regional narrative and created the ambivalent rhetorical architecture necessary for this vast geographical and human network. Yet given the TVA's scope and his own influence, Lilienthal remains conspicuously absent from environmental discourse in southern studies. Born to immigrant parents who were small-business owners in Illinois at the turn of the century, his childhood only vaguely gestured toward his rise to power under Franklin Delano Roosevelt's administration and his expansive work in the American public sphere. Prior to joining the Tennessee Valley Authority, his work in the Wisconsin Public Service Commission (WPSC) was often professionally frustrating and undermined by the nation's deep economic depression and political divisions. Republican incumbent Philip La Follette's defeat in the 1932 gubernatorial campaign signaled the conclusion of Lilienthal's work in Wisconsin. His subsequent transition out of the WPSC in late 1932 paralleled FDR's presidential campaign and election to the White House in 1933. Already known to Roosevelt and his advisors, Lilienthal's reputation and political ideology matched the energetic approach to the early months of Roosevelt's presidency in addressing the immediate need for economic reform and revitalization.[1]

By the summer of 1933, Lilienthal was tapped to join a three-person leadership team for the new TVA, and from the outset he recognized the challenge of gaining entry into the regional structures of the US South.[2] Already possessing a reputation for reimagining public utilities and being willing to engage with expansive restructuring, Lilienthal took a job many thought him still ill equipped for at the age of thirty-four and unprepared for as a nonsoutherner. In a journal entry on June 22, 1933, Lilienthal recalls a meeting with three members of the House Military Affairs Committee—John Jackson McSwain of South Carolina, Lister Hill of Alabama, and W. Frank James of Michigan—who appeared "obviously disappointed in what the President drew out of a bag," with James unable to "refrain from showing his disillusionment" (*The Journals* 37). Yet the new TVA chairman Arthur E. Morgan described Lilienthal as "brilliant, accurate, aggressive, fair, loyal, and committed to public service," as well as a "fresh, young, vigorous person" (qtd. in Neuse 62–63).[3] Amidst the mixed reception, two things become quite clear. First, Lilienthal's age and zeal, married with an energetic agenda of economic and regional reform from the White House, made for a potent combination in the late years of the Great Depression. Second, the dilemma of persuading individuals in the South to accept the policies and projects of the TVA would require all of his rhetorical nous and vigor. The broader conversation of water politics and environmentalism in the South requires a closer examination of Lilienthal's rhetorical strategies in order to expand traditional ecocritical discourse and encourage a more robust eco-rhetorical analysis in southern studies.[4]

In his biography of Lilienthal, Steven M. Neuse describes his view of the TVA as a "righteous sword to revolutionize ratemaking and energy consumption practices throughout the nation" (71). Neuse's provocative simile of a "sword" correctly reflects both Lilienthal's view of the TVA's purpose and informs my own view of his rhetorical strategies as both incisive and persuasive in their force and effectiveness. This chapter examines three examples of this swordlike rhetorical quality in the recurring tropes of refrigerators, mosquitoes, and phosphates. Each of these Lilienthal employs in speeches, transcripts, and other uncollected papers housed in the David E. Lilienthal Papers at Princeton University's Seeley G. Mudd Public Policy Library and in his polemical memoir and history *TVA: Democracy On the March* (1953). I argue that he distills his broad environmental policy of problem solving with technological solutions into these three tropes as a means of identifying with his disparate audiences and persuading both individuals and communities as to the purported effectiveness and long-term necessity of the TVA's large-scale damming and anthropocentric repurposing of flowing water.[5]

The distillation of Lilienthal's environmental rhetoric as a means of identification draws upon, and nuances, Kenneth Burke's term "identification" within a "rhetoric" that he defines as "the use of words by human agents to form attitudes and induce actions in other human agents" (*A Rhetoric of Motives* 41). Identification, then, "is compensatory to division" and offers the rhetorician the means of pulling together disparate or divided individuals and communities toward a shared purpose or use (22). To overcome these divisions and accomplish his agenda, I argue that Lilienthal's rhetoric manifests as *concentric spheres of identification* emphasizing the agent-to-agent/community rhetorical exchanges that occur on multifaceted fronts of persuasion. Together these refrigerators, mosquitoes, and phosphates operate as concentric spheres of persuasion, beginning in the local sphere, moving outward to the regional space, and finally connecting with a national identity.

Each trope functions as a site of identification between the TVA's rhetorical representative Lilienthal and various individuals and communities across the South. Each trope also presents an environmental problem Lilienthal proposes to solve through technological or mechanical means, therefore mobilizing these symbols as different forms of communal imaging. Each reinforces again and again the anthropocentric identification between the interests of the local, the regional, and the environmental policies of the TVA in order to imagine a productive, healthy, and sustainable human experience. *Refrigerators* function as a material representation of the electrification of the rural farmer's home. Time and time again Lilienthal speaks directly to the local "farmer's wife" and details the domestic advantages of refrigeration, while simultaneously positing refrigeration as a means of expanding the farmer's agricultural profit margin. Second, the pesky *mosquito* and its accompanying malaria operate as a metonym for the presumed social and medical malaise in the region. Lilienthal positions the mosquito as both a real and fictive threat, while consistently arguing that proper application of scientific manipulation and technocratic medical intervention will eradicate the disease carriers. Lastly, *phosphates* serve as an intriguing duality in Lilienthal's writings. As a product of factories built by the TVA and powered by hydroelectric energy, phosphates simultaneously improve soil quality, increase agricultural production, and ease US reliance on imported fertilizers. Yet phosphates also provide a vital element of the US military's armament during preparation for and participation in World War II. Refrigerators, mosquitoes, and phosphates, in sum, position the TVA as the means of access for the South to economic prosperity, social and physical health, and national pride.[6]

"REFRIGERATION PLANTS"

The refrigeration plant and in-home refrigerator symbolized social and economic progress in the local sphere and a potential position in the burgeoning
American middle class for the rural southern farmer. The ability to preserve
food for distribution dramatically shifted the scale of a farmer's agricultural
production and profitability.[7] President Roosevelt's signing of both the Tennessee Valley Act on May 18, 1933, and the Executive Order 7037 on May 11,
1935—creating the Rural Electrification Administration—signaled a concerted
effort to electrify the poorest and most rural portions of the US South in the
1930s in order to ensure the long-term agricultural and economic viability of
the region.[8] The localized problem of food preservation, contended Lilienthal,
could be solved by the use of refrigeration plants and refrigerators within
the home and local community. He rendered the material artifact in the local
imagination as a mechanical solution to the organic problem of rot. But the
acceptance of this solution demanded the acceptance of electricity produced
by damming the Tennessee River for hydroelectric power.

In one of his earliest radio addresses for the Columbia Broadcasting System's (CBS) national network on the afternoon of January 20, 1934, Lilienthal
animates the local sphere of concentric identification and links the preservation of food through refrigeration and the improvement of the home economics to the water management and the redevelopment projects of the TVA. "I
want to talk to you this afternoon," he begins, "about that which I suppose is
closest to the heart of every man and woman—the home" (1). Through the
technological mediation of the radio, Lilienthal simultaneously enters the domestic space and appeals to listeners' inherent self-preservation and value of
the home. The local "home" functions as the central sphere of control for the
listener. Furthermore, he specifically emphasizes the anthropocentric core of
the "home." In other words, those listeners "who have the responsibility of
guiding and caring for the home" and desire to "lighten the [domestic] labors"
will inevitably choose their own preservation. To direct more energy toward
the betterment of their children, husbands, and agricultural profits thereby
reimagines their local interests as the primary concern.

For Lilienthal, the "home" or the local sphere becomes the originating
space of anthropocentric imagining. The technological artifact of the refrigerator functions as a metonym for the much larger issue of electrification of the
region. Only a small percentage of homes in the rural South possessed access
to electricity, and of those, Lilienthal offers, only a small number makes full

use of the resource, including refrigeration. "Twenty million housewives now have electric lights in their homes, but only a small percentage of these have the other equally important advantages which electricity brings," he states. "Only a few have the advantage of electric cooking and of electrically heated water; relatively few enjoy the benefits of such other mechanical aids to the housewife as electric refrigeration" (1). Therefore, TVA policy related to electricity rates during the early years confirms that Lilienthal delivered on this rhetorical identification. By disseminating the energy, the TVA and its subsidiaries increased the number of first-time-use homes and farms. While the home is posited as the space of anthropocentric values, the refrigerator is the emblem of the individual's complicity in both the economic and energy agenda of the TVA.

Furthermore, the refrigerator functions as a material representation of the larger national dichotomy between rural and urban communities. In another address, this one given to the American Farm Bureau Federation in Nashville, Tennessee, on December 12, 1934, Lilienthal identifies with the dilemma of the rural poor and locates the problem in the much larger landscape of the national transition from decentralized rural communities to large, centralized cities. "I don't see how you and I can discuss rural electrification here tonight, or how we can consider the place of the farm, and of farm life in the America toward which we are all working," he states, "unless we recognize this domination of the big city and its ideals over the earlier ideals of American life" (1). The problem is the erosion of the "earlier ideals of American life"—i.e., the farm—and Lilienthal proposes that electricity and the preservation of food via refrigeration are the solution to staving off cultural decline.

First, note the pronoun shift from "you and I" to "we" within the opening sentence of the address. As the son of an itinerant midwestern small-business owner and graduate of DePauw College and Harvard Law School, Lilienthal's own identity was certainly not that of the rural southern farmer. Yet he links their strife with his purpose and creates a sense of identification between himself and his listeners. The plural pronoun remains throughout the opening comments: "For a quarter of a century we have witnessed in the United States the steady decline of the farm income, and with it the decline of the influence of farm life upon the standards of the American people" (1). Lilienthal's clear gesture toward the "earlier ideals" of Jeffersonian agrarianism emphasizes his need for rhetorical solidarity with his audience.[9] The subtle anachronistic blend of Jeffersonian ideals with modern capitalism allows Lilienthal to maintain his progressive purpose of damming the Tennessee River, while not alienating the cultural bedrock of the agricultural community.

Striding forward with an ardent tone, he asserts, "The spectacle of subsistence farming in the shadow of skyscrapers is grotesque, but no more so than the conditions that brought such a situation about" (3). The "spectacle" Lilienthal describes is the dramatic economic and population shift to urban spaces that leaves the farmer disenfranchised in the changing cultural landscapes. The "condition," in Lilienthal's speech, is the direct result of disparity in electricity usage in the home and on the farm. The refrigerator, then, operates as a synecdoche for rural electrification and possesses the potential to resurrect the "subsistence farming" from obscurity back to prominence in American culture. The weighted language of the "grotesque" and the stark delineation between rural and urban demonstrates Lilienthal's ability to identify with an audience already cognizant of these differences. To emphasize his argument, Lilienthal's marginalia indicate that he wants to "slow" down the pace of his speaking voice and then add handwritten slashes between the opening words of this statement. "There is no / single / thing / we could do toward restoring the American farm and American farm life to its proper and rightful place than to bring electricity to every one of the farms of the country" (3). The refrigerators and the necessary electricity symbolize the progress of the American farm in order to restore the balance between rural tradition and rampant urban development.

The affect of his notation and the repetition of the word "American" creates a punctuated cadence resulting from a slowed rate of speech. The elongated pacing and annunciation of these three words—"no," "single," "thing"—creates a forceful effect that asks the listener to imagine that there may, in fact, be nothing else that can accomplish these grand ideals set out by the speaker. Lilienthal argues that the electrification of the farm and the use of refrigeration are not only basic necessities, but also an "American" necessity that will provide the catalyst to push the farmer and farm out of the past to their "proper and rightful" place in the American industrial economy.

The farmer is simultaneously enlightened and empowered to regain his position as a primary economic and agricultural force. He continues with a quotation from President Roosevelt to again align his local work with the national agenda: "[electricity] can relieve the drudgery of the housewife and lift the great burden off the shoulders of the hard working farmer."[10] Relieving the weight allows for the "convenience and comforts, which have long been customary to the townsmen" and is now a "means of increasing the income of the farmer"—for example, "a small electric refrigerating plant" (4). The "refrigerator plant" offers a provocative polysemantic moment in Lilienthal's speech. The "plant" is first the organic substance at the core of the problem to be solved by electricity and refrigeration. The "plant" is also the mechanical site where hydroelectricity is produced in an attempt to solve the organic problem with technological solutions. The juxtaposition of these meanings within "refrigerator plant" presents Lilienthal's environmental duality. The "plant" conflates both the anthropocentric and economic problem of agricultural preservation *and* the technological solution that both preserves the produce and offers to preserve the agrarian way of life. Lilienthal's recurring tendency to leverage the refrigerator as a symbol of progress and preservation allows him to simultaneously establish a local identification with individuals and communities without forsaking the broader regional agenda of the Tennessee Valley Authority.

"A COMMON MORAL PURPOSE"

The building of dams for the creation of hydroelectricity to power these refrigerators created another significant environmental problem—among several— for TVA officials, engineers, and scientists. As dams closed, large bodies of water began to form, flooding fields and valleys and displacing numerous communities.[11] These same bodies of water increased breeding grounds for malaria mosquitoes (*Anopheles quadrimaculatus*), which were already endemic in the region. After an organism is bitten and injected by an infected mosquito, the parasite Plasmodium enters the red bloods cells and spreads through the host. Malaria caused fevers, nausea, and chills, as well as the possibility of pulmonary edema, and, in some cases, death.[12] The stagnant shorelines of these lakes brought new attention to a regional biohazard and propagated the spread of the disease.

Lilienthal viewed this human-induced environmental dilemma as an opportunity to create a unified front against a common enemy, a problem to be solved through mechanical processes, and a means of regional identification. While the possibility of improving communal health in the region is certainly laudable, Lilienthal's use of the mosquito connects diverse and divergent interests in the region by providing a common opponent to rally the support of disconnected communities. In *TVA: Democracy On the March*, Lilienthal posits

the malaria dilemma as a unifying force and calls for "the common moral purpose of benefit to the people" (72). In a talk to the Outdoors Writers Association in Chattanooga, Tennessee, on May 29, 1946, he tells a story of experts
coming together to balance the need for specific water levels in the reservoirs
and the fluctuating of these levels to remove the perfect conditions for mosquito larvae. He recounts an almost identical scenario in *TVA* wherein experts
participate in a "chance to broaden their view of their own special fields and
to relate them to the other areas of knowledge" (72). Both stories tout the
"common moral purpose" that he later praises in his article "TVA Pioneers" in
the September 1946 edition of *The New Republic* as the "TVA's successful battle
against malaria" (406). The combination of "moral purpose" and obvious allusion to the "pioneering spirit" embedded in American exceptionalism frames
malaria as a frontier to be conquered and brought to heel in the name of righteous intentions.

In both *TVA* and "TVA Pioneers," Lilienthal's rhetoric employs economic
and philanthropic ideas to justify the eradication of mosquitoes through the
manipulation of water levels and the spreading of DDT (dichlorodiphenyltri-
chloroethane) and other pesticides throughout the region.[13] The specificity of
the mosquito as a regional blight and the subsequent rhetoric of its eradication forms a sort of environmental demagoguery. In other words, Lilienthal
identifies with the regional fears of disease and exploits them to harness the
full human potential of the region. "To minimize this danger and if possible to
drive malaria entirely out of the valley is plainly, of course, part of the obligation of TVA," he writes, "for the disease is a drain on its human resources—the
South loses a substantial part of its working time to the malaria mosquito"
(73).[14] Here again Lilienthal's tendency for polysemantic words appears in "resources." The word operates throughout his written and oral texts to describe
the natural subjects to be employed by humans, but in this instance the meanings slip to include humans within the region as an additional "resource" to be
made more productive through the technological and chemical eradication of
a disease.

Lilienthal's rhetorical tendencies reveal a constant ambivalence between
his ongoing and necessary concentric identification with local and regional individuals and agendas sometimes in tension with the economic, political, and
technological agendas of the TVA. Emphasizing the threat of malaria and the
power of the TVA to provide a technological solution obfuscated the TVA's responsibility for the increased threat. And words such as "plant" and "resource"

work to maintain the identification necessary for persuasion. The mosquito, then, provided the rallying regional symbol for Lilienthal to assert this regional sphere of identification and a larger anthropocentric perspective concerning the region's relationship to water and insects, thereby foregrounding the need for a "common moral purpose" intended only to better the humans within the region.

The reality that these malaria management practices actually resulted in increased human morbidity and mortality rates between 1933 and 1955, according to Carl Kitchen's article "A Dam Problem: TVA's Fight Against Malaria 1926–1951," published in the *Journal of Economic History* in 2013, is both ironic and less than useful. Focusing specifically on data from Alabama and Tennessee, Kitchen's findings complicate the accepted history of the TVA's eradication of malaria, but it is unlikely that Lilienthal would have been aware of the data Kitchen gathers for his analysis. The false presupposition of success in Lilienthal's early speech has much less to do with truth or blurring the facts and more to do with establishing the mosquito as a persona non grata within the region. After identifying with the local fear of cultural erasure and agricultural ruin, the regional adversary found in the mosquito identifies an enemy to the social, economic, or environmental health of the region that requires a swift and unified action, elevating human health over environmental impacts.

"THE LAST BEST HOPE OF FREEDOM"

The early focus of Lilienthal's discussion of phosphates addresses the threat of soil depletion and the salvation of the "almost magical mineral." But the impending American participation in World War II required the TVA and Lilienthal to adapt in real and rhetorical ways to shifting geopolitical dynamics both foreign and domestic. Therefore, I am focusing on the transition in two speeches from a conservation-focused soil rejuvenation program to anthropomorphized military munitions. Throughout his address "Nutrition and Soil Conservation," delivered on October 18, 1937, to the American Dietetics Association in Richmond, Virginia, Lilienthal repeats the statement, "As the soil is, so are the people" (1). Inverting the simile's standard structure requires the listener to ponder the import of the mantra for an extra moment. The sentence emphasizes the ecological interconnectedness between the health of communities and the health of their lands. The simile expands as the speech continues, and Lilienthal posits a string of possible causes and effects associated with soil health, as he moves from agricultural benefit to social progress. "A deficient soil is a cause of low income, of a deficient nutrition, and of a deficient social order," he states. "An inadequate nutrition in turn leads to further exhaustion of the soil, which in turn cumulatively means an increased impairment of our human and natural resources" (3). The deficiency and "disregard of land" are connected to the social ills that negatively impact the positive social order and cripple any attempt at a nutritious diet, income, and community. The employment of an ecological concept allows for a slippage between soil health and human health that works to persuade an audience of dietitians as to the value of phosphates produced as part of the TVA's expansive regional redevelopment.

The rhetorical pivot from soil to social health enables the stakes of the problem to grow inordinately high in Lilienthal's polemical presentation and makes the need for a solution all the more pressing. In response to his own question "What is phosphorus?," he responds with a lengthy "slippery slope" of problems that mirrors the linear string of causes and effects above:

> It is, of course, one of the mineral elements to be found in the soil and through the soil in all living things, in plants and in human beings. Take away phosphates entirely and life ceases on this globe. If the soil is deficient in phosphorus, our food supplies are immediately threatened. Without adequate phosphorus in the soil and hence in the plant life, the life of the animals and of human beings would rapidly deteriorate and would proceed on a halting and pitiful basis. (4)

The problem, writ large, is the annihilation of humankind, but the solution is a bit different in this instance. Unlike the refrigerator as a solution for preservation or mechanical manipulation as a solution for malaria mosquitoes, since phosphates occur naturally, they must be processed from the ground and reintegrated into the soil. More specifically and more relevantly, it is the deficiency—not the absence—of phosphates that concerns both the TVA and dietitians. "The dire consequences of deficiency of phosphorus in the soil is not an academic question, nor is it simply a wild imagining," he continues (4). The question is one of quality of life and, within his logic, a quality of social order and community.

Both of these statements presume two counterarguments received from local farmers and farming consortiums during the early years of the TVA: 1) a mistrust of scientific intervention in traditional agricultural methods within the region, and 2) the miscalculation of predicated declines. "The fact," Lilienthal states, "is that most of our land in this country east of the Mississippi River is fast becoming deficient in phosphorus and unless this deficiency is met, unless the supply in the soil of these millions of acres is supplemented, the lands east of the Mississippi cannot long support agriculture" (4). Clearly, his argument is in line with the contemporary assessment of soil health, and the predicted catastrophe requires the listener to consider the implications. While phosphate supplements are one of many necessary adjustments—others include crop rotation and allowing land to remain fallow—Lilienthal needs the impending agricultural collapse to predict both an economic decline and loss of the agrarian culture.

He completes the argument by offering a final question and answer: "Now, where are the available phosphorus supplies for this life-preserving replacement? Virtually the only source of phosphorus for replenishment of the soil lies in the deposits of so-called phosphate rock. No nation which does not have access to large quantities of these deposits of phosphate rock can permanently endure" (5). The full argument is now present and accounted for in Lilienthal's rhetoric concerning phosphates and the necessity of the TVA to identify, research, and then solve the dilemma of phosphate decline and soil depletion through the increase of dam construction to prevent soil erosion and the increase of chemical plants for phosphate supplementation. But by extending the problem to the level of the nation-state, Lilienthal reveals his blend of liberal progressivism and American exceptionalism. According to his data, the United States holds more than one-third of the world's phosphate rock and, therefore, stands the best likelihood of outlasting most other nation-states. The possible erasure of healthy soil and the agrarian ideal—the independent and financially solvent individual farmer—demands a reimagining of the identification between farmers and the national agenda. But the link will not arrive until several years later.

By 1942 America is engaged on both the European and Pacific fronts of World War II. These developments clearly inform the tone and passion of Lilienthal's work as he prepares the text titled "Phosphorus: Key to Life—Weapon of Death" for the American Institute of Cooperation delivered in Atlanta, Georgia, on January 12, 1942. After opening with a brief statement that he will be discussing the proposed chemical processing plant on the Gulf of Mexico in Mobile, Alabama, he offers this statement of intent: "That factory, if funds are appropriated, will produce elemental phosphorus to burn and harass the enemies of our country; and it will produce fertilizer to increase the yield of food to feed those armies and peoples the world over who are the last best hope of freedom" (5). The absence of a hopeful turn-of-phrase like "As the soil is, so are the people" is striking in his opening remarks. While a revised version of environmental conservation and degradation prevention will return, the opening remarks are defined by a jarring juxtaposition that expands on the title's parallelism and complicates the dual agendas of the speech. Lilienthal is selling the idea of a Mobile plant, while also promoting the role of the TVA phosphorus-processing facilities in the current global crisis (not to mention the continued necessity of phosphates to replenish home soils and generate greater crop yields).

The conflict is no longer a regional one; instead, it has been replaced with a national problem. The tone of his address is angry ("burn and harass") and fearful ("last best hope"), as Lilienthal and the TVA come to terms with recent national and global developments and their impact on the ongoing work of the Authority. The Atlanta address redefines the phosphate trope and reemploys it to better serve the national interest in winning the new war by urging regional listeners to identify with the national stakes and connect the health of their soil to the health of the nation-state. While Lilienthal still manages to present the positive impact of phosphates on agricultural practices in the South, the more provocative aspect of this speech is his seamless navigation of the juxtaposition of life and death, peace and war. He recognizes that the audience that makes up the American Institute of Cooperation is primarily interested in the agricultural work of the TVA:

> And there are other matters that would interest this audience: the rapid growth of navigation on the river channel created by these dams, a traffic that includes huge shipments of agricultural products from the Middle West; the reduction of flood dangers; the fight against malaria; the protection of eroded lands by the planting of 135 million trees; and the development of a sustaining agriculture—these are some of the activities of the nearly 35,000 men and women workers who carry on this regional development agency. (3)

But he rather unemotionally couples the list of the TVA's projects with another list of phosphorus's effective uses in theaters of war:

Spattered from high explosive bombs [speaking of phosphorus] it sets fire to property and burns and maims human beings. It produces smoke screens to conceal battleships at sea and troops on land. In peacetime, when suitably combined with other elements, it becomes available as a needed nutrient of the plants of the field. War multiplies the burden carried by phosphorus. (4)

The anthropomorphization of "phosphorus" as a beast of burden or, more accurately, an overworked human being, creates an intriguing rhetorical situation. Phosphorus is both life-giving and life-taking work, and in both forms provides technological solutions to the problems of soil degradation and national defense.

Phosphorus morphs, in Lilienthal's speech, into a piece of the natural world working diligently to support the Jeffersonian agricultural ideal here at home, while dispensing death and pain as a means of protecting the democratic capitalistic social project continents away. The "magic" of phosphorus is the great tension between its agricultural and military uses and its ability to become representative of American domestic and international policies. Moving from the large-scale production and processing of phosphates, Lilienthal also emphasizes its intimate qualities: "The framework of our bodies, our bones are composed almost entirely of phosphorus in combination with calcium. . . . Indeed, phosphorus is necessary in the life processes of every living cell" (7). Again, the listener is caught between the "burn[ing] and maim[ing] of human beings" and the "life processes of every living cell" (4,7). The tension is not one that Lilienthal seems particularly concerned about, but the duality of phosphates emphasizes Lilienthal's ability to use these tropes for multiple purposes. The polysemanticism of "plants" and "resources" is now coupled with the ambivalent uses of phosphates.

The last sphere of concentric identification reveals the essential anthropocentrism of Lilienthal's environmental rhetoric in phosphorus that can both rejuvenate life-giving soil and destroy the human body. He connects the very cellular structure of the individual's bones with the military munitions necessary to destroy the most basic bodily structures of bones and blood. The national interest in the defense of "freedom," democracy, and capitalism weave together in this speech with the production of phosphates, which are integral to the health of the human cellular structure and necessary for the disintegration of that same body in war. Throughout the speech, Lilienthal removes large and significant portions of detailed text related to the production of phosphates, the geological and environmental impact of phosphate production, and the statistical analysis of the new facilities necessary in both the domestic and military function. His substantial subtractions between the draft and the delivered speech indicate an orator more focused on the large ideas within the text, rather than detailed support. The stripping down of the text and the body create a persuasive symmetry. The fewer details offered, the more willingly one accepts the identification between agricultural phosphate production and war munitions.

The problematic duality of Lilienthal's anthropocentrism woven throughout his environmental discourse in these speeches is perhaps most striking in an address following the end of World War II, and it offers a fitting conclusion. During his 1945 Radcliffe College commencement address, titled "Machines and the Human Spirit," Lilienthal proclaims, "the great Tennessee River is now changed, twenty-six huge dams make it do what it's told to do" (4). The TVA dams, much like many others within the southern bioregion, have done what they have been told to do in allowing the TVA's massive water development projects. The river is rendered as an unruly child being chastised by an all-knowing parent to correct its behavior. And each problem that arose was met with a technological or mechanical solution predicated on assuring the greatest benefit to the human inhabitants of the Tennessee Valley. A year later, Lilienthal writes in "Science and Man's Stewardship" that the "river, once a scourge and wastrel, now is productive" (*Zion's Herald* 891). The problem for Lilienthal, perhaps all along, was a greater and greater need for productivity dependent upon the expansion of electricity usage within the South. Each environmental concern was subservient to this larger local, regional, and national anthropocentric agenda. While there are certainly positive aspects to the TVA's environmental legacy in the South, Lilienthal's rhetoric frames a narrative throughout the bioregion emphasizing the power of identification through a fear of economic, cultural, and national erasure in order to achieve the TVA's purposes. The river does "what it's told to do" only when the individuals and communities that make up the bioregion acquiesce to the supremacy of their own anthropocentric needs and forsake the complex ecological implications of these decisions, actions, and words.

* * *

NOTES

1. Lilienthal worked for the Wisconsin Public Service Commission from 1931 to 1933, and then for the Tennessee Valley Authority from 1933 to 1946, and next as the first chairman of the Atomic Energy Commission from 1946 to 1950, before transitioning into the private sector until his death in 1981.

2. Several key texts are valuable resources concerning the origins of the TVA: Preston J. Hubbard's *Origins of the TVA: The Muscle Shoals Controversy, 1920–1932* (1961), Roy Talbert's *FDR's Utopian: Arthur Morgan of the TVA* (1987), Arthur E. Morgan's *The Making of the TVA* (1974), and Marguerite Owen's *The Tennessee Valley Authority* (1973), to name just a few.

3. It is necessary to note that while Morgan's initial impression of Lilienthal may have been positive, the relationship between the two quickly became adversarial. It deteriorated to such a degree that Morgan's work and name are thoroughly absent from Lilienthal's book *TVA: Democracy On the March.*

4. The 1992 publication of Killingsworth and Palmer's *Ecospeak* catalyzed an ongoing discourse concerning the presence and analysis of eco-rhetoric. While the work is primarily concerned with the disconnect between scientific, political, and local conversation and language surrounding environmental issues, it informs my own analysis of Lilienthal's eco-rhetoric and the role of the TVA in shaping environmental discourse in the South.

5. Archival research was made possible through a generous grant from the Friends of the Princeton Libraries Research Grant.

6. A more robust discussion of David E. Lilienthal's rhetoric can be found in my dissertation "Damming the American Imagination," completed in the Spring of 2018.

7. According to the 1950 TVA *Annual Report,* 250 community refrigeration plants were serving approximately 950 families, up from just 19 in 1941, as cited in Anderson's *Refrigeration In America* (1972). In addition, Lilienthal notes in a speech to the Todhunter group on 22 Nov. 1937, that approximately "one hundred thousand pounds of fruit were processed" through a quick-freezing method developed by the TVA, and in one Georgia farming community "11,100 pounds of pork, 3,435 pounds of beef, and 675 pounds of miscellaneous products" were saved from early rot due to refrigeration, thus allowing for greater quantities for market and greater profits for the farmers.

8. One simple statistic indicates the swift and significant change in rural electrification during Lilienthal's tenure at the TVA: "The number of homes and farms that are using electricity *for the first time:* from 225,000 in 1933 to 1,065,000 in 1951. This is an increase of 375 per cent. In the same period the increase for the nation was slightly less than 100 per cent" (*Democracy* 22).

9. Jeffersonian agrarianism references a long tradition of valuing the single, land-owning, and rural farmer as the bedrock of American democracy. These principles play a significant role in *Notes on the States of Virginia* (1781–1785) and reappear in *I'll Take My Stand: The South and the Agrarian Tradition* (1930).

10. Here Lilienthal is quoting from FDR's campaign speech on 21 Sept. 1932, in Portland, Oregon, addressing public utilities and hydroelectric power. Notably, the subtitle of

his speech, "A national yardstick to prevent extortion against the public and encourage the wider use of the servant of the people—electric power," employs the same language of ownership and manipulation later employed by Lilienthal.

11. See Michael J. McDonald's book *TVA and the Dispossessed: The Resettlement of Population in the Norris Dam Area* (1981).

12. In his book *TVA's Public Planning: The Vision, the Reality,* Walter L. Creese notes that these "physical afflictions that caused lethargy [were] regularly discussed in premedical and sociology courses in northern universities. The general condition of widespread illness," he writes, "was sometimes blamed for what was occasionally termed the 'analgesic subculture' of the Appalachian area" (93).

13. One would be remiss not to mention Rachel Carson's landmark text *Silent Spring,* published in 1962. Her incisive and persuasive book brought the scale of environmental degradation attributed to DDT to the attention of the general public. The TVA's role in the spread of DDT use throughout the world only heightened the necessity of Carson's intervention and the part her book played as a catalyst for late twentieth-century environmental policies.

14. In addition, the TVA labored diligently to train pilots from around the world to refurbish military aircraft to properly spray and spread DDT in the Pacific, Greece, and the Balkans.

WORKS CITED

Anderson, Oscar Edward. *Refrigeration in America: A History of a New Technology and Its Impact.* Princeton UP, 1953.

Burke, Kenneth. *A Grammar of Motives.* U of California P, 1945.

———. *Language as Symbolic Action: Essays on Life, Literature, and Method.* U of California P, 1966.

———. *The Philosophy of Literary Form: Studies in Symbolic Action.* U of California P, 1973.

———. *A Rhetoric of Motives.* U of California P, 1950.

Carson, Rachel. *Silent Spring.* 1962. Houghton Mifflin. 2002.

Chandler, William U. *The Myth of the TVA: Conservation and Development in the Tennessee Valley: 1933–1983.* Ballinger. 1984.

Clapp, Gordon. *The TVA: An Approach to Development of a Region.* U of Chicago P, 1955.

Colignon, Richard A. *Power Plays: Critical Events in the Institutionalization of the Tennessee Valley Authority.* SUNY P, 1997.

Creese, Walter L. *TVA's Public Planning: The Vision, the Reality.* U of Tennessee P, 1990.

Davidson, Donald. *The Tennessee: Civil War to TVA.* Rinehart P, 1948.

Freidberg, Susanne. *Fresh: A Perishable History.* Harvard UP, 2009.

Hargrove, Erwin C. *Prisoners of Myth: The Leadership of the Tennessee Valley Authority, 1933–1990.* 2nd edition. U of Tennessee P, 1994.

Hubbard, Preston J. *Origins of the TVA: The Muscle Shoals Controversy, 1920–1932.* Vanderbilt UP, 1961.

Killingsworth, M. Jimmie, and Jacqueline S. Palmer. *Ecospeak: Rhetoric and Environmental Politics in America*. Southern Illinois UP, 1992.

Kitchens, Carl. "A Dam Problem: TVA's Fight Against Malaria, 1926–1951." *The Journal of Economic History*, vol. 73, no. 3, 2013, pp. 694–724.

Lilienthal, David E. "American Farm Bureau Federation, Nashville, Tennessee, 12 Dec. 1934." David E. Lilienthal Papers, 1900–1981. Speech.

———. "The Armament of a Democracy." University of Minnesota, 16 Jan. 1941. David E. Lilienthal Papers, 1900–1981. Speech.

———. "The Bridge of Understanding." Chattanooga Chamber of Commerce, 18 Apr., 1941. David E. Lilienthal Papers, 1900–1981. Speech.

———. "The Electrification of the American Home." CBS Broadcast, Washington, DC, 20 Jan. 1934. David E. Lilienthal Papers, 1900–1981. Speech.

———. "Even the Experts Have Fun." The Outdoor Writers Association of America, Chattanooga, Tennessee, 29 May 1946. David E. Lilienthal Papers, 1900–1981. Speech.

———. "Farm Women Meeting, Knoxville, Tennessee, 27 Aug. 1935." David E. Lilienthal Papers, 1900–1981. Speech.

———. *The Journals of David E. Lilienthal: The TVA Years 1939–1945, Volume 1*. Harper and Row, 1964.

———. "Little Drops of Water—." September 1946. David E. Lilienthal Papers, 1900–1981. Draft of article.

———. "Machines and the Human Spirit." Radcliffe College, 27 June 1945. David E. Lilienthal Papers, 1900–1981. Speech.

———. "A New National Conservation Policy." International Congress of Women, Chicago, Illinois, 18 July 1933. David E. Lilienthal Papers, 1900–1981. Speech.

———. "Nutrition and Soil Conservation." Annual Meeting of the American Dietetic Association, Richmond, Virginia, 18 Oct. 1937. David E. Lilienthal Papers, 1900–1981. Speech.

———. "Phosphorus: Key to Life—Weapon of Death." American Institute of Cooperation, Atlanta, Georgia, 12 Jan. 1942. David E. Lilienthal Papers, 1900–1981. Speech.

———. "Research Has a Moral Responsibility." *The Christian Century*. July 1945. David E. Lilienthal Papers, 1900–1981 (mostly 1950–1981), Public Policy Papers, Department of Rare Books and Special Collections, Princeton University Library.

———. "Science and Man's Stewardship." *Zion's Herald*, 10 Sept. 1946. David E. Lilienthal Papers, 1900–1981.

———. *This I Do Believe*. Harper and Row, 1949.

———. "Todhunter School Group, Norris, Tennessee, November 22, 1937." David E. Lilienthal Papers, 1900–1981. Speech.

———. *TVA: Democracy On the March*. Quadrangle, 1953.

———. "TVA Pioneers." *The New Republic*, 30 Sept. 1946. David E. Lilienthal Papers, 1900–1981.

———. "Who Says It Can't Be Done." Rotary Club, Knoxville, Tennessee, 27 May 1941. David E. Lilienthal Papers, 1900–1981. Speech.

Neuse, Steven M. *David E. Lilienthal: The Journey of an American Liberal*. U of Tennessee P, 1996.

Roosevelt, Franklin Delano. "Campaign Address On Public Utilities: A national yardstick to prevent extortion against the public and encourage the wider use of the servant of the people—electric power." *The Public Papers and Addresses of Franklin D. Roosevelt*, vol. 1, *The Genesis of the New Deal, 1928–1932*. Random House, 1938, pp. 733–34.

Selznick, Philip. *TVA and the Grass Roots*. Harper and Row, 1949.

"TVA at a Glance." *About TVA*. Tennessee Valley Authority, www.tva.com/About-TVA. Accessed 30 July 2018.

Wengert, Norman. *Valley of Tomorrow: The TVA and Agriculture*. U of Tennessee P, 1952.

Flooding Mississippi

Memory, Race, and Landscape in Twenty-First-Century Fiction

CHRISTOPHER LLOYD

Flooding saturates southern history and the regional imagination. From the devastations of the Great Mississippi Flood in 1927 to the tragic impacts of Hurricane Katrina in 2005, the South is a particularly waterlogged region in the United States. Broadly put, "What could be more southern than disaster?," Robert Jackson asks (555). From colonial contact to the present day, "one way to tell the story of what is now the U.S. South is a series of disasters—natural, man-made, and otherwise" (Jackson 555). The ways in which these catastrophes have been mediated is at the heart of what Jackson calls the "southern disaster complex." In terms of flooding, southern literature has consistently responded to the watery locales of the region. From the treacherous river in William Faulkner's *As I Lay Dying* (1930) to the life-changing hurricane in Zora Neale Hurston's *Their Eyes Were Watching God* (1937), and from the destruction of a town in Robert Penn Warren's *Flood* (1963) to the swift, near-biblical flooding in Cormac McCarthy's *Child of God* (1973), these literary works depict floods both as disastrous to landscapes and giving rise to events that spark personal, social, and cultural change. In short, floods are transformative.

This large corpus of floods mediated in southern writing continues into the twenty-first century. It is as dominant an imaginary today as it ever was, coursing through works like Ron Rash's *One Foot in Eden* (2002), in which a small Appalachian town is about to be flooded after the introduction of a dam. The impending waters threaten to displace an entire community and history as well as bring a hidden, murdered corpse to light. Similarly, Jayne Anne Phillips's *Lark and Termite* (2009) features a flood that wipes out a family's past and ushers in a new and potentially redemptive future. In a different vein, Ann Pancake's *Strange as This Weather Has Been* (2007) details the life of a coal-mining family whose locale is steadily being torn apart by mountaintop removal. The destruction of the mountain creates black floods that steadily overwhelm all kinds of human and nonhuman life. On through the work of Tim Gautreaux, Karen Russell, Michael Parker, Jesmyn Ward, and the numerous writers who have responded to Hurricane Katrina, southern literature to-day is frequently invested in watery spaces, events, locales, and processes.

To narrow the scope of this chapter, I will focus on the ways in which the state of Mississippi and the river that bears its name are figured in contemporary fiction as sites of flooding and memory. In particular, the chapter examines Bernice L. McFadden's *Gathering of Waters* (2012) and to a lesser extent Tom Franklin and Beth Ann Fennelly's *The Tilted World* (2013), both of which feature the Great Flood of 1927. These novels are significant for their attentiveness to the specifics of place and landscape. Mississippi (and neighboring Louisiana) are central to Thadious Davis's influential study *Southscapes: Geographies of Race, Region and Literature* (2011), because they are "two of the southern geographical spaces with the most fascinating connection between land, space, and social place" (4). While not exceptional—Davis sees the issues at the heart of these states across the South and the United States at large—Mississippi and Louisiana enfold histories and memories of race relations into their physical and psychic spaces. Mississippi's place in the deepest of deep Souths makes it an especially charged site of national and regional imaginaries. Following Davis's lead, this chapter explores the relation between place and memory, especially as they intersect with conceptions of watery environments.

In "The Site of Memory" (1995), Toni Morrison entangles the work of the literary imagination and the potency of memory. A key comparison comes late in the essay:

> . . . the act of imagination is bound up with memory. You know, they straight-ened out the Mississippi River in places, to make room for houses and livable acreage. Occasionally the river floods these places. "Floods" is the word they use, but in fact it is not flooding; it is remembering. Remembering where it used to be. All water has a perfect memory and is forever trying to get back to where it was. Writers are like that: remembering where we were. . . . [A] rush of imagination is our "flooding." (99)

The central simile is that the writer's imagination is like an altered river re-membering its past route; therein, however, lies another metaphor. Rivers cannot remember in the way we usually use the word, but Morrison makes a river's flooding a kind of memory. If the writer—for our purposes, the southern writer—recalls the past affectively through writing, they do so in a way akin to a river's overflowing of its banks. When writers utilize southern spaces and waterways like the Mississippi or the Tallahatchie to remember events like the Great Flood of 1927, or the drowning of Emmett Till's body, or Hurricane Katrina, they are doubly recollecting in both form and content: the river is overflowing. Morrison's use of the Mississippi in her reflective essay is no surprise, considering the role the river has had on the US imagination, not least in the South. As Thomas Ruys Smith outlines, the Mississippi River has numerous lives in cultural and literary representation: through the eighteenth and nineteenth centuries, the river "was a powerful symbol of both America's conception of itself, and the world's conception of America" (2). It was "connective tissue, borderline, and crossing point; a channel of slavery and a path to freedom; a lonely wilderness . . . ; a pastoral paradise and an industrial powerhouse; a place of salvation, and a notorious underworld" (3). In short, Smith writes, "It was America's river, physically and culturally at the heart of the nation" (3). As a literal and metaphorical American artery, the river enables various kinds of remembrance of where the country has been, and where it might be going.

The growing field of memory studies theorizes the ways in which the past is refracted in the present. The field, in Pieter Vermeulen and Stef Craps's words, "has predominantly studied the representation and mediation of memories and their circulation in society," even into the ways that "memories circulate and migrate in and between cultures" (224). Memory studies alerts us, in terms semantically linked to Morrison's essay, to the way that "memory fundamentally means movement" and is always "border-transcending" (Erll, "Travelling" 15). This movable, shifting, *flooding* of memory (sometimes, even, back to an origin, like the river) is not simply a way of responding to past events, but a form of engaging with how this past affects and lingers in the present, and how we might look toward a future. Memory is as much forward- rather than merely backward-looking. In the era of the Anthropocene, when climate change is ever more visible, the dominance of US writing that remembers landscapes and ecologies (especially as it was, is, and might be) is fitting. Novels like Barbara Kingsolver's *Flight Behavior* (2012) and Annie Proulx's *Barkskins* (2015) are but two broad examinations of the intertwining of human and nonhuman subjects, caught in a period of dramatic and widespread planetary change. As Kate Marshall argues, "Contemporary US fiction seems quite clearly to be responding to the pressures of the larger anthropocentric imagination by staging its own temporality within increasing time scales and geologies" (524–25). These temporalities are registered most vividly in literatures of cultural memory. As a recent special issue of *Textual Practice* on "planetary memory" attests,[1] it is through remembrance of the past, present, and future at local and planetary scales that our current condition can be imagined.

Though Ursula K. Heise tells us that the ecocritical turn in American studies frequently begins at the local level (384), she argues that a focus on broader transnational, hemispheric, and planetary frames is more useful to understanding our world. However, localism—"an emphasis on the body and sensory experience, as well as on small-scale communities and economies" (Heise 385)—is still visible in fiction from the US South. My central examples (in addition to *Flight Behavior* and others) often invest in the local alongside the national or transnational. And if southern studies is to keep pace with American studies more broadly in unpacking diverse ecologies in cultural texts, then, as Jay Watson asserts, "we need the combined conceptual resources of southern and environmental studies to unpack the thick layers of meaning that accrue when southerners write ecologically and environmental thinkers write about the South" (159). That interdisciplinary work is a difficult, yet important direction for the field to take.

In a review of recent novels about the 1927 flood (including *The Tilted World*), Robert H. Brinkmeyer Jr. sees their publication as "significant," especially because the event "remains today a buried cultural memory," which the novels may "help recover" (207). Brinkmeyer echoes Franklin and Fennelly who, in the preface to *The Titled World,* argue that the flood "seems largely forgotten" (xii) even though it, among other things, "flattened almost a million homes," "caused an estimated one billion dollars' worth of property damage" (in 1927 money), "permanently chang[ed] the landscape of the South," and "permanently altered race relations and American politics" (xi). Many poor African Americans were forced to migrate to northern states after their homes were wiped away, recalling so many disasters (natural and man-made) in the region that have catalyzed the involuntary relocation of the poor and people of color. In addition, Herbert Hoover became president in 1929, "cementing the belief that the federal government—which had done nothing to help the flood victims—should create an agency to prevent emergencies and assist recoveries" (Franklin and Fennelly xii). The flood thus became a crucible of national politics and environmental issues. According to Brinkmeyer, *The Tilted World* and another "great flood narrative," Bill Cheng's *Southern Cross the Dog* (2013), reveal ways to begin imagining "the scope of the great flood's destruction." He does not think the "great novel of the great flood" (211) has yet been written, but these twenty-first-century texts are attempts at grasping this partially drowned memory.

The Tilted World opens with an image of something once buried emerging, a trope deeply entrenched in novels of flooding and memory (*One Foot in Eden*, for example).[2] Dixie Clay, the novel's protagonist,

> was squelching through the mud along the creek's swollen banks, shooing mosquitoes with her hat, when she saw a baby coffin bobbing against a sycamore snag. For a second the idea that her son, Jacob, buried two years back might have come home nearly collapsed her . . . . She was crashing hip-deep through the foamy, coffee-colored water when she got hold of herself. It wasn't Jacob. . . . Wasn't, in fact, a coffin. (1)

That materialization of the past (a kind of physical memory) may seem an obvious image of history manifesting in the present, but as the editors of *Undead Souths* (2015) tell us, "the dead contain cultural vibrancy in the present": in short, "To see dead people is to face the past and its many cultural irruptions in the present" (4–5). *Undead Souths* rethinks the parameters of southern gothic imaginaries by attending to the ways that the past impacts us now. Dixie Clay's vision of her dead child unearthed from the ground is prescient, for the novel considers the ways that secrets and histories cannot be kept hidden. As Brinkmeyer notes, "for all the interest in the larger politics and history of the flood," *The Tilted World* is principally "a love story" in which the flood brings together an "unlikely couple" and even "washes away all the constraints and difficulties that might drive them apart" (210).

Though there are critiques of environmental fictions which focus on human narratives rather than those of the planet,[3] the personal *and* emotional center of *The Tilted World* draws us deeper into the people and landscapes of the South in the early twentieth century. Its depiction of the flood itself, and the devastation wrought, is vivid and visceral. Dixie sees the water rising and rivers bursting their banks: "a stream become a river filled with things that were not water. A church steeple. A brace of mules. A mailbox. A tree, a tree, a tree, lifted and thrown" (240). As she clambers to safety, she watches a deer and a coyote scrabbling to find some elevated land. She hears trees collapse (it "boomed like a cannon and thundered into the water"), and a "huge wave soared over her" as Dixie thinks, through free indirect discourse, "How much water was in the Mississippi anyway, yet it kept coming." Seeing a landscape "wholly alien" and otherworldly, Dixie rephrases her statement: "No, not a landscape, a seascape" (259). Franklin and Fennelly make the setting strange (things where they should not be, vistas transformed from solid to liquid, a limitless river) in order to transport readers back to the melee of the disaster. Recovering the memory of this moment means, for the authors, delving into the effects on particular characters in the region.

At the novel's end, Dixie imagines a future moment when she would have to explain the flood to her young child. "How big . . . was the area that was drowned?" (331–32), she rhetorically asks. "About the size of Connecticut, New Hampshire, Massachusetts, and Vermont. Of course, if it *had* been those states, we'd have had help right quick. . . . Later, chapters in history books. Monuments everywhere. But it was Delta dirt." "This flood," she continues, "now forgotten by much of our nation, changed what our nation became" (332). Here, Franklin and Fennelly are most explicit about the novel's politics. Whether this veers into sermonic territory is debatable, but the significance of remembrance—of combating the lack of national memories of the event, the scarcity of memorialization or monuments—is foregrounded most precisely here. If literature can succeed in raising the past to the floodwater's surface, cultural memories of the flood may yet survive. Activating and imagining memories of the flood can help ensure that the cultural, political, and regional/national coordinates of the disaster are not forgotten or overlooked. A novel, which is perhaps even more complexly invested in these issues, and which opens out to a larger historical canvas, is Bernice L. McFadden's *Gathering of Waters*.

Gathering of Waters spans a vast history from colonialism to the twenty-first century but is focused on the town of Money, Mississippi. McFadden's narrator is a life force that is embedded in the town itself: "I am Money" the book opens (15). Having been "many selves and many things" brought into being through "growing, stretching, and expanding" (15), the narrator is an everlasting "soul," which, we are told, Native peoples and Africans believe "inhabit all objects, living things, and even phenomena" (16). Souls, however, bring along "baggage," which can often be memories (16). The memory-work of McFadden's novel begins with a Native past: "before white men came [to Money] . . . this place that I am was inhabited by . . . Choctaw Indians." Those Indians named the river and state of "Mississippi—which means *many gathering of waters*" (15). The novel then hurtles forward through generations to events like the 1927 flood and the murder of Emmett Till in 1955, and on to

Hurricane Katrina in 2005. The gathering of waters in this novel (so rooted in the spaces and geographies of Mississippi) might be reformulated as a gathering of memory.

Although Till's murder is at the heart of this novel—the narrator tells us that the story "begins not with the tragedy of '55 but long before that" (17)—and the place where his body is dumped in the Tallahatchie is one watery locale among many, the novel is clearly interested in the broader meaning of landscape and ecology. In 1900, the narrator tells us, a construction company built some "clapboard homes" on the land that would become Money. To do so, they "dug up the bones of the Choctaw Indians and the Africans" along the Tallahatchie River and "tore from their roots" (18) many trees, plants, and flowers. The northern shore, for instance, "was cleared of most of the ancient, towering long-leaf pines" (19), to make room for human settlement. Such deforestation and land-clearing are, for McFadden, violent acts that undergird Money: the founding of the town is one of erasure. Environmental disaster is deeply entangled in colonial and settler histories, but in charting a long sweep of Money's past, McFadden may be suggesting the network of events that enmesh in a specific regional memory. The novel overflows with this difficult history.

Early in the novel, we learn of a key character, Doll, who is a "thief" and a "bandit," though none of this apparently is "her fault—the spirit of a dead whore had taken root in Doll's body" (22). Esther, the spirit inside Doll, had been "half-buried for a decade" after a life of prostitution and violence; the men that lusted after her, and did all kinds of things to have sex with Doll, eventually "beat the goodness and the sweetness out of her" (24). Because of Esther's spirit, Doll "didn't make a good wife or a good mother" (51), and though considered scandalous in the local community, she marries a reverend. The presence of Esther is a complicated one; indeed, Doll's behavior is always shaped by the spirit inside her, or so the omniscient narrator tells us. That the driving force of "evil" in this novel is a dead prostitute's spirit is troubling; the way in which a sex-worker is cast into such a villainous role is not even tempered by the short explanation, quoted above, of how she is abused by the men around her.

Esther's spirit impacts not only Doll's life, but also the entirety of the region. For instance, when the torrential rains of 1927 begin to fall, Doll's husband August imagines that the community's sins are to blame; however, even this thought might be an unconscious response to his suspicion that Doll is sleeping with other men. The flood of 1927 is a major historical marker in the novel's memory-work. As the weather becomes increasingly inclement, "most folk in Mississippi couldn't think of anything but rain, mud, mosquitoes, and flooding"; "Bullet rain. Bucket rain. Rain as soft as rose petals" (103). The weather is keenly evoked through the fragmented sentences and alliteration, but the source of the rain is unclear. As the narrator says, focalized through August, the rain and floodwater did not wash "the stench of sin right out of the air" but rather "infused it, transforming it into an invisible vapor" (103) that seemingly has disastrous effects. Along with the changing weather, the "sinful air" triggers attacks and fights, and even impacts the killing of black people in the state: "MISSISSIPPI LEADS IN NEGRO LYNCHINGS" (104). It is as if the water, imbued with so-called sin (originating with Esther), is a dark and dangerous presence across the South. The flooding eventually worsens, "rising through the seams of the floorboards" (120) in a church, and upriver the levees break "and the Mississippi and all of her arteries breached their shores" (121). The surge destroys towns "like a beast" and kills many across the region. Doll, for instance, is killed in the flood—she "disappear[s] beneath the water" (123)—yet Esther lives on, falling into the "open mouth" of a young boy, J. W., who is near death. When the waters die down, "the riverbank looked like a battlefield," and the landscape is littered with people and detritus: "Floating bodies. Bodies in trees, trapped in houses" (128, 132). One cannot but see the flooded streets of New Orleans after Hurricane Katrina in this description; so many bodies, mainly black, were left dying and abandoned in the streets, on rooftops and elsewhere. The connection is underscored when the novel ends with Katrina's disastrous movement through the Gulf of Mexico.

Like the imaginative work of recalling the flood that McFadden's novel carries out, Susan Scott Parrish's book *The Flood Year 1927: A Cultural History* (2016) expansively considers the significance and role of the 1927 flood in the regional and national imagination. In short, it was a "major cultural phenomenon" that "was arguably the most publicly consuming environmental catastrophe of the twentieth century in the United States" (4). Indeed, the "nation's multifarious responses to the flood" (4) tell us much about the early 1900s and, of course, our current time. Connecting the flood, as McFadden also does, to Katrina in 2005, Parrish argues that "disaster-intensive periods . . . can both be placed along a continuum within the new planetary epoch . . . dubbed 'the Anthropocene'" (5). "The contours of the 1927 disaster," Parrish goes on, "its racial and regional manifestations, its political and media handling, its repercussions to human conceptions of self—show us what life within the Anthropocene has become" (7). It is uncertain, though, whether McFadden wants us to see the flood in this larger planetary framework. While it is certainly book-ended by other acts of environmental disaster (clearing, logging, storms, and so on), the sinful heart of Esther is central to the storm's path of wreckage.

The problematics of this notion continue as Esther's soul courses through J. W.'s body. Once a "sweet child," J. W. becomes, after the resurrection experience and Esther's habitation, incredibly violent. He is "suddenly fond of torturing living things: cats, puppies" and even ties up his baby sister's "ankles and wrists" to a tree, setting it ablaze (153). Though his mother makes excuses for him, "dub[bing] him extraordinary" because he seemingly came back to life from the dead, he nonetheless pursues his "burgeoning passion—murder" in World War II (153, 154). Esther's evil pushes J. W. to commit all kinds of atrocious acts, none more infamous and shocking than the murder of Emmett Till. The stories surrounding Till's killing—his visit to Mississippi from Chicago to stay with relatives; his supposed "wolf whistle" at a white woman; his vicious beating and murder; the dumping of his corpse in the Tallahatchie River; the open casket at his funeral, photographed and then disseminated worldwide; his mother Mamie Till Mobley's public response to the killing— are widely known and frequently remediated in works of fiction.[4] McFadden's representation of these events joins books like Lewis Nordan's *Wolf Whistle* (1993), for example, in thinking through the complexities of Till's death. At the time of his murder, as Thadious Davis explains, reflecting on "the image of [Till's] brutalized body became the new language to signify the treatment of black people under segregation and the place Mississippi held as the most vicious site of that treatment" (88). It is clear that even in the twenty-first century, the significance of remembering Till is keenly felt in the South, and in Mississippi particularly. McFadden interestingly addresses the wolf whistle by having shopkeeper Carolyn ask, "Do that whistle for me again, would you?" because "it made her feel included in something free and forbidden" (170). Here, the whistle is put squarely in Carolyn's, not Till's, hands, thus undermining the moment that ignites the violence thereafter. Conversely, McFadden undermines the racist killing of Till by locating the murderous agency of J. W. in Esther's spirit. I am troubled that Esther is the cause of his death, that when J. W. and Roy "Shot [Till] through the temple, tied him to a cotton gin fan, and tossed him in the Tallahatchie" (185), it is because of a haunting prostitute.

If we are able to put aside this problematic element of the plot, McFadden's novel still overflows with memory and its relation to water. As Till's body is dumped in the Tallahatchie, Roy (one of the killers) realizes he has "left his voice near the river, and when it finally found him again, it spewed out of his mouth in great, sorrowful wails of regret" (181). The liquidity of that wail is intimately connected with Till's watery grave and the memories of him that stubbornly persist. His memory lives on in the other characters' worlds, too. Tass, a local girl who falls in love with Till, always thinks about their time together: how "could she forget him?" (209). Moreover, other subsequent hate crimes, such as those targeting Medgar Evers and other civil rights workers in Mississippi, similarly "brought Emmett Till back to the forefront . . . [of] the minds of many people all around the world" (209). Till lives on in various recollections. Near the end of the novel, when Tass returns to Money, she sees Bryant's grocery store: it was "still standing" fifty years later, but it is "Vacant and ghostly," the narrator tells us, "surviv[ing] high winds and treacherous storms, holding onto a life that no longer wanted it" (237). The building's vitality is part of its role as a *lieux de mémoire* (or "site of memory"), in Pierre Nora's terms. The store lingers "as a sort of artificial placeholder" (Erll, *Memory* 23) for memory that might otherwise disappear. Bryant's store "stood as a reminder of the then and the now; refusing to die, it clung stubbornly to this world always, loudly insisting upon itself" (237). Loudly insisting, the spirit of Esther also continues to haunt this region of the United States.

At the very end of the novel when Tass dies, and Till's ghost takes her to the afterlife, Hurricane Katrina is gathering on the horizon. People begin to board up their homes and fill their cars with luggage, ready to leave the town. The narrator explains that "*she* . . . started to form over the Bahamas. . . . In the Gulf of Mexico, *she* suddenly turned furious. Draped in black clouds, blowing wind, and driving rain, *she* charged into Louisiana like a bull and fanned her billowing dark skirts over Mississippi" (252). While people called the storm Katrina, the narrator says, "I looked into the eye of that storm and recognized her for who she really was: Esther the whore, cackling and clapping her hands with glee" (252). The violent and malevolent spirit that contributed to the rise in lynchings and violence, the 1927 flood, and the death of Emmett Till is now also responsible for Katrina. McFadden's literary device is a dubious one; while she invokes African American and Native American conceptions of a spiritual life that might exceed so-called "rational" explanation, the shifting of blame onto a dead prostitute still rankles. It is as though, regardless of the imaginative leaps McFadden takes, the novel still must fall back on stereotypical villains: the jezebel figure has to embody a multitude of social forces for the narrative to move forward. Tacking on a final note, the narrator says, "Whether you have embraced this tale as truth or fantasy, I hope you will take something away from having read it. I pray you will become more sensitive to the world around you, the seen and unseen" (252). What is unseen, in this light, might just be malevolent spirits, rather than deeply rooted racism and inequality or climate change and environmental disaster. The "moral" message of *Gathering of Waters* is hazy. In one sense, the novel's attention to the role of memory in relation to a specific place allows us to formulate clearly rooted and emplaced visions of the past. In another, McFadden offloads a myriad of complex socio-historical forces relating to race and place onto an undead figure.

While McFadden as well as Franklin and Fennelly recollect memories of the southern past through their novels, this literary remembrance is always a process of (re)mediation, forever shaping the ways in which the past is presented. In turn, this affects the ways that memory is activated by us as readers. How these novels invoke the past in the present and then apply it to an unknown future is deserving of more attention. Both novels are interested in casting memories forward, proleptically imagining a time when the 1927 flood might be forgotten; this is a common feature of climate change fiction today.[5] In *The Titled World* and *Gathering of Waters,* the authors reimagine the southern past, and the southern landscape, to the same end: to retain, and to continue recollecting, memories that might otherwise be washed away either now or in the future. Though Franklin and Fennelly's text is more interested in textures of the local—people, towns, landscapes, wildlife—and McFadden's is more concerned with a deeper sense of time and space—from colonialism to the present—both books are deeply concerned with the imbrication of people and environment. Such an ecological vision is illuminated in very different ways by the texts. *The Tilted World* and *Gathering of Waters* are exemplary literary mediations of the South's precarious ecologies and environments.

In a *New York Times* article from August 2016, Jonah Engel Bromwich argues that "Climate change is never going to announce itself by name. But this is what we should expect it to look like": a growing number of deadly and widespread floods around the United States, especially in southern states like Louisiana and South Carolina. As the article's title simply puts it, "Flooding in the South Looks a Lot Like Climate Change." While flooding dominates literary reflections on the southern past and present, the future of the region's landscapes remains uncertain. Literary scholars of the South, in attending to floods of memory, can look forward and backward to old and new transformations of southern place. The Anthropocene demands multitudinous modes of writing that attempt to describe and evoke the short and long histories of environmental change, especially when they are embroiled in questions of race, poverty, place, and politics. *Gathering of Waters* and *The Tilted World* are small attempts at scaling that imaginative challenge.

NOTES

1. "Planetary Memory in Contemporary American Fiction," special issue of *Textual Practice*, vol. 31, no. 5 (2018). Edited by Lucy Bond, Ben De Bruyn, and Jessica Rapson.

2. See Christopher Lloyd, *Rooting Memory, Rooting Place: Regionalism in the Twenty-First-Century American South,* Palgrave Macmillan, 2015, pp. 53–84.

3. See, for instance, Timothy Clark, *Ecocriticism on the Edge: The Anthropocene as a Threshold Concept*, Bloomsbury, 2015.

4. For incisive interpretations of this field, see Harriet Pollack and Christopher Metress, editors, *Emmett Till in Literary Memory and Imagination*, Louisiana State UP, 2008.

5. For more on this mode of thinking in relation to climate change, see Sebastian Groes, "Introduction to Part III: Ecologies of Memory," 141.

WORKS CITED

Anderson, Eric Gary, Taylor Hagood, and Daniel Cross Turner. "Introduction." *Undead Souths: The Gothic and Beyond in Southern Literature and Culture,* edited by Anderson, Hagood, and Turner, Louisiana State UP, 2015, pp. 1–9.

Brinkmeyer, Robert H. Jr. "New Fiction on the Great Flood of 1927." *Virginia Quarterly Review,* vol. 90, no. 1, 2014, pp. 207–11.

Bromwich, Jonah Engel. "Flooding in the South Looks a Lot Like Climate Change." *The New York Times,* 16 Aug. 2012, https://www.nytimes.com/2016/08/17/us/climate-change -louisiana.html?_r=0. Accessed 26 Jan. 2017.

Davis, Thadious M. *Southscapes: Geographies of Race, Region and Literature.* U of North Carolina P, 2011.

Erll, Astrid. *Memory in Culture.* 2005. Translated by Sara B. Young, Palgrave Macmillan, 2011.

———. "Travelling Memory." *Parallax,* vol. 17, no. 4, 2011, pp. 4–18.

Franklin, Tom, and Beth Ann Fennelly. *The Tilted World.* 2013. Pan, 2014.

Groes, Sebastian. "Introduction to Part III: Ecologies of Memory." *Memory in the Twenty-First Century: Critical Perspectives from Sciences and Arts and Humanities,* edited by Sebastian Groes, London: Palgrave Macmillan, 2016, p. 141.

Heise, Ursula K. "Ecocriticism and the Transnational Turn in American Studies." *American Literary History,* vol. 20, no. 1–2, 2008, pp. 381–404.

Jackson, Robert. "The Southern Disaster Complex." *Mississippi Quarterly,* vol. 63, no. 3/4, Summer/Fall 2010, 555–70.

Marshall, Kate. "What Are the Novels of the Anthropocene? American Fiction in Geological Time." *American Literary History,* vol. 27, no. 3, 2015, pp. 523–38.

McFadden, Bernice L. *Gathering of Waters.* Akashic Books, 2012.

Morrison, Toni. "The Site of Memory." *Inventing the Truth: The Art and Craft of Memoir,* 2nd edition, edited by William Zinsser, Houghton Mifflin, 1995, pp. 83–102.

Parrish, Susan Scott. *The Flood Year 1927: A Cultural History.* Princeton UP, 2017.

Smith, Thomas Ruys. *River of Dreams: Imagining the Mississippi before Mark Twain.* Louisiana State UP, 2007.

Vermeulen, Pieter, and Stef Craps. "Introduction." "The Future Dynamics of Memory Studies—A Roundtable." *Memory Studies,* vol. 5, no. 2, 2012, pp. 223–26.

Watson, Jay. "The Other Matter of the South." *PMLA,* vol. 131, no. 1, 2016, pp. 157–61.

"I Want My City Back!"

The Boundaries of the Katrina Diaspora

EVANGELIA KINDINGER

In *Treme*'s third episode, "Right Place, Wrong Time," the character Davis Mc-Alary (Steve Zahn) is put in jail for insulting a National Guard officer in the city of New Orleans, shortly after Hurricane Katrina. Unable to comprehend why he is punished in such an exaggerated manner, he desperately tells his attorney Toni Bernette (Melissa Leo), "I want my city back!" (*Treme* 1.3). The episode's title reflects McAlary's demand: he might be in the right place, his hometown of New Orleans, yet three months after Hurricane Katrina hit the Gulf Coast, this is not his city anymore. The time is wrong; not so much the hurricane, but rather its aftermath has shifted the dynamics of the city and has turned its residents' lives upside down. McAlary's feelings of loss, separation, and loyalty are strikingly reminiscent of those experienced and voiced by diasporans, people who have had to leave their homes in order to seek a safe and fulfilling life elsewhere. However, McAlary has not left his home; he is still in New Orleans. His experiences, as well as those of other characters in *Treme,* suggest that the boundaries of diaspora need to be redrawn in order to grasp the effects Hurricane Katrina had for the residents of New Orleans.

Eric Overmyer and David Simon's critically acclaimed ensemble drama that ran from 2010 until 2013 on HBO covers the first three-and-a-half years after the storm and narrates a diverse group's personal stories of recovery, as well as "the city's grueling journey back" (Leyda 244). *Treme* is both appreciated and criticized for its play with authenticity and the tourist gaze, for its focus on the New Orleans artist-intellectual community and the city's rich cultural heritage. It circulates southern (or rather New Orleanian) exceptionalism and simultaneously tries to grasp the complex interplay of race, class, culture, and politics in the city. "[A]s a televisual belonging quiz" (Fuqua 235), and with its expansive references to local culture and its use of local celebrities, *Treme* works as a didactic text for outsiders and a nostalgic text for those familiar with the city and its people. It addresses belonging, not only that of its viewers, but of its characters as well—specifically their struggles to foster and reclaim their belonging to the beloved hometown that changed significantly after the storm. The alienation and the consequential attempt to recover and reunite the self, communities, and the city are central to the appeal of *Treme*'s post-Katrina narrative. Looking at belonging and questions of home in more detail, I propose reading *Treme* as a diaspora text that examines geographical and emotional separation, trauma, longing, recovery, and return.

DIASPORA STUDIES AND THE KATRINA DIASPORA

As a response to the increasing transnational mobility of peoples across the globe and the often diffuse circumstances that inform or cause this mobility, "diaspora" has gained considerable momentum since the 1990s. A term "derived from the Greek verb *speiro* (to sow) and the preposition *dia* (over)" (Cohen ix, emphasis original), historically "the Diaspora had a very specific meaning: the exile of the Jews from their historic homeland and their dispersion throughout many lands, signifying as well the oppression and moral degradation implied by that dispersion" (Safran 83). While this traditional understanding of diaspora is based on forced dispersal and its traumatic effects, the term was revived and reconceptualized in recent decades to describe different kinds of dispersion from an imagined or real homeland. As Khachig Tölölyan explains in the first edition of *Diaspora: A Journal for Transnational Studies* (1991): "We use 'diaspora' provisionally to indicate our belief that the term that once described Jewish, Greek, and Armenian dispersion now shares meanings with a larger semantic domain that includes words like immigrant, expatriate, refugee, guestworker, exile community, overseas community, ethnic community" (4). These "words"—or rather, various forms of existence caused by transnational migratory movements—have turned diaspora into a more inclusive concept that always needs to be contextualized and particularized in order to be accurate about the impacts these movements have on identity and the nation-state. There is no ideal diaspora, only characteristics of diaspora communities that can be utilized to draw comparisons and understand the role of diaspora in a global context.

One unifying feature of most diasporas is the role of the original homeland for the creation and sustainment of diaspora communities. Even after generations "all diasporic communities settled outside their natal (or imagined natal) territories, acknowledge that 'the old country'—a notion often buried deep in language, religion, custom or folklore—always has some claim on their loy-

alty and emotions" (Cohen ix). Diasporans display a "dual orientation" (Werbner 5) to the place of settlement and the so-called natal territories that goes
along with a continuous investment in both places. Robin Cohen suggests that
this orientation or investment in the "old country" is nurtured by a "myth
about the homeland" (184), which William Safran specifies as a myth about
the homeland's "physical location, history, and achievements" (83) that creates
unity even within very heterogeneous diaspora communities. This myth about
the homeland is expressed through longing, specifically longing to eventually return to this place that is a diasporan's emotional anchor. The narrative
of return implies that diasporans "regard their ancestral homeland as their
true, ideal home and as the place to which they or their descendants would (or
should) eventually return" (83). While definite return is seldom performed,
the imaginative return affects diaspora consciousness and communities, and
strengthens the transnational ties diasporans foster.

Yet diaspora is not solely a transnational phenomenon; it can refer to an
intranational dispersion that is marked by an orientation toward a "homeland"
that is localized or regionalized. Although diaspora scholars like Tölölyan have
criticized the seemingly never-ending flexibility and inclusivity of the term
as "conceptually untidy" ("Contemporary Discourse" 648), non-transnational
dispersion can also be classified as diasporic if it fulfills core characteristics
of traditional diasporas, such as the journey and settlement "from a specific
original 'center' to two or more 'peripheral,' or foreign, regions" (Safran 83),
the continuous loyalty for and orientation toward this "center," and the importance of the narrative of return. Despite its occasional untidiness, "it may
be best to think of diaspora not as the name of a fixed concept and social
formation but as a process of collective identification and form of identity"
(Tölölyan, "Contemporary Discourse" 649–50). For the people who had to leave
New Orleans before and after Hurricane Katrina hit the city, this catastrophic
event has become decisive for their identification with the US South, the nation, and the city itself. Shortly after the storm, and even a decade later, New
Orleanians, especially black New Orleanians seeking shelter, were labeled "refugees" by mainstream media outlets (cf. *Fox News,* the *Wall Street Journal, USA
Today*). Quickly, this was deemed a highly problematic term, because it "helped
construct a view of the victims as undeserving of government and resources"
(Fox Gotham and Greenberg 71). Because Hurricane Katrina evacuees were
labeled "refugees," these American citizens' fates were discarded as not being
of national concern. "Refugees" expressed "a deep unease with the notion that

African Americans might need to look to anything other than their citizenship in order to legitimate their rights" (Hartnell 24). In addition, "the displaced population was also figuratively construed as outside the norm of middle-class white citizenship—and indeed, a threat to it" (Kish 672). While limitations of space preclude an extensive discussion of the validity of the term "refugee" and the ways in which it was both racialized and classed, what is most pressing for the current argument is that "diaspora" was utilized as a term to counter "refugee," despite the terms' complex conceptual intersections.

The Katrina Diaspora was, like most diasporas, "born out of catastrophe" (Tölölyan, "Contemporary Discourse" 649)—in this case an environmental catastrophe that was worsened by human habitation and ecological manipulation of low-lying lands in southern Louisiana. This catastrophe caused intranational dispersion and generated a "rhetoric of restoration and return that, in practice, takes the form of a sustained and organized commitment to maintaining relations with kin communities" (649). This commitment, I argue, whether organized or not, facilitates the myth of home. Diaspora is more than a term descriptive of dispersion; it is, as Steven Vertovec has argued, a consciousness,

> a particular kind of awareness said to be generated among contemporary transnational communities. . . . Its particularity is variously described as being marked by a dual or paradoxical nature. It is constituted negatively by experiences of discrimination and exclusion, and positively by identification with an historical heritage . . . or contemporary world cultural or political forces. (281)

Its paradox lies in the investment diasporans have in their home(lands) while living, or having settled, outside this mythical place. *Treme* is a product of this consciousness, as it participates in the "rhetoric of restoration and return" and responds to what Helen Taylor described as "the refrain in the years since the 2005 catastrophe": "'Home' and the desire to 'go home'" (486).

In August of 2015, the *Times-Picayune* published an interactive map to display the diasporans, who are termed "post-Katrina transplants" (Swenson). While New Orleans residents are shown to return gradually, approximately 65,000 households have "transplanted," according to these maps, somewhere else. One of the few publications dedicated solely to these "transplants," *Displaced: Life in the Katrina Diaspora* (2012), edited by Lori Peek and Lynn Weber, offers relevant insights into the concrete processes of the Katrina Diaspora;

yet it falls victim to the untidiness Tölölyan ascribes to many works about the diaspora. The editors miss the chance to establish their understanding of diaspora, abandoning the term in the course of their introductory remarks in favor of "internally displaced persons" (2). This kind of displacement refers to displacement within one's supposed home, in this case the Gulf region, the South, or the United States and is thus a paradox as such, because the traditional understanding of home suggests belonging, not displacement. The language used to describe the condition of Katrina diasporans—displaced, dislocated, dispersed, or transplanted—indicates the spatial dimension of diasporas. The title of Peek and Weber's volume, for instance, suggests that people live displaced *in* the diaspora, as if this were an actual physical space. And indeed, especially Avtar Brah has stressed the importance of space for diaspora theory and experiences, and refers to diaspora as a space: "the intersectionality of diaspora, border, and dis/location as a point of confluence of economic, political, cultural and psychic processes" (181).

These processes did not suddenly surface after the hurricane hit New Orleans and the Gulf Coast; the Katrina Diaspora is the result of long-established and institutionalized economic and political processes, which deemed some residents more vulnerable to dislocation and trauma than others. Particularly poor New Orleanians—some white, but predominantly people of color—were exposed to the destruction of the hurricane and the subsequent breaking of the levees to a greater extent than other more affluent residents. The Katrina Diaspora is a victim diaspora, "a social formation engendered by catastrophic violence" (Tölölyan, "Contemporary Discourse" 648). However, the violence caused by Hurricane Katrina—the loss of life, property, home, and humanity—was quickly exposed as more than the "side effect" of a natural disaster. Despite the spectacular images of winds, rain, and flooding, Hurricane Katrina resulted from what Rob Nixon calls "slow violence," the consequence of climate change that does not have the "sensational visibility" (2) of other forms of violence, but rather "occurs gradually and out of sight, a violence of delayed destruction that is dispersed across time and space, an attritional violence that is typically not viewed as violence at all" (2). Hurricane Katrina, as an outcome of the Anthropocene, of an age in which the invasive human influence on the world's climate cannot be countermanded or undone anymore, is symptomatic of an age in which the natural and the social are irreversibly intertwined:

Katrina is a natural phenomenon that is what it is in part because of human social structures and practices. Seeing through the eye of Katrina reveals no hard-and-fast divide between natural and social; rather, they are seamlessly swept together in its counter-clockwise rotation. Katrina came into being because of a concatenation of phenomena—low pressure areas, warm ocean waters, and perhaps swirling in that classic cyclone pattern are the phenomena of deforestation and industrialization. (Tuana 192)

The natural phenomena Nancy Tuana mentions conglomerated with "the failure of human technology and the collapse of an engineered levee system designed to protect residents" (Picou and Marshall 2). Yet not only "human technology" failed the residents; they fell victim to more than a faulty levee system. The deep-rooted racism and classism that structured the New Orleans "cityscape" for centuries placed the most disenfranchised residents in the most undesirable and vulnerable positions within the city, close to the levees. Hurricane Katrina was an "unnatural disaster" (cf. Dyson; Hartman and Squires; Levitt and Whitaker), or a "natural-technological . . . disaster" (Picou and Marshall 5) that led to the traumatic dispersion of residents, the formation of a diaspora, and a consequent consciousness that is based on these experiences of violence, vulnerability, and negligence.

THE KATRINA DIASPORA IN *TREME*

Treme can be read as an extreme weather text (cf. Leyda and Negra), because all actions are motivated by the outcomes of Hurricane Katrina. It is also an ecocritical text in that it responds to the environmental crisis that culminated in Hurricane Katrina. This response is highly anthropocentric; while it visualizes the catastrophic violence laid bare by Hurricane Katrina, *Treme* focuses on how individuals and human communities deal with this violence instead of explicitly addressing climate change and the concurrent vulnerability of New Orleans and its surrounding environment. *Treme*'s anthropocentric approach is mirrored in the series' interest in the Katrina Diaspora, which is represented through various story lines. As Kevin Dowler has observed, for instance, the numerous scenes of encounter, in which the protagonists and minor characters ask each other about the whereabouts of other people, "serve . . . to remind everyone, including the show's audience, of the forced distribution of bodies to various sites: Baton Rouge, Houston, and places beyond, stretching across most of the continental United States" (151). The story lines, which exemplify the burdens of diaspora most explicitly, are those of jazz musician Delmond Lambreaux (Rob Brown) and chef Janette Desautel (Kim Dickens) who, despite differences in race, gender, and class, share a diaspora experience. For various reasons, they have both decided not to live solely in New Orleans, but rather to travel back-and-forth between there and New York City, a "serialized coming and going" (Fuqua 236), which also addresses the imagined and long-established tensions between the so-called North and South.

Traditional conceptualizations of diaspora rely on the separation of those who left or have had to leave and those left "behind." Outside of the homeland/ hometown is the diaspora. Yet as Brah has persuasively argued, diaspora space is more inclusive than former definitions suggest: "diaspora space as a conceptual category is 'inhabited' not only by those who have migrated and their descendants, but equally by those who are constructed and represented as indigenous" (181). Inspired by Brah's breaking open of diaspora boundaries, I argue that more important than those "represented as indigenous" in the places of new settlement are those who stay behind; they, too, are participants and makers of diaspora space. Consequently, diaspora is inclusive of those who left and those who stayed behind, because both groups feel absence and dislocation, and develop a nostalgic longing for restoration and completeness. If "a diaspora that is born out of catastrophe inflicted on the collective suffers trauma and usually becomes a community to which the work of memory, commemoration, and mourning is central" (Tölölyan, "Contemporary Discourse" 649), then the community that dwells in the place considered home is also engaged with the memory and mourning of times and people lost. They share diaspora space with those who have left. *Treme* is a diaspora text, because all characters who define themselves as New Orleanians share this diaspora space, regardless of whether they stay or leave.

One of the most popular characters of the first season, Creighton Bernette (John Goodman), is exemplary of this inclusive understanding of diaspora: although he remains in the city with his wife Toni and daughter Sofia (India Ennenga), he is part of the Katrina Diaspora, because he is as dislocated from what used to be a familiar and homely place as those who had to leave. He mourns the loss of his city to such an extent that he decides to take his own life in Season One. As a fierce nonnative lover and defender of his chosen home, and a "member of the [white] middle-class elite" (Leyda 246), his suicide might appear alienating, exaggerated, and unnecessary, because he lives in relatively safe and prosperous circumstances compared to other characters of the series. Yet while Creighton's loss is not material as such, it is distinctively psychological; he has developed a diaspora consciousness. In his seminal essay "Diasporas," James Clifford defines diaspora consciousness as "[e]xperiences of loss, marginality, and exile," and "constitutive suffering" that "coexists with the skills of survival" (312). Creighton, unlike the rest of the characters, feels loss and believes he lives in internal exile; as a result, he gives in to the suffering and does not survive the catastrophe.

In the episode "All on a Mardi Gras Day," Creighton and his daughter Sofia look at the ruins of the city as he points out buildings and institutions that do not exist anymore. In this haunting scene, Creighton is shown to feel the buildings' absence and the loss more urgently than his daughter. In self-made YouTube videos, he seeks an audience with which to share his anger about the government's mismanagement of the city; in one video, he states, "Living here now is like a dream, the way that everything in a dream is the same yet not the same. Familiar yet strange. Not quite right, but you just can't put your finger on it. . . . Whatever comes next is just a dream of what used to be" (*Treme* 1.8). As one of those who stayed behind, he feels the absence of people and buildings to be devastating, because it transforms "home," a supposedly familiar place of comfort, into a strange, unrelatable place. Restoring the city as he knew (or rather imagined) it seems impossible—New Orleans will never be the same again. The "Katrina fatigue" he accuses the nation of, in the end, is also his own fatigue. The loss he feels is existential, and he ultimately gives himself up to the city by jumping into Lake Pontchartrain. As Tuana has stated, "Katrina . . . is emblematic of the viscous porosity between humans and our environment, between social practices and natural phenomena. . . . [T]here is no sharp ontological divide here, but rather a complex interaction of phenomena" (193). Creighton's death powerfully visualizes this porosity.

Like Creighton, Delmond and Janette represent the complexity of diaspora life, which Cohen has structured by means of nine features, among them "(4) an idealization of the supposed ancestral home; (5) a return movement; (6) strong ethnic group consciousness; (7) a troubled relationship with host societies; (8) a sense of solidarity with co-ethnic members; and (9) the possibility of a distinctive creative, enriching life in tolerant host countries" (180). Delmond's and Janette's story lines support the perseverance of the myth of home and the myth of the exceptionalism of pre- and post-Katrina New Orleans, and their story lines also display a strong local *and* diaspora consciousness that results from a troubled relationship with their host city, New York City.

Similar to Creighton, Janette feels defeated by New Orleans. Not only has she had to close down her restaurant in Season One, but after heavy rains, her rooftop caves in and the water drenches everything. Reading it as a cosmic sign, she tells her then-boyfriend Davis, "The thunderstorm cleared things for me. . . . [T]his town beat me. As much as I love it, I'm not trying to fight it anymore" (*Treme* 1.9). She personifies the city as her personal antagonist and decides to leave it, lamenting that all it offers are beautiful moments but not a life. In search of "life" and in order to push her career forward, she moves to New York City. Davis, next to Creighton probably the most insistently comic, adorable, and annoying advocate of New Orleans's culture, announces that her moving to "the North" is not a good idea; he tries to sell New Orleans and its merits—a four-hour lunch, Second Line parades, beignets, music, po' boys, afternoon naps, partying. In the end, though, he fails to convince Janette to stay.

In Season Two, *Treme* paints a disheartening image of life in the diaspora, away from New Orleans. It creates a version of New York City along the lines of common stereotypes about the city as tough, unforgiving, and anonymous. Janette is shown to have "a troubled relationship" (Cohen 180) with her new home, and instead of being her own boss, she works for a tyrant chef. Her unhappiness is visualized by typical New York iconography and cacophony; permanent traffic noise, sirens, high-rises, inclement weather and cold, and the blue lighting she is shot in all reflect her disposition. Shots of her alone in New York are interrupted by warm-colored images of New Orleans leisure activities, primarily music sessions that are utilized to create a contrast between the cities. A shot of a crowded and ecstatic New Orleans gig is immediately followed by images of Janette, drinking alone in a New York bar. Despite her resignation and the rather sobering trips back to New Orleans, she voices her belonging to the city, and thereby her nonbelonging to New York, proudly. In an act of local and personal emancipation, she throws a Sazerac (a signature New Orleans drink) into food critic Alan Richman's face, as she was enraged by his dismissive and snobbish *GQ* article on New Orleans cuisine, "Yes, We're Open," which was in reality published in 2006 and incorporated into the narrative. In reaction to his outrageous claim that Creoles "are a faerie folk, like leprechauns, rather than an indigenous race," and that "New Orleans was always a three-day stubble of a city" (Richman), she tells him, "Excuse me. This is how we Creole faerie folk back home cure their three-day stubble" (*Treme* 2.4).

Janette certainly displays a "strong ethnic consciousness" (Cohen 180) in this scene. Moreover, she displays a diaspora consciousness: away from home she feels her city's pull and loyalty to its people, history, and customs.

Delmond's diaspora experience seems different at first; he left before Hurricane Katrina and only reluctantly returns to help out his father, Albert "Big Chief" Lambreaux (Clarke Peters), after the storm. Still, witnessing his father's resilience turns him into a diasporan. As a jazz musician, he sought distance from New Orleans "trad jazz," only to discover a longing to grapple with the city, as well as with his father's Indian traditions. His version of New York is screened primarily through his performances in upscale, rather sterile-looking large venues that are cut by images of sweaty, crowded, loose performances in New Orleans, which in their own way reproduce common tropes about the city and its people before Katrina. As Kim M. Leduff puts it rather exaggeratedly, "[p]rior to Katrina, New Orleans and its residents had a reputation: they party . . . they let the good times roll! . . . ; and they eat well" (136). *Treme* tries to balance out this reputation with distinctive story lines about police violence and corruption, while it still portrays what Taylor calls "the city's cultural heritage . . . its cuisine, music, parades, gardens of scented blossom, eroticism, sexual transgression and sheer hedonism" (501). This heritage is not trivialized, though, but rather is deemed essential for the survival of the city and its residents, whose heritage was almost washed out.

Delmond also gets his own emancipation scene, defending his hometown and proudly declaring himself part of the New Orleans diaspora. At a New York party, people ask him about New Orleans, suggesting it will never again be the same. In this conversation, New Orleans outsiders are represented as pretentious, "[f]ucking know-it-all New Yorkers" (*Treme* 2.1), as Delmond explains to his girlfriend, enraged by their attitude. The New Yorkers at the party think they praise Delmond when they suggest his music is of value exactly because "it transcends New Orleans," is not so-called "Dixieland shit," and is not "caught in that tourist economy, like a minstrel show" (*Treme* 2.1). Delmond reacts very strongly to this comment before storming out to the balcony, which stands—in order to stress the location of such ignorance—right in front of the Empire State Building. Like Janette, he declares his belonging to New Orleans and its traditions to oppose outsiders' presumptions about his hometown.

Both characters, while successful in New York, are established as foreigners in the city, surrounded by a more or less hostile environment, which pushes them back to New Orleans and its musical and culinary traditions. Their emancipatory moments are those in which they stand against New York, the so-called beacon of culture. Delmond turns his back on modern jazz and, inspired by more traditional jazz and Indian calls and drums, decides to bring both together, trying to capture the essence of New Orleans. He ends up recording a jazz/Indian fusion album with his father and fellow New Orleans musicians, the first project that seems to make him happy and that brings him closer to the Big Chief. The separation from New Orleans and the perceived continuing loss of local music and cultural traditions lead to the discovery of his roots.

Janette, on the contrary, is always depicted as an advocate for and connoisseur of local cuisine. Unlike Delmond, though, she has not found her own style yet. Interestingly, she finds it in New York. Working in a liberating environment, the Lucky Peach, chef David Chang (appearing as himself) asks her to do "Southern food. New Orleans food": "Do your own take on it. Our own take on it" (*Treme* 2.10). This is not enough, though; in Season Three, she returns to New Orleans to open her own restaurant. New York, while depicted as an undesirable place, is also the setting that opens "the possibility of a distinctive creative . . . life" (Cohen 180). As diasporans, Janette and Delmond are among "alien host societies" (Tölölyan, "Contemporary Discourse" 648) in which they not only try to hold on to their old identities, but try to generate new ones that encompass their diaspora experiences. New York liberates them to find their own style, which is highly inspired by "home," the place they return to. *Treme* clearly reproduces a diaspora "rhetoric of restoration and return" (649).

CONCLUSION

The diaspora narratives in *Treme,* I suggest, have different effects. For one, they certainly promote New Orleans's positive and negative exceptionalism, the ways the city has been historically constructed and imagined as an exceptional place within the South and the nation. "[S]omehow outside the American mainstream" (Keeble 55), New Orleans "has long maintained a distinctive status within the national imaginary" (Negra 2), an imaginary based on "European-American cultural affinities . . . a 'Carribeanized' site of flamboyance, multiculturalism, and multiracialism" (2). This exceptionalism, according to Leyda, was functionalized after the storm: "Mainstream America's paradoxical love and disdain for New Orleans became particularly clear in media representations of Katrina and its aftermath, underscoring the city's exceptional status" (244). In *Treme,* this status is supported by the staging of New York City as a place opposed to and decidedly different from New Orleans. Herman Gray, referring to the contrasts created by means of music between the two cities, observes that in the scenes in which the music "moves between New York City and New Orleans," the latter is "authentic, pure, origin, uncontaminated, a wellspring of precious traditions," while the former is "the place of success, of headlines, and recognition" (274). I agree, yet Delmond's and Janette's stories also suggest that success and recognition can eventually result from these "precious traditions."

Although *Treme* does not necessarily idealize life in post-Katrina New Orleans, laying bare stories of loss, violence, and corruption, these stories are always countered by what Delmond calls the "joy and life" of the city. And indeed, one common and necessary narrative of exceptionalism circulated post-Katrina has been that of perseverance and support. In *Treme,* the people "persevere; they overcome; and they triumph in the face of the storm" (Leduff 136). Taylor's emphasis that the survival of the city is based on a "fiercely loyal" (486) population in and outside the city is clearly shown in the series. The diasporans, Creighton, Janette, and Delmond, among others, idealize their hometown and cultivate its mythic status as a city "of new starts, transformation, destruction and rebuilding" (485). Janette experiences numerous new starts: after her second attempt at owning a restaurant fails in Season Three, her former business partner symbolically exiles her when he forbids her to use her own name for a new restaurant. She is back home, yet still internally displaced. Like the city, it seems, she perseveres, though, and in Season Four's final episode, we see her looking proudly at her new restaurant's sign "Desautel's on Dauphine." As a diasporan, she has returned from New York, has fought for her identity and her name, and has succeeded. Delmond ends up leading a diaspora life: after the birth of his child, he decides to live both in New York and New Orleans, or, as he formulates it, to "keep a foot in both places" (*Treme* 4.5). This diaspora life promises to be full of departures, arrivals, and returns.

As these story lines show, the boundaries of the Katrina Diaspora need to be understood as flexible. Interestingly, this flexibility counters the exceptionalism promoted in the series. The Katrina Diaspora is not unique; it is a result of slow violence, and it displays features common to most modern diasporas and thus joins the members of other intranational and transnational diaspora communities who were dispersed from their center, who retained a collective memory of home, who feel alienated in host environments, who wish to return, who believe in the maintenance and restoration of the original home, and who feel solidarity with other members of the diaspora. Post-Katrina narratives are necessarily concerned with diaspora consciousness, diaspora spaces, and their boundaries, albeit some more than others. Beyond the importance these narratives, and the Katrina Diaspora as such, have for the region and the nation, they also need to be evaluated within a global network of diasporas that have resulted from violence, forced expulsion, government negligence, and the changes in climate that dictate life in the twenty-first century.

WORKS CITED

Brah, Avtar. *Cartographies of Diaspora: Contesting Identities.* Routledge, 1996.

Clifford, James. "Diasporas." *Cultural Anthropology,* vol. 9, no. 3, 1994, pp. 302–38.

Cohen, Robin. *Global Diasporas: An Introduction.* U of Washington P, 1997.

Dowler, Kevin. "Dismemberment, Repetition, and Working-Through: Keeping Up in *Treme.*" *Canadian Review of American Studies,* vol. 43, no. 1, 2013, pp. 145–63.

Dyson, Michael Eric. *Come Hell or High Water: Hurricane Katrina and the Color of Disaster.* Basic Books, 2006.

Fox Gotham, Kevin, and Miriam Greenberg. *Crisis Cities: Disaster and Redevelopment in New York and New Orleans.* Oxford UP, 2014.

Fox News. "Half Katrina Refugees Have Records." foxnews.com, 22 Sept. 2005, http://www .foxnews.com/story/2005/09/22/half-katrina-refugees-have-records.html. Accessed 26 Mar. 2017.

Gray, Herman. "Recovered, Reinvented, Reimagined: *Treme,* Television Studies and Writing New Orleans." *Television & New Media,* vol. 13, no. 3, 2012, pp. 268–78.

Hartman, Chester, and Gregory D. Squires, editors. *There Is No Such Thing as a Natural Disaster: Race, Class, and Hurricane Katrina.* Routledge, 2006.

Hartnell, Anna. "'When the Levees Broke': Inconvenient Truths and the Limits of National Identity." *African American Review,* vol. 45, no. ½, 2012, pp. 17–31.

Keeble, Arin. "Won't bow: Don't know how: *Treme,* New Orleans and American Exceptionalism." *European Journal of American Culture,* vol. 35, no. 1, 2016, pp. 51–76.

Leduff, Kim M. "*Down in the Treme* . . . Buck Jumping and Having Fun? The Impact of Depictions of Post-Katrina New Orleans on Viewers' Perceptions of the City." *Watching While Black: Centering the Television of Black Audiences,* edited by Beretta E. Smith-Shomade. Rutgers UP, 2012, pp. 121–37.

Levitt, Jeremy I., and Matthew C. Whitaker, editors. *Hurricane Katrina: America's Unnatural Disaster.* U of Nebraska P, 2009.

Leyda, Julia. "'This Complicated, Colossal Failure': The Abjection of Creighton Bernette in HBO's *Treme*." *Television & New Media*, vol. 13, no. 3, 2012, pp. 243–60.

Leyda, Julia, and Diane Negra. "Extreme Weather and Global Media." *Extreme Weather and Global Media*, edited by Leyda Julia and Diane Negra, Routledge, 2015, pp. 1–28.

Negra, Diane. "Introduction: Old and New Media after Katrina." *Old and New Media after Katrina*, edited by Diane Negra, Palgrave Macmillan, 2010, pp. 1–22.

Nixon, Rob. *Slow Violence and the Environmentalism of the Poor*. Harvard UP, 2011.

Peek, Lori, and Lynn Weber, editors. *Displaced: Life in the Katrina Diaspora*. U of Texas P, 2012.

Picou, J. Steven, and Brent K. Marshall. "Katrina as Paradigm Shift: Reflections on Disaster Research in the Twenty-First Century." *The Sociology of Katrina: Perspectives on a Modern Catastrophe*, edited by David L. Brunsma et al., Rowman & Littlefield, 2007, pp. 1–20.

Richman, Alan. "Yes, We're Open." *GQ Magazine*, 2 Nov. 2006, http://www.gq.com/story/katrina-new-orleans-food. Accessed 22 Mar. 2017.

Safran, William. "Diasporas in Modern Societies: Myths of Homeland and Return." *Diaspora: A Journal of Transnational Studies*, vol. 1, no. 1, 1991, pp. 83–99.

Swenson, Dan. "Hurricane Katrina Migration: Where Did People Go? Where Are They Coming from Now?" *The Times-Picayune*, 26 Aug. 2015, http://www.nola.com/katrina/index.ssf/2015/08/hurricane_katrina_migration_di.html. Accessed 26 Mar. 2017.

Taylor, Helen. "After the Deluge: The Post-Katrina Cultural Revival of New Orleans." *Journal of American Studies*, vol. 44, 2010, pp. 483–501.

Wall Street Journal. "Hurricane Katrina Refugees Sink Deep Roots in Houston a Decade Later." *wsj.com*, 27 Aug. 2015, https://www.wsj.com/articles/hurricane-katrina-refugees-sink-deep-roots-in-houston-a-decade-later-1440696252. Accessed 23 Mar. 2017.

Tölölyan, Khachig. "The Contemporary Discourse of Diaspora Studies." *Comparative Studies of South Asia, Africa and the Middle East*, vol. 27, no. 3, 2007, pp. 647–55.

———. "The Nation-State and Its Others: In Lieu of a Preface." *Diaspora: A Journal of Transnational Studies*, vol. 1, no. 1, 1991, pp. 3–7.

Treme. Season One, created by David Simon and Eric Overmyer, HBO, 2011.

———. Season Two, created by David Simon and Eric Overmyer, HBO, 2011.

———. Season Three, created by David Simon and Eric Overmyer, HBO, 2012.

———. Season Four, created by David Simon and Eric Overmyer, HBO, 2014.

Tuana, Nancy. "Viscous Porosity: Witnessing Katrina." *Material Feminisms*, edited by Stacy Alaimo and Susan Hekman, Indiana UP, 2009.

USA Today. "States Struggling with Katrina Refugees." usatoday.com, 5 Sept. 2005, http://usatoday30.usatoday.com/news/nation/2005-09-05-katrina-refugees_x.htm. Accessed 26 Mar. 2017.

Vertovec, Steven. "Three Meanings of 'Diaspora,' Exemplified among South Asian Religions." *Diaspora: A Journal of Transnational Studies*, vol. 6, no. 3, 1997, pp. 277–99.

Werbner, Pnina. "The Materiality of Diaspora—Between Aesthetics and 'Real' Politics." *Diaspora*, vol. 9, no. 1, 2000.

The Universe Unraveled

Swampy Embeddedness and Ecological Apocalypse in
Beasts of the Southern Wild

SARAH E. MCFARLAND

A friend warned me when I first moved to Louisiana from the Pacific Northwest that I had to be careful: there is something about this place that oozes in.
She was right. Like heat and wet, it sneaks past the hard vowels and demean-
ored defenses into your very blood, coursing through each cell until you find
yourself part of the humid hot moistness, grown into the live oaks dripping
with Spanish moss, the slow bayous with their brown water and cypress knees
as familiar as the old penny color of a proper roux no longer being cooked for
you but bubbling in gumbo on your own stove. And like the fusing of "this
and that" in gumbo, there is no sharply demarcated "wilderness" in Louisiana,
at least not in the sublimity of the western sense: there are no vast expanses
of untrammeled land, no thrilling mountain views, no separate civilization
against which wildness can be opposed. Instead, blended together are green
spaces and small towns, agriculture and agrarian living interlaced with swamp-
lands, pine forests, hunting leases, and kitchen gardens. Black bayous mirror
clear blue skies peppered with eagles, hawks, herons, uncountable songbirds,
and, inevitably, vultures circling some freshly dead treasure.

As is true everywhere but obvious here, then, nature and culture do not
occupy separate domains. All the same, it was not so long ago in history that
we humans considered ourselves a separate and superior creation divinely
granted authority over the natural environs, at least in the Western tradition.
Even after Darwin's evolutionary theory forced us to accept that we are related
through descent to other animals, we have maintained a polite fiction that preserves a comfortable distance, entrenching human exceptionalism within our
humanist philosophies and environmentalisms: humans are intelligent and
extraordinary, and, therefore, we will survive the consequences of our ecological exploitation, a deeply felt anthropocentrism that is hard to fight. Yet we
are nonetheless animals, as embroiled in environmental change as any other
creature.

That change is significant in Louisiana, where even the state's silhouette constantly evolves, the coastline's twists and bends melting inland so rapidly that printed maps cannot possibly reflect an accurate seaboard. Estimated to be utterly gone by 2050 at current rates of loss, Louisiana's coastal wetlands have been transformed into open water largely because of erosion and greatly hastened by canals cut by oil and shipping industries,[1] and the wetlands were also forever changed by environmental disasters, including the horrific wreckage caused by Hurricanes Katrina and Rita in 2005 and the Deepwater Horizon oil gush in 2010. Another major factor contributing to Louisiana's coastal erosion and environmental destruction is the Mississippi River-Gulf Outlet, the shipping channel in St. Bernard Parish that has allowed marsh-killing saltwater to invade more than 27,000 acres of wetlands since the 1960s when it was completed. Oil companies dredged canals through the wetlands on exploratory missions that actually increased in number after Hurricanes Katrina and Rita, despite the fact that wetlands decrease wind speed and would shield coastal Louisiana from the full force of future hurricanes. There is some good news, though: on January 3, 2017, the Louisiana Coastal Protection and Restoration Authority released its master plan for wetland restoration and coastal protections, although it is unclear at this point whether the plan includes new protections or only funds repairs of current levee systems, or whether it will be ignored entirely at the federal level by the new presidential administration.[2] As Paul Sutter points out, "In a disproportionately poor and rural region renowned for being friendly to migrating industries and slow to regulate environmental impacts, southern environmentalists have had a hard time getting traction" (4). As a state with a permissive regulatory culture and with populations of people who lack political power and experience substantial poverty, it is most likely that Louisiana will continue to bear the brunt of wetland loss, air and water pollution, industrial and military waste disposal, and other environmental degradations. There is a twisted social, political, and religious Gordian knot of issues at play here.[3]

Thus, in this chapter, I analyze the complicated environmentalisms in Behn Zeitlin's postdiluvian film *Beasts of the Southern Wild* (2012), which is about agency and empowerment in times of ecological uncertainty and promotes a type of storytelling that is attentive to the ecological fabric of the entire coastal ecosystem and all species living there. Importantly for considerations of the future of southern studies, I argue, *Beasts* leaves readers and viewers aware that it is too late for the swamp communities featured there to remain unchanged, much as it is too late for the real residents of Isle de Jean Charles. That community is moving north, the entire tribe relocated by the US government as the first American climate refugees because their wetland marsh has eroded into open water (Davenport and Robertson). As Hushpuppy says in *Beasts*, "Sometimes you can break something so bad that it can't be put back together." Instead of arguing for an impossible "putting back together" of global ecosystems, I show how ecologically embodied storytelling as a form of community defiance, resilience, and agency is the only meaningful way for the human species to endure and adapt to climate crisis. Perhaps southern literatures, so full of examples of endurance and adaptation in the face of innumerable challenges, can reposition our thinking about what ethical interactions with human and nonhuman others look like in the inevitable ecopocalypse of our near future.

Set in the Bathtub, a fictional community modeled after real wetland neighborhoods in south Louisiana below the levee, Zeitlin's *Beasts of the Southern Wild* has been lauded by reviewers and audiences alike for its surreal mythology and post-Katrina critique of climate change. As Roger Ebert says in his July 4, 2012 review, "Hushpuppy is on intimate terms with the natural world, with the pigs she feeds and the fish she captures with her bare hands. . . . She is like a new generation put forward in desperate times by the human race." The young African American female protagonist of the film, Hushpuppy becomes a prophet of the destruction facing not only her fragile community but the whole human and nonhuman world. The titular "beasts" are imagined aurochs, a species of game animal that evolved in the Pliocene alongside the earliest hominids and were hunted to extinction by their *Homo sapiens* descendants, the last recorded aurochs dying in 1627. But there were never aurochs in Louisiana (they were a European species), and the "beasts" of the film parallel the people of the Bathtub, also going extinct. Rather than positing ecological catastrophe as an event in a far-off future, then, Zeitlin has the extinct aurochs symbolize current ecological anxieties in *Beasts of the Southern Wild*, representing for Hushpuppy how, as one character puts it, "the fabric of the universe is coming unraveled. Gotta learn to survive now." Rejecting the consumer-driven capitalistic social and economic structures of twenty-first-century America, residents of the Bathtub demonstrate that skills, not things, matter.

Thus, their ethical philosophy is one based on multispecies community, abundance, celebration, and recognizing that bad comes with any good. The film opens, for example, with a scene of Hushpuppy moistening a mud and moss nest and carefully placing a young chick on the handmade microcosm of the Bathtub wetlands. Hushpuppy and her father Wink recognize that all the animals, human and otherwise, are in it together, sharing food and living where they please, unlike "on the dry side" above the levee where restrictions define everything: the "fish in plastic wrappers, babies stuck in carriages." The film is awash with images of abundance and community: shrimp, fish, crawfish to share; colorful found items to repurpose; a school filled with young children. Hushpuppy's mother has "swam away," as Wink puts it, and her primary maternal figure is Bathsheba, the community's schoolteacher and wise woman who instructs her that "every animal is meat—I'm meat, your ass is meat, it's called the buffet of the universe" and that the most important thing is "you gotta learn how to take care of people smaller and sweeter than you are." Hushpuppy's father Wink is dying—his "blood's eatin' itself"—reminding viewers that humans have very vulnerable animal bodies. Wink thus personifies the only meaningful test of moral action: we can die at any time, but do you want to die doing *this*?

Wink's poor health and eventual death have important ecocritical impacts, whether he dies from toxic pollution from living downstream of the entire US agricultural runoff into the Mississippi, from leptospirosis carried by mud-borne bacteria from the nearby oil refining and petrochemical production, or from some other cause. First, no one is immune from toxic pollution, regardless of race, gender, or social class. Second, should Wink's disease be bacterial rather than cancerous, we know we are not immune from that either: with our overuse of antibiotics in the United States, we are complicit in creating the drug-resistant superbugs that are now mortal dangers for those infected. And, finally, who knows what a warmed climate and stronger storms will stir up?[4] But rather than focus on the harsh realities of their lives below the levee, the Bathtub residents celebrate; in one early scene, Hushpuppy announces that "the Bathtub has more holidays than the rest of the world." When she gets spined punching a catfish, Wink reassures her, "Don't worry about that! That's all a part of it!," reasserting their attitude of ecological and psychological balance.

That balance is overturned not just by the devastating storm in *Beasts*, reminiscent of Hurricane Katrina, but also by the government interventions in the aftermath. For many Americans, Hurricane Katrina's destruction of the Gulf in 2005 was the first indication that environmental change might threaten the United States. For example, Roy Scranton, a war veteran, describes returning from Iraq to the relative safety of Fort Sill in Oklahoma only to watch Katrina flood New Orleans:

> This time it was the weather that inspired shock and awe, but I saw the same chaos and collapse I'd seen in Baghdad, the same failure of planning and the same tide of anarchy. The 82nd Airborne Division took over strategic points and patrolled streets now under de facto martial law. My unit was put on alert and trained for riot control operations. The grim future I'd seen in Baghdad had come home: not terrorism, not WMDs, but the machinery of civilization breaking down, unable to recuperate from shocks to its system. (14)

Once the floodwaters receded, New Orleans and other flooded coastal communities had to deal with disease; mold growth; polluted soils and waterways: destroyed buildings, roads, and bridges: and demoralized and traumatized populations. Many who evacuated never returned to the Crescent City, but the aftereffects of Hurricane Katrina and the Deepwater Horizon oil gush helped inculcate a sense of potential ecocatastrophe in the minds of Americans.

We can likewise see that the traumatization of subjects in *Beasts* is caused by the severing of important connections to place, people, and their ethical-ecological framework that accepts good with bad, and yet the sterile government rejects the modes of expression by which the Bathtub's human residents define themselves. Before the storm, Wink and Hushpuppy tour the neighborhood in their truck-boat and are angry that people are evacuating. They stay and nearly die, Wink cutting apart the roof to escape when the waters flood them out. As Hushpuppy says, "For the animals that didn't have a dad to put them in a boat, the end of the world already happened." However, the water does not recede, and those who stay face saltwater intrusion and the resultant death of their way of life—"everything started to die." But there is celebration in living too—an important lesson amidst our own climate change fatigue and learned helplessness in the face of catastrophe: Wink feeds everyone who stayed and lived through the storm during a party full of abundant food, music, drinking, and laughter. Hushpuppy's voiceover reminds us, "For the ones we never find, we have a funeral the Bathtub way, with no crying." Life includes death, just like catching catfish means getting spined, and we are all in this together.

In contrast to the community-based psychological response to the storm's damaging effects is the city above the levee. In *Beasts* the drylands above the levee are defined in opposition to the familiar wetland culture: from the perspective of Hushpuppy and her friends, "the dry side" is outside of time, outside of civilization, outside of the ordinary, and marked by intense fear and extreme danger. To the government, the wetlands function as a place of dangerous wilderness. The Bathtub residents blow up the levee to let out the seawater[5] and, as it drops, expose the detritus of consumerism (and more stuff for them to retrieve and repurpose), but then helicopters come and forcibly remove them to a "mandatory evacuation area." Wink receives unwanted medical care. Hushpuppy is washed and dressed and her hair forced into tight braids. She says the refugee center is "a fish tank with no water," and "when an animal gets sick here, they plug it into the wall." In one shocking scene filmed from Hushpuppy's height and point of view, viewers see her father Wink in a wheelchair, too drugged to do more than open his eyes with tubes sticking out of him: this is her story, after all, and we see her trauma in Wink's loss of agency and freedom.

Migration in apocalyptic fiction is a form of hope (think, for example, of the man and boy in Cormac McCarthy's *The Road* [2006]); however, here we see its rejection—going home instead—as a powerful form of agency and an outright disregard of the very capitalistic, consumeristic, and cultural factors that precipitate climate change in the first place. The residents of the Bathtub do not want government aid. They want to go back to their way of life off the grid and under the radar. They are determined to overcome the victimization imposed on them by the state police and National Guard (as well-intentioned and compassionate as those efforts might be). From their perspective, the people at the shelter are the enforcers of a culture of technology, "progress," and civilization, eating processed food in plastic wrap and demanding conformity. Externally imposed ideas of happiness, success, and safety are exactly that. At the first opportunity, Hushpuppy and her group force their way out, commandeer a bus, and escape back to the Bathtub, where their community is nearly ideal; it is integrated, the people work together, they self-police, and they are bound by friendship, familial ties, and shared celebrations. They refuse "refugee" status and just go home, challenging the seductive notion that "the environment" is a substrate of human culture and thus easily substitutable with another place when in fact human cultures exist in specific places, entangled in and of them.

Beasts' efforts to mark economic and social class as survival factors hint at the false hope that the very poorest might have the knowledge needed to adapt and survive the global climate crisis in the short term because they are less dependent on the easily broken systems of the highly developed world. Yoosun Park and Joshua Miller write that "ongoing environmental risks for poor people and people of color are consistently higher than for white people and those who are economically privileged," and they specifically demand that grassroots efforts take priority in disaster preparation and relief after lessons from Hurricane Katrina's aftermath (10). Mark Hertsgaard states that "although both white and black and rich and poor suffered grievously after Katrina, poor and nonwhite residents ended up losing a disproportionate share of their homes" (137). In *Beasts*, Wink's death and the storm's destruction name the lie: the poorest are already dying. Consequently, the film exposes the fantasy of typical postapocalyptic fiction's longings for a romanticized primitive Thoreauvian lifestyle that ignores the harsh realities of daily life for those without adequate food, clean accessible water, and decent shelter. However, some critics have accused Wink of being abusive or neglectful because Hushpuppy lived in a separate shack (away from his drinking) and burned her house down trying to heat up cat food; and yet his parenting is the equivalent of the catfish spine, part of the good and bad of the universe.[6] Hushpuppy is a fictional young black girl, but her story is a universal one of the struggle for existence and the persistence of even the smallest life. Is she not the little chick placed carefully on a wet mud nest to make her way in the world?

The future of these imagined crises will arrive sooner than we think: unpredictable shifts in formerly stable weather dynamics have touched every ecosystem worldwide. As I write this paragraph, the carbon dioxide in the atmosphere has reached 406 ppm, significantly higher than the 350 ppm considered a "tipping point" into runaway climate change.[7] According to NASA's Goddard Institute for Space Studies, the global average temperature has increased 1.5° Fahrenheit since the industrialization of the 1880s, and May 2018 marked the 401st consecutive month with global temperatures above the twentieth-century average.[8] Sea levels are rising already as arctic sea ice has declined to record low winter maximums each of the last 14 years and record high air temperatures in December, January, and February reached up to 10° Fahrenheit higher than average at the edges of the ice pack during the winter of 2015–2016.[9] The weather extremes called global climate "weirding" have become exceedingly commonplace: although Hurricane Katrina was the costliest environmental disaster recorded in North America, since then natural disasters have trended upward worldwide. There was "Frankenstorm" Hurricane

Sandy in 2012; a brutal Australian heat wave and massive wildfires in 2014; deadly rainfall and flooding in India and Pakistan in 2014; Hurricanes Irma and Harvey in 2017, South Asian flooding in 2017, and ongoing East African drought; even the ongoing Syrian conflict has roots in extreme drought that triggered mass migration, deteriorating Syria's economic stability and leading to civil war (Gleick 331). Winter precipitation swings from all-time records for snow one year to record warmth the next. Increasingly catastrophic floods, droughts, hurricanes, blizzards, and tornadoes point to an even more frightening future where humans and other animals face even greater temperature extremes, rising waters and droughts, shifts in growing seasons, food and water shortages, disease, overcrowding, and massive loss of life. Our species may go extinct, a possibility that demands we accept and embody our worldly entanglements before the human collective can begin to imagine and adapt.

I live in rural Louisiana in a town proudly known as the oldest permanent settlement in the Louisiana Purchase. We often open our home to evacuees and have watched with horror the aftereffects of repeated hurricanes, oil gushes, and flooding on the coastal ecosystem, as well as the shifts in demographics, loss of economic stability, devaluing of education, intensification of racial tension, and increase in conservative politics that seem to be an illogical response to these catastrophes. There is a hushed grieving in conversations about the Gulf, about the knowledge that oysters experienced up to 95 percent mortality rates, about the loss of wetlands and the looming hurricane seasons. There is a silent, brooding frustration with the larger discourse about the wetlands, continually damaged by pesticides from the Mississippi watershed, ripped by repeated hurricanes, and permeated by oil spills. Thus, Bill McKibben's charge in his 2010 book *Eaarth*—that it is too late to stop the weather extremes so we must adapt—makes a lot of sense to some of us here. But McKibben's recommendations will not really work in many communities: he suggests that we decentralize populations, infrastructure, government, and industry; return to a simple farming lifestyle; and reduce our impact on the already damaged ecosystem. Like many solutions to the climate change crisis, his is a form of primitivism that depends on a rural lifestyle most Americans do not know and cannot imagine, except when watching films like *Beasts of the Southern Wild*. Yet so many rural Louisiana residents—hunters, fishers, watchers of the land—have been adapting already. Locals have been observing the changes in weather, growing seasons, waterfowl migrations, and big game behavior for years and already endure environmental changes from within their embodied worlds.

David Abram suggests that "restorying" our landscapes is the first step toward "binding the imagination of our bodies back into the wider life of the animate earth" (290) by generating exactly the kind of resilient storytelling that Hushpuppy models for us. Countering a character's pessimistic view that the land and other animals have "only their silence left with which to confront us" in J. M. Coetzee's *The Lives of Animals* (Coetzee 25), Abram insists that the natural world is full of voices if only we listen—"becoming animal" and resituating humans within the animate world as eager members of the landscapes around us. For example, one of my most unforgettable experiences took place not with other environmentalists on an Oregon bike ride or an Alaskan hike but accompanying a Louisiana native—and no liberal preservationist—on a morning duck hunt. Crossing the moonlit dark of a cypress lake, the stars reflecting on the eerily invisible water with only the pirogue paddles and our breath to break the silence, it struck me how in tune with not only "nature" in the abstract but with a specific place my companion must be to know it well enough to hunt successfully; how much he must study the ducks and their habits to know where they roost, when they seek food and what it is, how high or low they fly, how well they have adapted to the hunting season itself, becoming temporary residents and learning where the hunting blinds are and from where the shots are fired. As I listened to his stories, I realized just how intimately he knows the changes in weather, not from a NASA chart but from his own life experiences embodied in a particular landscape with a particular ecosystem and all the other animals that share that space. These are the stories that matter: stories of ducks, of how the lake reflects, of wind and patterns of movement.

It is exactly these kinds of personal stories, meaningfully connected to our resident ecosystems, that have the power to counteract the powerful ideologues who, on the one hand, employ human exceptionalism to dismiss our responsibility to adapt to climate change, and, on the other, utilize fear tactics to construct false and disempowering solutions during ecocatastrophes like those that affect Wink and Hushpuppy. As Mark Hertsgaard argues in *Hot: The Next Fifty Years on Earth* (2011), "the ruination of New Orleans offers a lesson—a warning, really—about what can happen to people and places that fail to prepare for the impacts of climate change. At the moment, that includes most people and places on earth. At a time when weather-related disasters are projected to increase in severity and perhaps frequency, most people are waiting until disaster strikes before putting proper safeguards in place" (130). But

Katrina also taught those paying attention that the government was not the source of help and rescue. Rather, in the immediate aftermath of the storm surge and flooding, it was the thousands of other Louisiana residents who brought their boats and other equipment to rescue people off of rooftops, provide them water, food, and safe shelter, and in the next weeks, gut and begin rebuilding ruined buildings: the same community efforts we see in *Beasts*. Rebecca Solnit argues in *A Paradise Built in Hell: The Extraordinary Communities that Arise in Disaster* (2009) that altruism can abound in catastrophe (although so does elite panic). She quotes a Hurricane Katrina survivor:

> it turned into a community effort. Everybody cooked. They fed one another. They scavenged the food that they had from stores that had been vandalized, whatever, but they were really, really, really nice. I saw people being compassionate about people that they never met, people that they never saw, people that they never knew reaching out to them, feeding them, giving them clothes and the food. This was New Orleans everywhere. This was everywhere in New Orleans. (274)

Compassion and empathy are also everywhere in the Bathtub and within the larger story told in *Beasts of the Southern Wild*. Hushpuppy's vision of ecological interconnectedness foregrounds the embeddedness of human beings within a multispecies community while simultaneously decentering the human individual from its place of importance within that world. As Bathsheba tells Hushpuppy, the most important thing is "how to take care of people smaller and sweeter than you are"—kin relations of a greatly expanded sort, just as Hushpuppy's story is one of being "a little piece of a big big universe." Accordingly, the Bathtub inhabitants' behaviors stand in clear contrast to other psychological responses to catastrophe like learned helplessness or doomsday prepping efforts, which do not engage with dilemmas of speciest and anthropomorphic practices and retain a hierarchical relation with the environment and other people and nonhuman animals.

Beasts of the Southern Wild thus provides us with Hushpuppy's ecologically connected story filled with examples of an alternative community embedded in personal reciprocity and ecological interdependence to contrast with the individualism and hierarchy familiar to pull-yourself-up-by-your-bootstraps Americans. But reciprocity and interdependence are part of a cultural worldview that already accepts climate science as definitive and climate change as a high risk for our near future, according to Yale's Cultural Cognition Project (as portrayed in Naomi Klein's *This Changes Everything*): "Among the segment of the U.S. population that displays the strongest 'hierarchical' views, only 11 percent rate climate change as a 'high risk,' compared with 69 percent of the segment displaying the strongest 'egalitarian' views" (36). So while the resilience seen in *Beasts of the Southern Wild* and literature of the US South might be a model for us all, first we have to accept that ecological collapse and the grief that accompanies such massive loss also offers choices: to tell stories, to celebrate together, to support each other or to climb on the heads of neighbors while the rest of the world drowns.

NOTES

1. See coast2050.gov, which until January 2017 included detailed information about the causes of and potential state and federal responses to wetland loss on the coast of Louisiana; as of this writing, the website has remained unavailable but can be accessed using Google's archive search. See also Robert R. Twilley et al., "Co-evolution of Wetland Landscapes, Flooding, and Human Settlement in the Mississippi River Delta Plain," which models sediment loss in deltaic floodplains as a nonlinear response to capture how landscape degradation and increasing changes to the water-land ratio contribute to detrimental loss of the Louisiana coastline.

2. http://coastal.la.gov/. For a discussion of the proposals and controversies considered in debates about the master plan, see Chris Mooney, "The Next Big One," in the *Washington Post,* http://www.washingtonpost.com/sf/national/2015/08/21/the-next-big-one/.

3. In her 2016 book *Strangers in Their Own Land: Anger and Mourning on the American Right,* Arlie Russell Hochschild explores Louisiana as representative of the reddest of the red states to better understand why those demographics that would most benefit from progressive social and economic policies repeatedly vote conservative politicians into state and federal offices.

4. At least four ancient viruses have been exposed by melting glacial ice. See Rachel Feltman's "A Giant Ancient Virus Was Just Uncovered in Melting Ice," the *Washington Post,* 9 Sept. 2015.

5. In the real world, the only way to protect east Louisiana from becoming open ocean is also to blow the levee below New Orleans. The Atchafalaya delta dumps sediment into the Gulf of Mexico at Wax Lake, which is the only place with land growth amidst the wetland loss of east Louisiana and the Mississippi River delta plain. The Mississippi River dumps sediment right off the continental shelf, so it does not redeposit sediment to extend the alluvial fan.

6. Who decides what is good parenting in apocalyptic situations? For example, millions of destitute people worldwide live and work on garbage dumps, picking through refuse to

sort, reuse, and sell or eat what others have thrown away; their thousands of children live and labor on disgusting, dangerous mounds of rotting garbage. Interestingly, in many cases, volunteers from NGOs utterly failed to improve their living situations, and, globally, industrialized nations cannot seem to solve the problems of abject poverty or wealth inequality nor reduce consumerism and concomitant waste. See Poppy McPherson, "'Hell On Earth': The Great Urban Scandal of Family Life Lived on a Rubbish Dump," in *The Guardian*.

7. The 350 ppm goal was established in James Hansen et al., "Target Atmospheric CO_2: Where Should Humanity Aim?" *Open Atmospheric Science Journal*, vol. 2, 2008, pp. 217–31. The NOAA Earth System Research Laboratory "Global Monitoring Division" indicates CO_2 at 406.57 ppm on 3 Apr. 2016, and 406.38 ppm on 11 January 2017. See http://www.esrl.noaa.gov/gmd/ccgg/trends/weekly.html.

8. NASA/GISS, "Global Land–Ocean Temperature Index" (Latest Measurement: 2015). See also data.giss.nasa.gov for analysis showing monthly record temperature highs throughout 2016–2017 and the National Centers for Environmental Information for additional details about global temperature records.

9. Mari-Jose Vinas, "2016 Arctic Sea Ice Wintertime Extent Hits Another Record Low" (28 Mar. 2016), http://www.nasa.gov/feature/goddard/2016/2016-arctic-sea-ice-wintertime-extent-hits-another-record-low. See also http://climate.nasa.gov/vital-signs/arctic-sea-ice/.

WORKS CITED

Abram, David. *Becoming Animal: An Earthly Cosmology*. Vintage Books, 2010.
Beasts of the Southern Wild, Dir. Benh Zeitlin. Fox, Searchlight Pictures, 2012. DVD.
Coastal Protection and Restoration Authority. http://coastal.la.gov.
Coetzee, J. M. *The Lives of Animals*. Princeton UP, 1999.
Davenport, Coral, and Campbell Robertson. "Resettling the First American 'Climate Refugees.'" *New York Times*, 3 May 2016.
Ebert, Roger. "Beasts of the Southern Wild." 4 July 2012. Rogerebert.com.
Feltman, Rachel. "A Giant Ancient Virus Was Just Uncovered in Melting Ice." The *Washington Post*, 9 Sept. 2015.
Gleick, Peter H. "Water, Drought, Climate Change, and Conflict in Syria." *American Meteorological Society*, vol. 6, 2014, pp. 331–40.
"Global Land–Ocean Temperature Index." *NASA/GISS*. https://data.giss.nasa.gov.
Hansen, James, et al. "Target Atmospheric CO_2: Where Should Humanity Aim?" *Open Atmospheric Science Journal*, vol. 2, 2008, pp. 217–31.
Hertsgaard, Mark. *Hot: Living Through the Next Fifty Years on Earth*. Houghton Mifflin Harcourt, 2011.
Hochschild, Arlie Russell. *Strangers in Their Own Land: Anger and Mourning on the American Right*. The New Press, 2016.
Klein, Naomi. *This Changes Everything: Capitalism versus the Climate*. Simon and Schuster, 2014.

McKibben, Bill. *Eaarth: Making a Life on a Tough New Planet.* Henry Holt and Co., 2010.

McPherson, Poppy. "'Hell On Earth': The Great Urban Scandal of Family Life Lived on a Rubbish Dump." *The Guardian,* 11 Oct. 2016.

Mooney, Chris. "The Next Big One." The *Washington Post.* http://www.washingtonpost.com/sf/national/2015/08/21/the-next-big-one/.

Park, Yoosun, and Joshua Miller. "The Social Ecology of Hurricane Katrina: Re-Writing the Discourse of 'Natural' Disasters." *Smith College Studies in Social Work,* vol. 76, no. 3, 2006, pp. 9–24.

Scranton, Roy. *Learning to Die in the Anthropocene: Reflections on the End of a Civilization.* City Lights Books, 2015.

Solnit, Rebecca. *A Paradise Built in Hell: The Extraordinary Communities that Arise in Disaster.* Penguin Books, 2009.

Sutter, Paul S. "No More the Backward Region: Southern Environmental History Comes of Age." *Environmental History and the American South,* edited by Paul S. Sutter and Christopher J. Manganiello, U of Georgia P, 2009, pp. 1–24.

"Trends in Atmospheric Carbon Dioxide." *Earth System Research Laboratory: Global Monitoring Division.* https://www.esrl.noaa.gov/gmd/ccgg/trends/weekly.html.

Twilley, Robert R., et al. "Co-evolution of Wetland Landscapes, Flooding, and Human Settlement in the Mississippi River Delta Plain." *Sustainability Science,* vol. 11, no. 4, 2016, pp. 711–31.

Vinas, Mari-Jose. "2016 Arctic Sea Ice Wintertime Extent Hits Another Record Low." *NASA,* vol. 22, 2017. http://www.nasa.gov/feature/goddard/2016/2016-arctic-sea-ice-wintertime-extent-hits-another-record-low.

V

ECO-DYSTOPIAS

Grave Nature

Caroline Lee Hentz's Dead Slaves and the Eco-dystopia of the Old South

JOSHUA MYERS

Graves generally symbolize places where human bodies and nature coexist in a seemingly utopic state of tranquility; however, falsely representing gravesites as "natural" conceals environmental damage caused by coffins, embalming practices, and, most prominently, a long tradition of paternalistic ownership that has shaped funerary practices. As Kate Sweeney notes in *American Afterlife* (2014), burial profits have made "the funeral business grow into a twenty-billion dollar-a-year industry, one that profits mostly from a host of expenses that have nothing to do with a hole in the ground" (101). In the United States, these capitalist funerary practices are historically tied to ideologies of property and the ownership of bodies that bolstered slavery as an institution. As scholar Jamie Warren points out, the nineteenth century appears to be the first historical period in which white slave owners bought coffins for deceased slaves (122). However, this post-death assistance was often a way for white slaveowners to "express a paternalistic sense of ownership" (123). In *Arcadian America* (2013), Aaron Sachs explains that "the Civil War wrought broad, trenchant changes in the way Americans dealt with both the dead and the dying, ushering in the era of professional undertakers and embalmers and specialized surgeons . . ." (197). As this essay will show, the links between the antebellum and Civil War periods and the evolution of ecologically harmful funerary practices are reflected in the proslavery novels of Caroline Lee Hentz. In *The Planter's Northern Bride* (1854) and her lesser-known novel *Marcus Warland; or, The Long Moss Spring; A Tale of The South* (1852), Hentz uses gravesites that displace living slave bodies by burying them and thus cultivating a seemingly pastoral space to disguise the horrors of slavery.

Lucinda Hardwick MacKethan has identified the South's "Arcadian myth" that "the plantation provided the last and greatest bastion for the promotion of the pastoral ideal. Yet the planation regime was also founded upon an institution which made the innocence which we associate with a pastoral way of life impossible" (11). Hentz's depictions of tranquil graves similarly obfuscate the labor of slaves to create a seeming pastoral vision. Packing the earth with bodies and bodily containers reflects environmental violations that persist to our modern age and buries readers (and corpses) in the concealment of dystopic consequences, both human and environmental. In this essay, I examine three key depictions of burials and gravesites from Hentz's novels. Each scene reveals her attempts to present slavery as utopic by conflating the gravesites of slaves with idyllic nature. The first scene shows how Hentz's gravesites work as what I call "eco-miscegenation," a term I will define by exploring how interring a particular slave's racially mixed body diffuses it with nature to prevent changing land use and, by implication, any alteration to slavery and the plantation system. The second scene moves outside the plantation to reprise this postmortem captivity, suggesting that reenslaving African Americans through memorialization can colonize the entire southern landscape as a plantation that retains the use of slavery and adherence to private property. The third scene further develops this idea by situating the pastoral cemetery as a site that sanctions the perpetuation of slavery for the living, while linking insurrection, especially slave rebellions, to an uncontrolled environment.

A study of grave scenes must not overlook the politicization of buried bodies, and an especially important perspective for considering Hentz's fictional killing of slaves is scholar Russ Castronovo's idea of nineteenth-century "necro citizenship" and the abstract belonging that bodies attain through death. Castronovo suggests that physical bodies are requisitioned by governments, because "fear of the dissolution or death of the state creates the longing for an inactive, forever tranquil citizenry; meanwhile, the continued stable existence of government requires historically dead subjects" (8). Hentz's nationalistic concern about such "continued stable existence" of the Old South manifests in her dissolving the corpses' freedom—Castronovo's "forever tranquil citizenry"—into the environment where the grave is located, as her graves construct an artifice of so-called natural beauty dependent on manipulating the bodies of slaves to make the South look more utopic.

Examining the grave's paradoxical blending of utopic and dystopic qualities in relation to slavery necessitates expanding upon the traditionally denotative approach to utopia, as in *Utopia and Organization* (2002) where Martin Parker claims that "utopias are statements of alternative organization, attempts to put forward plans which remedy the perceived shortcomings of a particular present age" (2). Graveyards organize mortality through a means of remembrance, one that welcomes bodies suffering from the existential "shortcoming" of death. These imagined states of utopia, though, are muddled by the presence of slavery in southern graveyards, pushing the reshaping of graves into gardens toward Parker's description of dystopias that "do not propose anything but horror and scepticism" (5). The maintenance of gravesites meant slaves labored to create not just a pastoral image—MacKethan's notion of the "unique kind of Arcadia which forced human beings to labor in bondage for its support" (11)—but also to cultivate a garden space that augmented the beauty of the landscape as a justification for slavery.

To be clear, I do not suggest that Hentz viewed the South as flawlessly perfect, as per the generalized modern definition of utopia. However, using burial to commingle proslavery rhetoric with nature suggests that Hentz viewed slavery as a sustainable system capable of manufacturing a healthy society, one where idyllic grave spaces accentuated the beauty of the landscape regardless of environmental damage. Hentz locates that pastoral utopia in the graveyard rather than other spaces, because the plantation house and fields display too directly the dystopic and repulsive qualities of forced enslavement, as well as the devastating ecological harm caused by land development and monocrop agriculture. Burying the bodies of slaves in an idyllic, seemingly natural graveyard anchors the pastoral myth, while concealing the combined denigration of the enslaved human body and the overworked soil, a sort of eco-dystopia where so-called natural beauty is maintained only by the destruction of human beings and their environment. Thus, I argue that Hentz depicts grave scenes as utopic gardens using the death and interment of enslaved people to disguise the social and ecological damage of slavery.

Study of Hentz's work is often neglected due to her abhorrently racist rhetoric, which has caused scholars to miss the ecological impact of her novels and their revelation of slavery's negative effects on the environment. Certainly, we can accept that examining Hentz's work for its uses of death and burial is not unfounded, as Castronovo accurately identifies death as a common trope of nineteenth-century works: "With little connection to material life, an inert freedom fits the diverse agendas of black abolitionist, white antislavery activist, and slaveholder" (36). Since a primary facet of plantation novels was the rhetorical defense of slavery, we must accept the possibility that Hentz recognizes the capability of graves to contain the defiantly "inert freedom" of dead bodies, bringing the deceased slaves and their mourners under planter control.

In *Marcus Warland,* this power dynamic is reflected in the grave of a "mulatto" slave, Cora, admired by Hentz's other characters specifically for her mixed-race body until she dies unexpectedly in a tragic accident and her beauty becomes a part of her memorialization. Hentz writes, "There is a plain white slab in a green enclosure on Hickory Hill, sacred to the memory of Cora" (84). The unsurprisingly white grave-marker hides the intimacy between the environment and the "tragic mulatto" archetype, as killing the mixed-race character allows Hentz to transfer the beauty of Cora's "mulatto" body to the "green enclosure" with "sweet flowers and shrubs blooming around it," which is haunted by Cora's beautiful ghost, always dressed entirely in white "like a bride" (84–85). With the blackness of the body enclosed, its whiteness enhances nature at the gravesite—a use of a mixed-raced body in which the environment is utilized to propagate miscegenation to promote an increased slave populace, what I call "eco-miscegenation." This concept intensifies Castronovo's idea of "miscegenation without sex," in which miscegenation lacking a body "perfectly typifies a national utopia where African American citizenship is inert" (246). By blending the body of the "mulatto" slave with nature, Hentz forever traps the mixed-race body in the master's land. The horrors of miscegenation, such as the rape of black bodies by white masters, are concealed by nature and, in turn, whites feel justified in perpetuating miscegenation and, more broadly, the institution of slavery.

Greening the postmortem body of the "tragic mulatto" via this manner of eco-miscegenation also uses race to conceal environmental damage by deflecting attention from increasing human interference with the environment, so that additional land can be allocated for agriculture, property, and the cyclic memorialization of slaves. Beautiful spaces like the "green enclosure" of Cora's grave acknowledge slavery but symbolically disregard the treatment of slaves and the reshaping of the natural landscape, justifying the use of additional slaves to continually dominate nature. The "natural" beauty of the grave space is further accentuated by Cora's "mulatto" husband planting a weeping willow at her gravesite (84). Having a slave install a tree at the gravesite, as opposed to natural seeding, rearranges the landscape to remind living slaves that they and the dead are property whose location, like that of the tree, is determined by the dictates of the plantation owners. Thus, the gravesite encourages slaves' visitation and lessens the desire for escape by romanticizing or eliding the human and environmental costs of slavery. In *Marcus Warland,* this concept is exemplified by Hannibal, a slave who loved Cora and says he "gonter (sic) sleep where Cora sleep" and he is "willing to die, jist (sic) to be where she gone to" (259). Hannibal desires that his body be placed at the same plantation gravesite as Cora's. Since he is not of mixed race, described by Hentz as being of "Cimmerian blackness" (64), his body cannot participate in eco-miscegenation due to its lack of whiteness. Therefore, it would seem that Hannibal potentially fears that any separate resting place for him could not be as beautiful as that of Cora's. Thus, her grave makes Hannibal submissive and tied to the land, as his mind constantly returns "to the little green enclosure where Cora slept . . ." (258). His thoughts seem to be less of Cora than they are of the "green enclosure," suggesting a strong desire for the possibility of what seems a utopic setting surrounding their bodies, but what is actually a construct conceived by his master to ensure that those enslaved never leave the plantation, even in death.

The other primary setting of *Marcus Warland* is the Long Moss Spring, a site of bucolic nature located beyond the plantation. This setting is initially depicted using traditional pastoral conventions of beauty and innocence: the white protagonist Marcus sits there fishing with "the morning sunbeams glancing through the broad leaves of the magnolia and the brilliant foliage of the holly, and playing on his golden hair" (47). Later in the novel, Hentz turns this same area into a cemetery of the dead, yet the spring continues to retain pastoral elements even after it is converted into a burial ground. Hentz describes it as having clearly defined "borders" that consecrate the spring as a "sweet and hallowed spot" (259). Demarcating the spring-turned-graveyard invokes control and containment, utopic and dystopic characteristics of garden spaces, which scholars Gibson Burrell and Karen Dale discuss: "the production of organization along formal bounded 'lines' is to be found in very many utopian imaginings. . . . Every utopia is also a dystopia, for the first is predicated upon the second" (109). Utopic gardens, according to Burrell and Dale, depend on "the parallel production of the obscuring of the irrepressible, uncontrollable wilderness within which formality is valued" (109). If we apply these ideas to Hentz, we can see how she reshapes the previously wild spring into a cultivated garden using graves that purport falsely utopic principles of slavery, as the site becomes the burial ground of an elderly former slave, Simon, who is memorialized by Marcus: "There was a smooth white stone lying close to the grave, such as formed the basis of the fountain. Marcus knelt down, and taking his penknife, carved the name of the old [Christian] soldier on its yielding surface . . ." (187). The stone is "smooth" and "white," symbolically superior to other-colored, rougher stones; however, it is also "yielding," as if nature encourages and condones ownership by submitting freely to the desires of those who impose their will upon it. In essence, Marcus possesses the grave as master of nature *and* the body buried there; he determines who is forgotten or remembered.

Castronovo discusses the fading away of burial sites as represented in slave narratives to inquire: "Can a history that is not there have palpable consequences?" (195). *Marcus Warland,* a plantation novel not discussed by Castronovo, nevertheless seems to answer his question by suggesting that slaveholders feared such a history. The deceased body of Simon would return to a natural, untamed wilderness when buried at the Long Moss Spring *except that* he is memorialized as a slave, and the area where he is buried is remade as a cultivated garden by his memorial. Marcus places a stone strategically "at the head of the grave, [and] he pressed the earth against it, to prevent it from falling" (187). The white man places the white stone in a dominant position that uses the earth "to prevent it from falling," which remakes the grave as a space in which the black body is made submissive to the white man *and* his appropriation of nature. Hence, the plantation aristocracy uses the dead body of a slave, albeit one sentimentally honored, to ensure that the land is an unchangeable memorial to the plantation order instead of a more egalitarian space, especially since living slaves cannot "free" their buried ancestor.

Considering Burrell and Dale's idea of the garden as a utopic space, the similarly utopic design of graves is clear: ". . . we see the principles of boundary, formality, planning and design, *matter in its place,* control: in other words—management" (italics added, 109). Gravesites, like gardens, emphasize these utopic factors: if we consider the "matter in its place" as bodies, then we can see why Hentz buries slaves in the Long Moss Spring; to justify control of slaves and the environment, she remakes nature as a gravesite garden to sustain a utopic illusion. Thus, the elegiac "farewell" to one of the novel's primary settings: "Farewell, fair and peaceful waters. Farewell, ye green and silver-tinted plumes, ye bright-leaved, verdant hollies. Superb magnolia, sentinel of the lonely dead, we bid thee too farewell . . . perennial Spring, thou speakest of thrilling memories. We love thy name. It is embalmed in our recollection, and it sounds like music to our ears" (259). The reader regrets leaving such an idyllic scene of wondrous natural beauty full of "fair and peaceful waters" ringed by "bright-leaved, verdant hollies." The surrounding hollies act as the false utopia's guarding border to create "thrilling memories" that are "embalmed," recollections of the place as it *could be*—not as it is—an imaginary state of utopic bliss.

The most notable grave scene in *The Planter's Northern Bride* is that of the matriarchal slave, Dilsy: "On some graves, flowers were growing, showing that the taste which loves to beautify the places of death is sometimes found in the bosom of the African" (353). This unusual description oddly focuses on the body of the deceased slave to present a pleasing image of nature; it is "taste"— a human sense—that determines natural beauty. The description also implies that the flowers grow from the slave's corpse—"in the bosom of the African"— instead of from the soil. In this way, Dilsy's body becomes representative of nature, marking a shift in environmental awareness from an uncontrollable and abstract concept to an enslaved physical body. The flowers that are attracted to death, then, make it seem that nature condones slavery and the establishment of an eco-dystopic environment, one where flowers are not placed there to remember slaves, but where the bodies of enslaved people give us flowers. Similarly, John Michael Vlach analyzes an 1853 painting by T. Addison Richards to claim that Richards "read the scenic virtues of the natural landscape as indications of the potential for a 'higher and nobler civilization' and considered nature as a morally redemptive force" (28). In other words, the beautiful nature of the South is "morally redemptive" of any immoral happenings that occur there, a justification for slavery that suggests a possible utopia resulting from landscapes maintained by slaves. Much like Hentz's works, a nature shaped by slavery becomes the means by which Richards "create[ed] appealing images that would further his advocacy on behalf of the virtues of the South," which he guised "in the verdant cloak of nature" (Vlach 28). Thus, various antebellum works show that in the seemingly sacrificial act of slaves, nature is deliberately altered and environmental violations substitute for violations perpetrated against slaves. Hentz's novels function similarly to Richard's painting, as both cultural works present the South's proslavery agenda wrapped in a "verdant cloak of nature," but Hentz's ever-present theme of death and her frequent depiction of slave burial constantly remind us of the bodies buried beneath the surface of the pastoral landscape. What would otherwise showcase slave labor and remind readers of existential terror, is eased by the simultaneous and ubiquitous presence of cultivated nature surrounding the graves. Reading Hentz this way reveals how acts of consecration are usurped to serve a proslavery agenda that forgives atrocities committed on black bodies, the same bodies forced to drastically reshape the environment, an eco-dystopia where nature's ecological balance is destroyed for the sake of enslaving human beings.

Hentz further describes the cemetery in *The Planter's Northern Bride* as "the burying-ground of the plantation, surrounded by a neat, whitewashed paling . . ." (353). She clearly has the ground "surrounded" by a white fence, a racialized symbol constructed from the labor of slaves that reasserts ownership of the land and makes the graveyard seem not only like a pastoral landscape, but a space that actually possesses the utopic qualities of a garden. Burrell and Dale write of such qualities as often involving "boundaries [that] have frequently been the physical barriers of walls and fences. Both physically and symbolically, these landmarks protect boundaries from those outside and mark the limits of guaranteed safety for those within" (111). There is seeming "safety" in landscapes that can be viewed as pastoral and even more "safety" if those landscapes appear utopic. However, Hentz's reworking the graveyard into a type of garden does not belie the occurrence of death, nor the environmental happenings that result from the natural process of dying and the unnatural reshaping of the landscape as a monument to that process. As Castronovo writes, for people of various minority races sometimes death seemed preferable compared to "a life hemmed in by fences and property markers" (35). For slaves, death was desirable for its almost utopic state as the body returns to the land, a sort of ecological freedom obtained by decomposition. The imposed artifices of "fences and property markers" at the gravesite in *The Planter's Northern Bride* symbolically contain and imprison the body during the process of bodily decay, an attempt to negate any abstract views of freedom that may occur when considering the ecological cycle of death and decomposition. Thus, creating a garden from the burial site, with the fence as a man-made ecological determinant, reveals dystopic consequences of attempted human and environmental control.

The fence, then, additionally functions to separate buried slaves from slaves who envy the dead, as the latter are forced to labor outside the seemingly utopic space. Castronovo posits that "antislavery representations lovingly equate slave suicide to an emancipatory release from embodiment. . . . Here lies the ecstasy of death: the body's demise places the citizen beyond repressive forms of embodiment" (15). Such a notion is problematic for a proslavery stance, so Hentz inverts antislavery narratives by similarly establishing death as an alleged "freedom," but one that enslaves deceased bodies. She describes the fence as "shaded by evergreens and shrubbery" (353). Thus, Hentz uses nature, trees that appear to grow wildly, to cast the fence into darkness in a symbolic attempt to conceal the fence and make it seem part of the natural landscape, instead of an artifice erected by slave labor for the purposes of maintaining control over the deceased bodies within. This manipulation of nature imagery cultivates a falsely utopic graveyard constructed with the bodies of both living and dead slaves.

Interment as an extension of property is further seen in the interaction between slave and planter during Dilsy's burial. The gravesite presence of the planter, Moreland, is not unrealistic, as Warren suggests that changing ideas about slave ownership "encouraged masters to symbolically honor the corpses of their slaves" (113). Moreland seems to "honor" Dilsy in such a way by standing "with uncovered head, while they lowered the coffin into the deep, dark, narrow cavity scooped to receive it . . ." (353); however, describing the earth as "scooped to receive" the body makes the land seem welcoming of corpses, claiming the landscape should serve humanity as planters believed slaves should serve their masters—even in death. As Warren points out, death offered a "final stage for the master to act out his dominion over his bondspeople" (112), which we see in the particular manner that Moreland "threw the first shovelful of earth on the hollow-sounding lid . . ." (353–54). Moreland's symbolic gesture of grief and compassion attempts assurance of master/slave civility yet reasserts his possession of the soil and the bodies placed there. Holding the dirt in his hand becomes a symbolic extension of his body, and throwing the dirt on Dilsy's corpse ensures that she is covered by her master's body just as the earth and nature are subservient to all (white) bodies.

In the climactic scene of *The Planter's Northern Bride*, Moreland confronts his rebellious slaves at Dilsy's decaying gravesite buried in "autumn leaves [that] lay thick, damp, and rotting on the sods that covered them, choking the vines and plants, which, in happier hours, had been cultured there" (499). Natural decay suggests that the dead slaves that "cultured" the landscape fail to impose the desired control over living slaves. Sweeney writes that it was fashionable "for rural-style cemeteries to maintain a pastoral air . . ." (47); if we consider such American trends in relation to the proslavery South, then it fell to enslaved people to "maintain" such pastoralism and its common association with themes of innocence. The decaying gravesite is no longer pastoral, because Moreland's slaves have acted rebelliously: insurrectionist plots *and* nature mark the slaves as no longer innocent. To emphasize this, the novel gives a dystopic impression to the once beautiful gravesite: "As they walked through the place of graves, the long, dry yellow grass broke and crumpled under their steps, and the brambles twisted round their ankles. They had neglected their dead" (499). It is implied that what they really have "neglected" is the property of their master. The gravesite depicts tragedy befalling the landscape, creating a paradox in which living slaves are always needed to sustain and maintain the same property that contains and entraps them after death. In reality, the graveyard's decay merely returns to a more ecologically natural state where manicured grass is overgrown with "brambles twisted round," but the discordance of nature troubles control. As Burrell and Dale say, "the wilderness seems the antithesis of the garden. . . . But the garden may be associated with the free play of nature, with all its violence and abundance that might, one day, be domesticated" (121). Freed slaves act as nature's wild "abundance" in Hentz's works, so memorializing their corpses to prevent "violence" reaffirms the master/slave hierarchy and environmental conquest to link nature's resistant wilderness with slave insurrections.

The pastoralism of Hentz's works is irrevocably complicated by her using graves to disguise dystopic violations of nature that rework the landscape into a pristine falsity. The possible progression of further ecological damage with slavery's continuation suggests that we must consider slavery as more than pastorally false, a system that if left unchecked would have culminated simultaneously in bodily *and* environmental destruction. As Lewis P. Simpson claims of the Old South's "chattel slave society," the plantation "could *conceivably,* in a fuller realization of its essential nature than was permitted by historical circumstances, have found its representation in the industrial slave city" (80). Thus, it seems plausible that environmental harm would have been exacerbated by the addition of slavery to damaging practices of modern industrialization and capitalism, creating a dystopia that fortunately exists only as an imagined alternate history.

Nevertheless, graves continue to be sites where falsely cultivated nature clashes increasingly with modernization, becoming less enticing as population increases and urban development make environmental violations more evident. Our burial practices have far too often disguised the damage we do to each other and the world around us. Such practices have created, as they often do, a need to understand the past so that we may go forward. As Sachs suggests, "Environmentalists, of necessity, are future-oriented: the whole point is to cultivate modes of interaction with nature that can be sustained over time" (348). The environmentalist's role in death, then, might be further clarified by looking at the works of the antebellum South, as reading Hentz should make us think carefully about the environment of graves to ponder what else, besides bodies, those spaces might conceal.

WORKS CITED

Burrell, Gibson, and Karen Dale. "Utopiary: Utopias, Gardens, and Organization." *Utopia and Organization,* edited by Martin Parker, Blackwell, 2002, pp. 106–27.

Castronovo, Russ. *Necro Citizenship: Death, Eroticism, and the Public Sphere in the Nineteenth-Century United States.* Duke UP, 2001.

Hentz, Caroline Lee. *Marcus Warland; Or, The Long Moss Spring; A Tale of the South.* 1852. HardPress, 2013.

———. *The Planter's Northern Bride; Or, Scenes in Mrs. Hentz's Childhood.* 1854. Peterson & Brothers, 1870.

MacKethan, Lucinda Hardwick. *The Dream of Arcady: Place and Time in Southern Literature.* Louisiana State UP, 1980.

Parker, Martin. "Utopia and the Organizational Imagination: Outopia." *Utopia and Organization,* edited by Martin Parker, Blackwell, 2002, pp. 1–8.

Sachs, Aaron. *Arcadian America: The Death and Life of an Environmental Tradition.* Yale UP, 2013.

Simpson, Lewis P. *The Dispossessed Garden: Pastoral and History in Southern Literature.* U of Georgia P, 1975.

Sweeney, Kate. *American Afterlife: Encounters in the Customs of Mourning.* U of Georgia P, 2014.

Vlach, John Michael. *The Planter's Prospect: Privilege & Slavery in Plantation Paintings.* U of North Carolina P, 2002.

Warren, Jamie. "To Claim One's Own: Death and the Body in the Daily Politics of Antebellum Slavery." *Death and the American South,* edited by Craig Thompson Friend and Lorri Glover, Cambridge UP, 2015, pp. 110–30.

Sexual Assault and the Rape of Nature in
Child of God and *Deliverance*

JONATHAN VILLALOBOS

For Americans of the 1960s and early 1970s, environmental crisis was an everyday reality. *Silent Spring,* published in 1962, took the burgeoning environmental movement and pushed it into the mainstream, resulting in massive, widespread reaction and protest to the many environmental issues of the day. As an enormous number of Americans supported this nonpartisan concern, environmental protections and the creation of government departments and agencies flew through Congress, resulting in Richard Nixon's (1969–1974) signing more environmental legislation during his presidency than any other president until Barack Obama. The first Earth Day in 1970 saw more than 20 million Americans protesting around the country for environmental cleanup, safety, and protection; this first Earth Day remains one of the largest single-day protests in American history. As environmentalism came to the forefront of national dialogue, southern authors responded by penning works emphasizing and giving name to the imminent destruction of nature. In *Our South: Geographic Fantasy and the Rise of National Literature* (2010), Jennifer Rae Greeson argues that the region can be considered an "internal other" for the United States and that the nation used the South to define itself, with "America" being whatever the South was not (1). In an ecocritical sense, I work both with and against this argument, demonstrating that while the South may have served as a form of displacement for national fears about environmental catastrophe in a post–*Silent Spring* era, southern literature effectively convinced audiences that southern environments were in just as much danger as other regions of the country.

In this chapter, I specifically argue that the use of sexual assault in James Dickey's *Deliverance* (1970) and Cormac McCarthy's *Child of God* (1973) serves as a stand-in for the growing or looming destruction of southern nature as the region transitioned from a predominantly rural to predominantly urban economy in the second half of the twentieth century. Both novels were published in the early 1970s and are clearly responding to the fears of environmental catastrophe espoused by Carson and others in the early environmental movement. As a result, Dickey and McCarthy present the natural world as either pure but imperiled (the river valley about to be flooded in *Deliverance*) or corrupted by human presence and rotting from the inside out (the infected junkyard and near-collapsing cave system in *Child of God*). Moreover, the bodies who suffer assault almost always come from outside of the place that is threatened. In this way, both authors are reinforcing the fears of Americans and giving name to these fears, while simultaneously imploring these same Americans to help alleviate the suffering of rural communities and landscapes due to the growth and consumption of urban America during the baby boomer and suburban explosions of the 1950s and 1960s. In fact, *Deliverance,* despite its demeaning depiction of the people of this part of Appalachia, had a profoundly positive impact on the Chattooga River (which inspired *Deliverance*), mostly due to how the novel's readers sought to experience and eventually work to protect the Chattooga from development.

To make my argument, I must first emphasize the reaction (or affect) of horror that has been a part of southern literature since Edgar Allan Poe's earliest stories. This affect of horror has shifted throughout history to emphasize what national fears were most prominent: corruption, racial animosity, and conflict; the threat of the rural poor; and, in the late twentieth century, environmental devastation. The response of horror in general has been described in affect theory as being twofold: first, the reaction of disgust to the horrifying event, and second, a reaction of relief that the reader is not experiencing the event him- or herself. Building off of Greeson's argument, we can see that the vicarious experiences of disgust and relief that the reader encounters are ones that have existed throughout the purview of southern literature in encountering the shocking or frightening (perhaps the "un-American"). However, in the novels I analyze, these experiences also serve to remind all Americans that environmental catastrophe is lurking even in what seemed to be the most isolated and rural of places. In addition to the two responses of disgust (to the unclean, horrifying event of sexual assault or damaged environment) and relief (that the reader is not experiencing the violence or degraded landscape), this specific horror response also requires a mental connection that the devastation being wrought upon the body or bodies in question is linked deliberately to the devastation that is pending or which has already been perpetuated upon southern ecosystems.

Whether we see their perspectives as narrator or as tertiary characters, it is clear that the "outsiders" of these novels, those who either do not live in the threatened communities or do live there but in a way that disconnects them from the natural world, are unable to bring themselves to care about the impact their actions are having on nature. In *Deliverance,* when Ed and Lewis approach the small town of Oree to begin their fateful canoe trip, narrator Ed shows himself to be shockingly callous about the river's impending damming and the floods that will change life forever for the locals, claiming, "I don't mind going down a few rapids with you, and drinking a little whiskey by a campfire. But I don't give a fiddler's fuck about these hills" (40). Though Lewis tries to get Ed to appreciate the beauty and uniqueness of the northeastern Georgian mountains, he, like Ed, has no compunctions about the fact that Atlanta's growing population and need for energy has mandated the building of a new dam and hydroelectric plant that will destroy the exact environment he claims to appreciate. This purported appreciation, in fact, seems only to be aimed at *experiencing* the valley before it is altered, not *preventing* the alteration. Even in 1970, this message would have been tremendously clear due to the widespread protests, led by the Sierra Club, against damming in the Grand Canyon and other national parks. Moreover, protests against the TVA and its damming projects had been ongoing in the South since the 1930s.

Similarly, the lack of care that outsiders in *Child of God* show for the natural environment easily positions them as being enemies of the same nature they allegedly want to experience. The first couple Lester Ballard encounters in the mountains has asphyxiated on their car's exhaust fumes, demonstrating that while they were seeking to explore the countryside and enjoy a romantic interlude in nature, they still left their car running while they were doing so. As early as 1962, Congress was funding studies into whether car emissions were contributing to smog and acid rain, and the Motor Vehicle Pollution Act of 1965 set the first automobile emission standards. Therefore, readers of the time would likely be aware of the detrimental effects noxious car emissions would have. This hypocrisy, of wanting to experience nature but not considering the impacts of their actions upon it, shows that the visitors to these degraded or threatened sites are far more concerned with their own personal experience of nature than with the impact their sightseeing or consumption of nature will have. Bernice M. Murphy notes that in many southern-set horror films and novels (both very popular in the 1970s), "outsiders visit because they want to go hiking, or caving, or canoeing. There is an assumption that the local people do not experience the beauty of the wilderness in the same way our well-educated outsiders do" (154). Along these lines, we can see in both novels that those people who are "just passing through" are in actuality contributing to the devastation of the rural places they are in via their willful ignorance about how the people and landscapes they encounter will be impacted by their actions.

Viewing the novels through this lens allows us to understand them to be performing work similar to more environmentally canonical texts of the same era like Edward Abbey's *Desert Solitaire* (1968) and Gary Snyder's *Turtle Island* (1974), both of which also rail against the destruction of the American wilderness and lay blame with those whose selfish desires would put profits or progress over the needs of nature. Snyder's poem "Front Lines" demonstrates further the widespread use of the nature-as-body image, and his rape analogy for the logging industry could easily be out of either McCarthy or Dickey: "Ten wet days and the log trucks stop,/ The trees breathe./ Sunday the 4-wheel jeep of the/ Realty Company brings in/ Landseekers, lookers, they say/ To the land,/ Spread your legs" (7–13). Snyder's rage seethes out of these lines as he likens the developers, realtors, and potential clients to rapists of the land, for all of them are culpable in the vast wave of deforestation that spread across the United States at midcentury. If Snyder is performing a deadly serious version of the old chestnut that "Suburbia is where they cut down the trees and then name the streets after them," then certainly Dickey and McCarthy are performing equivalent versions incriminating casual campers, day-trippers, and would-be survivalists, who show up in their cars, lament that the beauty they encounter is so imperiled, and then drive back to their comfortable suburbia. As such, both nature and those who live in it can be seen in these novels to be striking back, imposing an assault on the interlopers that mirrors the assault on nature itself.

Ecofeminist scholars have long tied the concept of earth with the female body, demonstrating how the violation of the body and the violation of nature have been connected in literary texts. One of the most pointed ecofeminist claims comes from Andrée Collard's *Rape of the Wild* (1989), wherein she likens nature to a woman caught between two impossible dichotomies: "Nature has been blamed for being either seductive (and dangerous) or indifferent to man. Siren-like, she beckons and invites hooks and guns in the same way women are said to lure men and ask for rape. Or, like the cold, uncaring 'bitch,' nature does not respond to man's plight and must therefore be punished" (46). Throughout the South, this lose-lose scenario has emerged time and again and is emphasized in both *Deliverance* and *Child of God*. By the early twentieth century, vast tracts of land in the northern Georgia and eastern Tennessee regions of Appalachia that Dickey and McCarthy write about, respectively, had been heavily logged and deforested. The rich resources of coal, marble, and phosphate had not only resulted in extensive mining, but also tempted those who lived in these predominantly rural regions to abandon farming or other, less damaging forms of subsistence to take the quick money they could earn by stripping the land of its deposits. K. Wesley Berry argues that in the literature of the region, "Appalachia is revealed as a place both beautiful and ruined—a land of scant patches of virgin woodlands juxtaposed with the scars of over two centuries of pioneering" (61). His use of "virgin" to describe undeveloped land is no accident and helps again demonstrate the influence of the nature-as-body metaphor throughout both culture and literature; when a previously pristine landscape is subject to the demands of industry and economy, we no longer view it as being "pure" or, in other words, "virgin." Since nature cannot consent to its own development or use, this development is easily comparable to rape, especially when it leaves the landscape forever marred. This is similar to how Theda Wrede argues that nature "figures as both a metaphorically laden space and a separate, sensory, ecological reality," both a physical manifestation of the life on this planet and a deeply ingrained allegory for how we view that life as being manifested (178).

The rapes perpetuated by the rural characters in *Deliverance* and *Child of God* are both shocking and stomach-turning, further exacerbated by the graphic nature of the descriptions that Dickey and McCarthy use. Their proximity to the natural world, however, makes it clear that there is more going on than simple salaciousness; every action of sexual assault within these novels takes place out of doors and often in a landscape that is threatened, actively under assault, or already destroyed. The threat of assault, sexual or otherwise, lingers menacingly throughout the natural world, showing a southern landscape that is far from the bucolic idyll of stereotype. Berry notes that "violent acts run through the novels, dealt by humans, animals, and weather. Destruction to life is overbearing" (66). We can think of this "destruction to life" as being an analogy for the selfish and shortsighted use of the land.

Bobby's rape by the mountain men in *Deliverance* has dominated the novel's cultural impact, to the point where mere mention of *Deliverance* has become a punchline for male-male sexual encounter and the threat of sodomy. (As an example, upon learning of the existence of this chapter, a family member gifted me with a T-shirt that reads "Paddle faster—I hear banjo music.") The line "squeal like a pig" from the 1972 film adaptation (nowhere to be found in the novel) has taken on a valence of its own to the point where Ned Beatty, who played Bobby in the film, wrote an op-ed piece in the *New York Times* wherein he responded to the men who frequently shouted the line at him and speculated on the nature of how men feel about rape: "My guess is that we want to be distanced from it. Our last choice would be to identify with the victim" (qtd. in Barnett 157). Beatty's speculation has been echoed by scholars including Wrede and Pamela E. Barnett, who note how Ed, the only witness to Bobby's rape, seeks to both feminize Bobby and distance himself from the act even as he is similarly threatened by their captors. Bobby is presented as being soft and hairless, in stark contrast to Ed's heavy coat of body hair. The captors even note that the only place Ed has no hair would be in his mouth, which leads them to attempt forcing him to perform fellatio (116). Bobby's scream upon being penetrated is described as "higher and more carrying," his body as "plump and pink," and his underwear as "panties," all traditionally associated with the feminine (114, 113). The only thing saving Ed from forced oral sex is the arrival of Lewis, the pinnacle of masculinity, who shoots one of the captors with an arrow, sending the other fleeing into the woods. Lewis, whose nude body Ed has previously admired during a river bathing session, is the one responsible for the trip in the first place, and his carved musculature stands in stark contrast to the softer, fatter Bobby and Ed.

This feminization of Ed and Bobby serves, therefore, to link the assault and near-assault with the dominance of nature (traditionally rendered as feminine, e.g., "Mother Nature") and to transfer the assault onto the very people who are responsible for the looming loss of both the river valley and the way of life for those who live there. All four men on the canoe trip are from Atlanta, a city whose desperate need for more electricity has led to the imminent damming of the river, which will put everything currently in the valley underwater. When Bobby and Ed first encounter the mountain men, the latter's reactions are those of disbelief, an incredulous, "What the *hail* you think you doin'?" (108). The men do not immediately attempt to attack or assault Bobby and Ed, but once it is established that Bobby and Ed are outsiders from Atlanta, the spirit of vengeance appears to motivate their violent and depraved actions. As Murphy argues, it is "not difficult to see what happens on the banks of the river as at least in part an expression of contempt for the city folks whose desire for more air conditioning has hastened the destruction of a much older and more authentic way of life" (161). The threatened ruin of a home and land-scape where these people have lived and worked for generations is not unique to *Deliverance;* by the time of the novel's publication in 1970, the Tennessee Valley Authority had flooded twenty-nine valleys to create power-producing dams and was in the process of starting its thirtieth and final dam at Raccoon Mountain, just over the Georgia border in Tennessee. Though the dams were a tremendous boon to the cities that relied on the electricity generated by them, the people of the dammed regions suffered enormously as their way of life was cut off and they were forced to leave homesteads their families had in some cases lived on since close to the time of the Revolutionary War. The flooding of these dozens of valleys, besides being "a trope of colonization and oppression," was heavily detrimental to Appalachia's native species, many of which were displaced and forced to seek out new habitats (Wrede 188).

If *Deliverance* represents an environment in the process of degradation and destruction, then *Child of God* shows what happens to an environment after it is past the point of salvage. In the novel, the hills of Sevier County, Tennessee, are an ugly place, filled with scars on the land, felled forests, and deep, threat-ening caves that almost seem to be open wounds on the landscape. This is a South that has seen its best days long since gone. While the mountain people of *Deliverance* can at least hope to continue their way of life until the dam is finished, in *Child of God* there is no hope for any real kind of life to thrive. Chad M. Jewett argues that McCarthy emphasizes "both the passing days of subsistence agriculture and the idyllic values attached to it as well as the disso-nance of the violent, consumerist New South against the otherworldly beauty of the Appalachian hills" (87). It is in this hopeless countryside that we meet Lester Ballard, a ne'er-do-well whose first inclination is to lash out at anyone he encounters. Ballard's homestead is a fallow farm sold at auction in the nov-el's opening chapter for his failure to pay taxes—a difficult demand given the quality of the farm's soil and its lack of any timber. (Ballard's father sold the last woods on the property some twenty years prior and hung himself in the barn when, it is implied, this last money ran out.) Throughout the small towns and rural communities in McCarthy's novel, nature itself appears to be rotting from the inside out, and there is no longer any hope to be had in sustaining the land, a point made all the clearer by the fact that one of the few consis-tently employed characters we encounter is the dumpkeeper, one of Ballard's few friends. This damaged and putrid world is the backdrop, as Ballard turns slowly from being a social outcast to a necrophile, rapist, and serial killer.

Reflecting the degradation of the natural world, sexual activity and assault are rampant throughout *Child of God*. One of the earliest and most disturbing scenes in the book that evokes such assault surrounds the dumpkeeper and his daughters: nine gangly, malnourished girls who all gradually fall pregnant due to the excesses of boys coming around the dump and their father's own failure to set rules or enforce them, other than to beat the girls when they become pregnant. The brutal cycle continues through pregnancy, multiple infants, stillbirth, and the single trailer housing the family becoming full nearly to overflowing, a reflection perhaps of the initial successes of mining and industry in Appalachia leading to degraded land and little arable space. This pressure cooker explodes when the dumpkeeper catches one of his daughters having sex with a boy in the woods just outside the dump. Initially chasing the boy off and beating the girl with a branch, the dumpkeeper finds himself aroused by his progeny: "The air about him grew electric. Next thing he knew his overalls were about his knees and he was mounting her. Daddy quit, she said. Daddy. Oooh" (27–28). This scene manifests many of the stereotypical horrors of the backwoods: the incestuous, unwell family crammed into a single trailer, perpetuating a constant cycle of violence, poverty, and sex.

The sickliness of the dumpkeeper's family is likely a result of their environment: the girls are, after all, growing up in a junkyard without access to clean water or healthy food. Even their names (Urethra, Cerebella, Hernia Sue), which their father pulled from an outdated medical dictionary, reflect disease and a lack of wellness. As Murphy points out, however, this sickly stereotype has a basis in "the historical reality that the deprivation and economic marginality endured by the rural poor, particularly in the South, negatively impacted upon their physical appearance and health" (158). The prevalence of ringworm and other environmentally related diseases contributed tremendously to the negative impression most outsiders had of Appalachian people. The junkyard, which spills over into the surrounding landscape such that it is difficult to see where one ends and the other begins—"The mud packed with tins trod flat, with broken glass. The bushes strewn with refuse"—is further proof of the sickness of the surrounding environment and the violations it has endured over the years in the name of progress (26).

With this incident setting the scene for the multiple sexual assaults within the novel, the reader subsequently follows Ballard on a murder and necrophilia spree that begins with his discovery of the asphyxiated couple in their car, described earlier in this chapter. Ballard's lack of control over the direction of his life seems to drive much of his violence and depravity, especially after he is accused of rape by a woman whom he finds drunk and seemingly abandoned in the forest. Ballard spends a mere nine days in jail for the alleged assault. After this, his only sexual encounters are with dead women—first the woman he finds dead in her car and later with other women he kills and brings to a labyrinthine cave system in which he lives. If he cannot trust women to grant consent, Ballard will ensure there is no way for consent to even be an issue in the first place. His lack of control, beginning when he loses his family's land, shows that Ballard is desperate for some form of power over anyone or anything else. As Jewett argues, the deception that convinced many farmers to give up their lands and pursue the quick cash of mining or logging has culminated in Ballard being unable to do anything other than lash out at a world that has destroyed any potential for a meaningful relationship with the land: "What Ballard loses is the pastoral ideal of the rural, independent citizen working his own land for his own health and security. What he maintains is the violence that remains a part of the [Agrarian] ideal even as it continues to be pushed to the margins by a sublimated town-based Southern ethos" (Jewett 87). Similar to the mountain men from *Deliverance*, Ballard's anger at the loss of his way of life has manifested horrifyingly in his sociopathic rape and murder spree. Looking for someone to blame, Ballard primarily strikes out against those who have some connection with the destruction of nature, from couples having sex in their cars up in the hills to one of the dumpkeeper's daughters. Throughout the novel, consensual sex always seems to be interrupted and perverted into something grotesque, much like the shifting from early farming in Appalachia to mining, foresting, and other, temporarily more profitable occupations that led to more damaging and widespread impacts upon the environment.

Both novels demonstrate a rising sense of fear in the early 1970s throughout the South and the rest of America of environmental apocalypse through the destruction of what facets of the natural world seemed to remain. Lester Ballard and the mountain men of *Deliverance* are monstrous, of that there is no doubt, and nothing any of their victims has done is deserving of the sexual assaults and murders they suffer. However, by showing the impact of what urban and suburban America demanded of and took from rural America, Dickey and McCarthy demonstrate the burning anger felt by displaced rural Americans and environmentalists alike at what was happening to nature throughout the nation. The constant consumption and exploitation of nature, perpetuated full bore since the late nineteenth century, reached a point of unsustainability in the late twentieth century, particularly in communities that had been devastated by the heavy impacts of mining, quarries, and logging. Further exacerbating the problem were large southern cities like Atlanta and Knoxville, which demanded resources and energy from rural locales while simultaneously lamenting their degradation and longing for environmental protections. The cries of the NIMBY ("Not in My Backyard") movement echo hollowly in light of the heavy environmental destruction suburban America caused and the fact that rural communities struggled daily to continue to survive less than a hundred miles from most urban centers in the South.

The image of nature being subjected to rape, an invasion and exploitation against a subject's will, has always been a powerful one for the environmental movement, and an ecocritical reading of the sexual assaults in these two novels shows a similar parallel. The locations of the violence and depravity in these assaults—the banks of a river, the woods outside of a junkyard, an unstable cave system that collapses in *Child of God*'s final chapter—are not accidental. Each is a formerly pristine place, now ravaged (or about to be ravaged) by the gnawing demands of a greedy civilization. The links between sexual assault and the destruction of nature are consistent throughout these novels and emphasize once again what was happening to the environment of Appalachia and other southern regions. Yet these novels have not taken their place among other "environmental" American literature of the time because of the same horror within southern literature that has always served to displace national fears. If we accept Greeson's claims of the South being the internal other for the nation at large, it follows that a national audience would not respond to environmental destruction in the South as it would to that same destruction in the Northeast or West.

This argument, however, belies the truth that in at least one very real instance, literature did have a positive and meaningful impact on southern ecologies. In 1974, the Chattooga River (which Dickey based *Deliverance* on) was officially protected under the National Wild and Scenic Rivers System (Williams 3). This listing permanently kept the Chattooga from being dammed (which had been attempted four times, in 1935, 1944, 1968, and 1969), and the task force report concluded that "the benefit of protecting a free-flowing river outweighed the potential for hydroelectric power generation on the Chattooga River" (4). Readers of *Deliverance* responded to the threat against the Chattooga by visiting and rafting the river and fighting for its preservation; between 1970 and 1973, more than 1,000 individual statements were collected in favor of protecting the Chattooga and against its damming (4). This spike in popularity is directly linked to *Deliverance*'s publication, as before 1970 only a few hundred visitors came to the Chattooga each year, while in 1971, the river saw more than 50,000 visitors.

The publication of works like *Deliverance* and *Child of God* changed discussions about nature on a national basis and in the South worked directly to raise awareness of the threat many southern ecosystems were under in the mid-to-late century. Though literature was hardly able to stop all the destruction happening in the South, the fact that readers responded so overwhelmingly and enthusiastically to try to save the very nature they read about shows the power that these and other novels had during this time of increasing environmental awareness. Just as *Desert Solitaire* brought attention to the threat facing national monuments and *Turtle Island* railed against suburban sprawl, *Deliverance* and *Child of God* showed a national audience what was happening to previously pristine areas of the southern United States and demanded that these audiences do something to stop this imminent destruction. That the call was not only heard but followed demonstrates the power that literature had and continues to have in bringing natural crises to the attention of the people who read it.

WORKS CITED

Barnett, Pamela E. "James Dickey's *Deliverance:* Southern, White, Suburban Male Nightmare or Dream Come True?" *Forum for Modern Language Studies,* vol. 40, no. 2, 2004, pp. 145–59.

Berry, K. Wesley. "The Lay of the Land in Cormac McCarthy's *The Orchard Keeper* and *Child of God.*" *Southern Quarterly,* vol. 38, no. 4, 2000, pp. 61–83.

Collard, Andrée, with Joyce Contrucci. *Rape of the Wild: Man's Violence against Animals and the Earth.* Indiana UP, 1989.

Dickey, James. *Deliverance.* Bantam Doubleday, 1970.

Greeson, Jennifer Rae. *Our South: Geographic Fantasy and the Rise of National Literature.* Harvard UP, 2010.

Jewett, Chad M. "Revising the Southern Myth: Persephone Violated in Faulkner's *Sanctuary* and McCarthy's *Child of God.*" *The Faulkner Journal,* vol. 27, no. 1, 2013, pp. 77–96.

McCarthy, Cormac. *Child of God.* 1973. Vintage International, 1993.

Murphy, Bernice M. *The Rural Gothic in American Popular Culture: Backwoods Horror and Terror in the Wilderness.* Palgrave Macmillan, 2013.

Snyder, Gary. "Front Lines." *Turtle Island,* New Directions, 1974, p. 18.

Williams, Buzz. "The Wild and Scenic Chattooga River." *Chattooga Quarterly,* vol. 8, no. 3, 2004, pp. 3–4.

Wrede, Theda. "Nature and Gender in James Dickey's *Deliverance:* An Ecofeminist Reading." *The Way We Read James Dickey: Critical Approaches for the Twenty-First Century,* edited by William B. Thesing and Theda Wrede, U of South Carolina P, 2009, pp. 177–92.

Florida Man

Climatological Racism and Internal Homonationalism in US Political Satire

JOHN MORAN

Across news media, social media, and academic texts, Florida is considered "weird" and "wild," and Floridians are portrayed as exceptionally "crazy," criminally pathological, and dysfunctional. Although these terms are offensive, they often move through US public discourse as such. Increasingly called the "strangest of American states," as Diane Roberts writes in *Dream State* (2007, 26), Florida is recognized globally as the capital of "weird news" (Pittman 3–4), a category of entertainment news provided by major news outlets and content aggregators, consisting largely of reports of bizarre criminal behavior. These representations are so pervasive that making fun of Florida is a national pastime. For example, in August of 2015 on *Last Week Tonight with John Oliver* (Season 2, Episode 47), a chorus of children sings a song in favor of DC statehood with the lyrics: "And if you're totally convinced/ that there should be just fifty states/ Well then let's all kick out Florida/ 'cause no one thinks they're great."

Florida Man, the quintessence of such representations, is an internet meme associated with a Twitter account with an anonymous creator that debuted in January 2013 and, as of early 2017, had 380,000 followers (a larger account than Florida governor Rick Scott, with 85,000 followers, or Florida's leading newspaper, *The Tampa Bay Times,* with 200,000 followers). Florida Man's feed, joined by a similar but less popular Florida Woman account, is an aggregation of news reports of strange and often disturbing and violent, especially sexually violent, acts by men in Florida. Through the mug shots embedded in these linked reports and through his profile picture, Florida Man often appears as a middle-aged "white trash" man with grotesque facial features, suggesting methamphetamine addiction.[1] The name comes from evening news pronouncements, such as those recorded in *Esquire*'s "The 47 Wildest Florida Man Headlines of 2015," including "Florida Man Covers Himself in Ashes, Says He's a 400-Year-Old Indian, Crashes Stolen Car"; "Florida Man Tries to Sell 3

Iguanas Taped to His Bike to Passerby As Dinner"; and "Florida Man Goes on LSD-Fueled Naked Rampage, Bites Girlfriend's Finger."

Common wisdom and recent memory might trace the joke of Florida's dysfunctionality and unpopularity to the 2000 Presidential Election recount, or read it as an effort by northeasterners to ridicule the frivolity of the Sun Belt, with whom they are losing a demographic race. A historical perspective suggests, however, that the centuries-old, rather than decade-old, climatological and pathological depiction of Florida is rooted in climatological racism and can be understood by the analytical tools of whiteness studies and queer theory. The temperatist gaze of those in "civilized" temperate climates places the grotesque "white trash" criminal figures of "Florida Man" and "Florida Woman" outside of, and in opposition to, metronormative and homonational whiteness, or a properly civilized and socially inclusive urban whiteness. These associations between "white trash" and Florida Man erase structural inequalities; perpetuate a climatological racism that racializes degenerate, rural bodies as distinct from idealized, urban white bodies; and blames Florida Man on the excesses of US internal tropical space through insinuations of tropical degeneracy.[2] This temperatist gaze upon degenerate white bodies is symptomatic of what I have elsewhere termed internal homonationalism, a conceptual framework for understanding how rural, white southerners are represented as simultaneously perverse and homophobic.[3] The intervention of this essay is to consider internal homonationalism alongside climate. Attention to climate and ecology reveals the troubling underbelly of the sometimes admittedly funny Florida Man jokes: climatological racism.

Homonationalism, argues Jasbir Puar in *Terrorist Assemblages* (2007), is the inclusion of sexual minorities in America's imperial project. By reveling in the moral superiority of LGBTQ inclusion and women's liberation, the United States participates in "sexual exceptionalism" that justifies the continuation of "U.S. nationalism and imperial expansion endemic to the war on terror" (2). Homonationalism imagines a Muslim other that is not just homophobic, but also perverse—sexually repressed, lascivious, violating, and repulsive. Such representations of the bodies of homophobic others are similar to past representations of LGBTQ persons. While Puar wrote during the Bush era, the most virulent example of homonationalism emerged in 2016: the gay alt-right. These LGBTQ Trump supporters, largely white, gay men, associate their sexuality with Western civilization, relish authoritarianism as a style of gay male culture, and denigrate Muslims for homophobia.

At the Daddy Will Save Us art exhibition in 2016, which implied Donald Trump could be a gay "daddy" figure to a nation of submissive gay "sons," the media personality Milo Yiannopoulos evoked the Pulse massacre of forty-nine people in an Orlando gay club by a shooter who pledged allegiance to the Islamic State. Yiannopoulos said, "America is the kindest country to minorities. It treats women, blacks, gays, trannies, whatever minority you choose to identify with, it treats them the best out of any country anywhere in the world." He then bathed himself in pig's blood as a "a tribute to the suffering of those who have lost loved ones at the hands of illegal aliens and Islamic terrorists."[4] Many have found it easy to criticize Yiannopoulos. While the gay alt-right quickly demonstrates homonationalism as politics, homonationalism as a concept is not so easy to contend with, as it asks us to challenge more subtle, and cherished, representations and values, such as considering how projects of inclusion may also cover for, or become a tool of, violence, exclusion, and exploitation.

This challenge to received ideas of US nationalist heroics—which come packaged with complementary villains, such as the homophobic Muslim others and homophobic "redneck" others who serve as bigoted foils for US sexual exceptionalism—is also afoot in the new southern studies, whose scholars have taken their feminist, antiracist, antiessentialist stand with sectarian zeal. These scholars are unafraid to challenge problematic representations of the "South," unafraid to note comparisons between imperialism in the US South and the Global South, and unafraid to use terms like "orientalism" to describe the US South as an internal other.

An instantiation of internal homonationalism can be clearly seen on a January 13, 2015 episode of *The Daily Show with Jon Stewart* (Season 20, Episode 46). In preparing to introduce Florida senator Marco Rubio, Stewart goes on what he terms a "Florida Rant." This rant epitomizes the representation of Florida in contemporary US political satire. Stewart explains that same-sex marriage was ruled a constitutional right in Florida, and that in response, three clerks of court in northeastern Florida (Duval, Baker, and Clay Counties) ended their courthouses' optional service of performing, rather than only issuing licenses for, marriages; their rationale was to protect clerks from officiating ceremonies they might feel uncomfortable officiating. Stewart announces that this will be great news for "Duval County Cassanova Leland," a straight man who will thus not have to be tied down. Leland is depicted in a "wife beater" shirt and trucker hat, with "Jesus hair," in an obvious figuring of a "white trash" male whose southern accent and wolf howl Stewart satirizes.[5] Stewart then introduces the nongay Floridians that the county clerks are trying to protect from "reverse discrimination" with a montage of "Florida Man" and "Florida Woman" clips, such as a woman setting a man's car on fire after he refused to buy her a McFlurry, and a man charged with posing as a woman doctor and injecting cement into a woman's butt. "Florida," Stewart says, "you don't get to judge others when your state motto is, If Darwin was right, we wouldn't be here." This is a different take on the show's previous suggestion, after George Zimmerman's acquittal in the murder of unarmed African American minor Trayvon Martin, that the state motto should be "Florida: The Worst State" (Season 18, Episode 125).

After Stewart howls like "Duval County Cassanova Leland," he asks, "You're not going to perform weddings for these people?" The show displays wedding photos of same-sex, light-skinned men, evoking the upper-class habitus of metronormativity and the ideals of consumer perfection. He continues, "to preserve the sanctity of your courthouses for these people?" The show then displays six photos, presumably mug shots, of white men and women, including George Zimmerman, the infamous murderer of Trayvon Martin, evoking a different habitus and different bodies: long hair, prison and informal clothing, unkempt and extravagant facial hair, and expressions of aggression, confusion, and insanity. The bodies and sexualities of the six people in the mug shots are outside metro-heteronormativity and urban civility, because to be a good, heteronormative white person requires being LGBTQ-inclusive. The "white trash" Floridians are "smeared as queer" through internal homonationalism: they are depicted as perverse, sexually deviant, and violative, and their grotesque bodies index their bigotry. In queer theory, it is usually queers that do the queering; "queered" describes a space or relation being "queered" by queers who make it their own, or by a scholar who reads a text as queer. Describing the mug shots of supposed white trash Floridians as "smeared as queer," rather, is a queering more akin to the Smear the Queer game popular during my childhood, in which a ball is thrown at an unsuspecting child who catches it and is called out as "queer," and then must run for their life while others attempt to tackle them. Using queer broadly to describe nonnormative and marginalized sex and gender behavior and identification, as well as the readability of such qualities across bodily comportment, to be "smeared as queer" is to have your body—including bodily behaviors and qualities such as hygiene, gender expression, and attractiveness—marked and portrayed as nonnormative, especially repulsive, through the representational choices of particular images.[6] To say that representations of the white trash figure of Florida Man are both distinctly racialized and smeared as queer, is to bring two different, polemical approaches to the same thorny question of representations of bodily differences across groups of whites who live in different places.

The crux of Stewart's juxtaposition of idealized white, gay male couples against homophobic and grotesque "white trash" bodies that have been smeared as queer, including a montage of Florida Man's path of destruction, emphasizes the idealized gay couple's ability to reproduce society, and Florida Man's danger, lack of class, and inability to reproduce society. Eugenicist logic makes the joke funny—gay couples are the epitome of Saxon perfection, and Florida Man needs to be sterilized, or at least prevented from marrying. Stewart then concludes that we may have already found the "most Florida Man of the year": the man who hit his employees with a lizard at a reptile store where, if that was not enough, someone had recently choked to death in a cockroach-eating contest. Because the video of the incident was not released, Stewart uses his "Footage Faker 3000" to show a mock surveillance video created by *The Daily Show* of an obvious "white trash" woman in overalls, beating a "white trash" man with a lizard. "Stop, I beg you," the man screams. The woman, who began the clip barking almost like a dog, speaks in a difficult-to-understand southern "hick" accent: "I can't stop, I'm from Florida."

Like Stewart's mocking state motto, "Florida: If Darwin Was Right, We Wouldn't Be Here," which jests that Floridians are a distinct and inferior group that would be removed from history by natural selection, the lizard-wielding assailant's claim that she cannot stop because she is from Florida alludes to one of the foundational understandings regarding purportedly feebleminded poor whites during the eugenics movement in the early twentieth century: "they can't stop," as the lizard wielder puts it, because their condition is immutable and particularly hereditary.[7]

The key to that Florida joke, though, is the lizard; not just its absurdity, but its invocation of tropical wildness. Reptiles, like the weaponized lizard above, evoke the primitive, swampy, and even monstrous subtropical and tropical climates of Florida. Such associations suggest something beyond the workings of the poor white stereotype and the eugenicist thought that popularized it; they also suggest climatological racism. Climatological racism (which I distinguish from the more common term *environmental determinism*) is the belief that the world is composed of distinct types of peoples—races—that have differing abilities to succeed in the task of civilizing themselves, and that these differences result from the influence of climate. Climatological racism is also the institution of racist practices that depend on climatological thinking—such as when enslavement of persons has been justified by rhetoric that the enslaved may be biologically predisposed to work in the climate of the plantation zone. Climatological racism asserts a crude, temperatist dichotomy of a temperate North with tempered societies, and a tropical South with more primitive societies. We might also use the term in a looser sense, as I do here, to describe the linking of biases regarding what constitutes normal or extreme climates with assumptions regarding what constitutes normal or extreme (and thus, smeared as queer) persons. Internal homonationalist representations of simultaneously homophobic and perverse Florida Men and Women are most effective because associations with animality, primitivity, feral creatures, extreme climatic phenomena, and excessive and fecund ecologies draw on old imperial imaginaries that confront degeneracy, primitiveness, and others through fantastical travelogues, tropical gothic aesthetics, and exoticization.

We see the association between drug-addled behavior and reptiles again on *Last Week Tonight with John Oliver* (Season 2, Episode 7), when Oliver himself asserts:

> In 2012 in Florida, a staggering 88% of all license suspensions were due to failure to comply with summons or fines. Which is insane. It also leaves only 12% for Florida's other most common violations: accidently taking your golf cart on the freeway; feeding meth to an alligator; feeding an alligator to a meth dealer; and being an alligator meth dealer. Florida.

The screen displays a computer illustration of an alligator wearing a "wife beater" T-shirt. In Oliver's joke, an alligator meth dealer is the representation *par excellence* of Florida. At first, the figure of an alligator meth dealer (dressed in a "wife beater" just like Duval County Cassanova Leland) seems like an unmediated comedic escalation—through mutant combination—of the previous list of iconic figures that contribute to Florida's eccentricity. However, the alligator meth dealer evokes associations between alligators feeding at night and dealers engaged in illicit markets, as well as between the alligator's cold-blooded predation and the violence and exploitation of dealing. The meth-dealing alligator is also a coded evocation of white trash. A crack-dealing alligator would evoke inner-city blackness, a coke-dealing alligator might evoke upper-class whiteness, but a meth dealer draws on meth's associations with trailers, rural areas, and images of meth users' faces, which are disfigured by the drug, a disfiguration historically associated with poor "white trash."[8]

Florida Man relies on a longer history that involves the imagining of white degeneracy alongside climate and ecology. The genealogy of climatological racism and thought is beyond the scope of this essay; simply a comprehensive history of climatological thought regarding the US South would be a monumental undertaking. Such thinking had a long history before the colonial period and has continued into the present, where it is adopted in the discourse on global anthropogenic climate change, which preys on the fear of a planet degenerated by deadly heat and extreme weather. Although reference to the ancient Greeks as the origin of an idea in the United States is often less intellectual history than Eurocentric fantasy, the durability of climatic thinking is often flagged by reference to Hippocrates. "Greek scholars focused on climate to explain human intellectual difference," writes Nell Irvin Painter in *The History of White People* (5). Hippocrates believed that rugged and challenging climates, such as mountains and harsh winters, produced a temperament for imperial domination and manly beauty, and such thinking has been taken up variously across the centuries (10).

In *Ariel's Ecology: Plantations, Personhood, and Colonialism in the American Tropics* (2013), Monique Allewaert examines how in the seventeenth and eighteenth centuries, "Caribbean and North American intellectuals, naturalists, and politicians were particularly concerned about the impact of tropical climates on Anglo-Europeans as they moved from the temperate climates supposedly more suited to them to the tropical and subtropical climates supposedly better suited to Africans and Native Americans" (4). They feared that tropical heat and nature would weaken or kill them, and they dreaded the "revolutionary alliance between tropical elemental forces and subaltern persons" (7). Presaging representations of Florida Man's wildness through association with alligators, such as in the image of the Alligator Meth Dealer, was the threatening tropicality of the swamp: "There was perhaps no space more paradigmatically tropical and more threatening to colonials than the swamps" (33). Tropical excesses harbored not just danger but bounty, and some believed such bounty itself would degrade whites. William Byrd, in his account of the 1727 surveying of the Virginia and North Carolina border, "complains sardonically about the poor whites" and considers them a "distinct, inferior social group," as Wray notes in *Not Quite White* (21). Byrd suggests they labor less "by the great felicity of the climate, the easiness of raising provisions," and associates the warm sun with laziness. This focus on laziness was, for Byrd's worldview, a form of moral condemnation and extreme contempt (Wray 21–26). Louis D. Rubin Jr. saw Byrd as the forefather to the southwestern humor and local color traditions and to "the old Southern tradition of low comedy based on the peccadilloes and racy vigor of the poor whites" (28).

The mugshots of Florida Men and Women on *The Daily Show* evoke the nineteenth-century portraits of "poor white trash" and "dirt eaters" who engaged in the supposedly degenerate practice of eating clay, which served in the antebellum period as a disparaging image of the poor white in the South (Wray 41). Poor white trash, observed as Crackers and Lubbers in the colonial period, were widely recognized as a distinctive and biologically inferior group in the nineteenth century and into the early twentieth century, although there was much disagreement about the cause of such degeneracy, especially whether or not it was a product of the social and economic degradation of a slave society. During the eugenics movement, which peaked in the 1920s, "middle-class professionals constructed the degenerate poor white as a biologically inferior type" (83), and many middle-class professionals considered sterilization a humane way to allow the feebleminded to participate in society without fear of their reproducing.

In the early twentieth century, the most prolific advocate of climatological racism was the Yale geographer Ellsworth Huntington.[9] In *Climate and Civilization* (1915), Huntington argues both climate and racial inheritance influenced how far societies would develop along the road from primitive to civilized. Although confident in his scientific proof that "negroes" were mentally inferior to "Teutons" and that this difference was ineradicable (16), Huntington does speculate that hundreds of years in a more favorable temperate or less favorable tropical climate might change a race. Huntington also contends that the earth's climate changes, and that the flourishing of civilization in southern Europe and the Yucatan in antiquity was due to solar flares, which had increased stimulating storminess in the subtropics, making them more like the stimulating storminess of the contemporary temperate zone (263–70). Much like contemporary advocates for climate change mitigation who unwittingly produce a problematic fear of tropicality, one of Huntington's hypotheses for why he finds some people civilized and others not is "climatic changes"—extreme climate changes like droughts that are disproportionately the burden of less developed nations.[10]

Regardless, for Huntington, tropical climates are a great enervating handicap to thinking and laboring, and adverse tropical climates "set the wheel in motion" for the degeneration of the "cracker" type of "poor white trash" (52, 216). Huntington examines the influence of climate on productivity by studying factory workers in Florida, Maryland, and Connecticut, emphasizing the invigorating impact of a "stimulating" climate through daily and seasonal temperature fluctuation, especially sharp temperature drops. Huntington considers "tropical inertia" a "climatic handicap" of the US South (Ring 619). Furthermore, Huntington presages the association between angry outburst and tropicality in the Florida Man meme, as well as themes of inebriation and sexual excess, when he writes, "Almost any American or European who has traveled or resided within the tropics will confess that he has occasionally flown into a passion, and perhaps used physical violence, under circumstances which at home would merely have made him vexed . . . [in the tropics] their power of self-control is enfeebled" (43). Huntington wrote as US imperial tropical medicine, whose practitioners often rotated between US imperial holdings abroad and the South, "framed the South as an infectious primitive space . . . in need of colonial uplift, much like the tropical possessions acquired as a result of American imperialism" (Ring 620–27).

The dichotomy of developed temperate and undeveloped tropical zones continued through the midcentury, where boosters of US tropical development abroad, such as Douglas Lee (173–74), argued that while tropicality was not the exclusive factor in underdevelopment, peoples in tropical areas suffered "disadvantageous handicaps" compared with temperate-zone dwellers. At the same time, real estate boosters such as those in Florida tried to reframe tropical and subtropical land holdings as healthful, rather than harmful, to white bodies, and tropical beaches became sites of leisure where the vigor of white bodies could be demonstrated.[11] Promotion of leisure could also reinforce the dichotomy of wintry industriousness and tropical sloth. In his 1876 Florida travelogue, which devoted a chapter to climatology and the benefits of Florida's climate for consumptives, Sidney Lanier writes that Florida could enlarge pleasure against "that universal killing ague of modern life—the fever of the unrest of trade throbbing through the long chill of a seven-months' winter" (13). The success of the Florida Man meme is still reliant on a belief in the relationship between climate and societal productivity. When Stewart's Florida Man rant is accompanied by clips of hurricane winds and coastal flooding, the suggestion that Florida is not normal because of extreme weather brings up the association between the destructive power of such disasters and the destructive power of Florida Man's actions. Florida Man's bizarre criminality is, like a tropical hurricane, antithetical to economic productivity. The flip side is that such destruction is economically productive as clickbait.

Four centuries of what I call climatological racism have catalyzed and sustained the stereotypes and imagery that give Florida Man life. Florida Man would not be as funny, as legible, or as compelling to internal homonationalists if not for the old imperial, global trope of the white man degenerating in the tropics. Fueled by media representations of climate change that rightly warn of a warming planet, but unfortunately draw from older fears of tropical degeneration, this temperatist gaze producing Florida Man may become more pronounced in our climatic future.

NOTES

1. Criminal images, especially mug shots circulated in anti-methamphetamine campaigns, are a key site where the trope of the "white trash meth head" is circulated and articulated as a threat to "the supposed purity of hegemonic whiteness" (Linnemann and Wall 317–18).

2. Using the terms "racism" and "racialization" to describe representations of certain white bodies highlights the connection between such representations and blatant climatological racism against people of color, demonstrates how insinuations of tropical degeneracy rest on representations of bodies, and follows a tradition in whiteness studies of recognizing the unique history of "white trash" as "not just a classist slur—it's also a racial epithet that marks out certain whites as a breed apart, a dysgenic race unto themselves" (Newitz and Wray, "Introduction," 2).

3. Moran, "Queer Rednecks."

4. http://www.breitbart.com/milo/2016/10/08/milo-unveils-angel-mom-piece-at-new -york-art-show/.

5. On the TV show *Atlanta* (Season 2, Episode 1), one character explains Florida Man in a montage that similarly includes an image of a white man in a trucker hat and "wife beater" shirt.

6. "Smeared as queer" builds on the use of queer to describe representations of grotesque homophobes in Moran, "Queer Rednecks," 96–98.

7. *The Kallikak Family* by Henry Goddard was a study published in 1912 that exemplified such hereditarian belief; see Painter, *The History of White People*, 273.

8. Social psychologists suggest that across Anglophone nations, white trash subjects are sometimes imagined as bestial and incompletely human; see Loughnan et al., "Dehumanization and Social Class." "Racialities, animalities, and sexualities interplay," writes Mel Chen

in *Animacies*, departing from the recognition in animal studies of the "profound interconsti-tution of animal and human identities" (99) to consider how, while stereotypes of animality become attached to specific races, this "animality can shift, attaching itself to different kinds of groups" and that the "white man at the top" of the hierarchy "can be dragged down by his own queer association" (115).

9. While Huntington's work is often referred to as "environmental determinism" (see Aresenault, "The End of the Long Hot Summer," 598), I use "climatological racism" to avoid confusion with writing on the determining influence of social environment in personal de-velopment. Climate also evokes the tropics and particularly heat, which are central to such imperial imaginaries, while environment may allude to a less crude understanding of cul-tural difference as proposed by early Boasian anthropology or by environmental historians. I use "racism," not determinism, because such thinking was raciological and racist.

10. Oddly, one of the most highly cited articles in the humanities concerning climate change, "The Climate of History" by Dipesh Chakrabarty, appears to unwittingly share a title with "The Climate of History," a chapter in Huntington and Visher's *Climatic Changes: Their Nature and Causes* (1922). For examples of climate change reporting that rely on tropicalism, see discussion of "sweltering tropical rainforests" (http://www.bbc.com/earth/story/201511 30-how-hot-could-the-earth-get) and the association between "civilization" and a moderate climate (http://www.cnn.com/2015/01/14/opinion/co2-crisis-griffin/index.html).

11. See Cocks, *Tropical Whites*. Of course, Huntington's hope that man would "conquer climate," especially regarding labor environments, has been largely borne out in the South by air conditioning. See also Arsenault 616. Koeniger, in "Climate and Southern Distinctive-ness," asks, "is it merely a coincidence that the first generation in the history of mankind freed by technology from virtually all unwanted contact with climatic environment was the first also to dismiss the importance of climate?" (30).

WORKS CITED

Allewaert, Monique. *Ariel's Ecology: Plantations, Personhood, and Colonialism in the American Tropics.* U of Minnesota P, 2013.
Arsenault, Raymond. "The End of the Long Hot Summer: The Air Conditioner and Southern Culture." *The Journal of Southern History*, vol. 50, no. 4, 1984, pp. 597–628.
Chen, Mel Y. *Animacies: Biopolitics, Racial Mattering, and Queer Affect.* Duke UP, 2012.
Cocks, Catherine. *Tropical Whites: The Rise of the Tourist South in the Americas.* U of Penn-sylvania P, 2013.
Huntington, Ellsworth. *Civilization and Climate.* Yale UP, 1922.
Huntington, Ellsworth, and Stephen Sargent Visher. *Climatic Changes: Their Nature and Causes.* Yale UP, 1922.
Koeniger, A. Cash. "Climate and Southern Distinctiveness." *The Journal of Southern History*, vol. 54, no. 1, 1988, pp. 21–44.
Lanier, Sidney. *Florida: Its Scenery, Climate, and History.* J. B. Lippincott & Co, 1876.

Lee, Douglas. *Climate and Economic Development in the Tropics*. Council on Foreign Relations. Harper and Brothers, 1957.

Linnemann, Travis, and Tyler Wall. "'This Is Your Face on Meth': The Punitive Spectacle of 'White Trash' in the Rural War on Drugs." *Theoretical Criminology*, vol. 17, no. 3, 2013, pp. 315–34.

Loughnan, Steve, Nick Haslam, Robbie M. Sutton, and Bettina Spencer. "Dehumanization and Social Class: Animality in the Stereotypes of 'White Trash,' 'Chavs,' and 'Bogans.'" *Social Psychology*, vol. 45, no. 1, 2014, pp. 54–61.

Moran, John. "Queer Rednecks: Padgett Powell's Manly South." *Southern Cultures*, vol. 22, no. 3, 2016, pp. 95–122.

Newitz, Annalee, and Matt Wray. "Introduction." *White Trash: Race and Class in America*, edited by Annalee Newitz and Matt Wray, Routledge, 1997, pp. 1–14.

Painter, Nell Irvin. *The History of White People*. W.W. Norton & Company, 2010.

Pittman, Craig. *Oh, Florida!: How America's Weirdest State Influences the Rest of the Country*. Macmillan, 2016.

Puar, Jasbir K. *Terrorist Assemblages: Homonationalism in Queer Times*. Duke UP, 2007.

Ring, Natalie J. "Inventing the Tropical South: Race, Region, and the Colonial Model." *Mississippi Quarterly*, vol. 56, no. 4, 2003, pp. 619–32.

Roberts, Diane. *Dream State: Eight Generations of Swamp Lawyers, Conquistadors, Confederate Daughters, Banana Republicans, and Other Florida Wildlife*. Simon and Schuster, 2007.

Rubin, Jr., Louis D. *The Literary South*. 1979. Louisiana State UP, 1986.

Wray, Matt. *Not Quite White: White Trash and the Boundaries of Whiteness*. Duke UP, 2006.

New Orleans in the Twenty-Second Century

ROBERT AZZARELLO

The future holds a simple promise.
—VALERIE MARTIN, *A Recent Martyr*

By the end of Valerie Martin's 1987 novel *A Recent Martyr,* the narrator has survived a number of disasters both large and small: a dead-end job, an unhappy marriage, a sadomasochistic relationship that turns into rape, bubonic plague, forced quarantine, and the loss of a friend who is a young Catholic nun murdered on her way back to the convent. New Orleans grounds and enlivens all this action, and yet the narrator chooses in the novel's denouement to remain in the city. "It's an odd sensation to recognize in oneself the need to be in a particular physical environment," Martin writes, "when one longs for the home ground no matter how terrible the memories it holds, no matter how great the efforts made to leave it behind" (204). When the narrator does make those efforts to leave the city, she thinks herself "lucky to escape its allure, for it's the attraction of decay, of vicious, florid, natural cycles that roll over the senses with their lushness" (204). But try as she might, her efforts to escape always end in the same way: with her return to New Orleans. "Where else could I find these hateful, humid, murderously hot afternoons," she asks, "when I know that the past was a series of great mistakes, the greatest being the inability to live anywhere but in this swamp?" (204). For Martin's narrator, as well as for many New Orleanians, the decision to stay or go is caught up in this kind of circular dynamic between attraction and revulsion, topophilia and topophobia, in determining oikos, or one's place within a vast network of built and nonbuilt environments.

This circular dynamic between philia and phobia plays out not only according to topos—in responses to the physical environment—but also according to chronos—in responses to time. Indeed, the novel's denouement is best understood as a conjunction between topophilia-topophobia and chronophilia-chronophobia. For the narrator, there is pleasure and danger in "the threatening encumbrance of moss on trees, the thick, sticky plantain trees that can grow from their chopped roots twenty feet in three months, the green scum that spreads over the lagoons and bayous" (204). But the pleasure and danger she finds in the place, and the specific life-forms contained therein, are also caught up in the narrator's sense of time. After focusing on the past, especially how New Orleans is associated for her with bad personal and social memories, a long "series" of haunting "mistakes," the narrator then moves outside that temporal frame. In the last three sentences of the novel, Martin writes the following: "The future holds a simple promise. We are well below sea level, and inundation is inevitable. We are content, for now, to have our heads above the water" (204). While the novel's denouement remains fixed in one place, the city of New Orleans, it moves temporally from the past to the future, and then it backpedals into the present. The conditional contentment "for now" that ends the novel in 1987 seems especially poignant, almost prophetic, looking back from our own now in the present. Its mood, a kind of good-enough-for-now apathy, recognizes a certain environmental disaster looming on the horizon without having the will to do anything about it.

Eighteen years after *A Recent Martyr* appeared in 1987, the inevitable happened. During the devastating floods of Hurricanes Katrina and Rita in August and September 2005, the conditional contentment "for now" came to an end. The future's simple promise, that which was sent forward ahead of itself, became actualized in the present. A poem by Katie Ford called "Earth," quoted in full from her book *Colosseum* (2008), describes that moment just before the future keeps its promise, just before the inevitable inundation will come. The poet writes,

> If you respect the dead
> and recall where they died
> by this time tomorrow
> there will be nowhere to walk. (13)

Written in the wake of the 2005 hurricanes but seemingly set the day before the waters began to rise, "Earth" presents a haunting vision of tomorrow in the form of a syllogistic proof. If A (one has respect for the dead), and B (one is capable of memory), then C (within the next twenty-four hours, all ground will become unwalkable). Like all syllogisms, the poem works through a kind of rational clarity and certainty. As Ford writes it, the conclusion cannot help but to follow from the combination of the two propositions. The logic, therefore, seems inevitable. As in Valerie Martin's novel, human agency seems to be rendered powerless to effect change within the span of the next twenty-four hours.

Such a view of the world is dark, but there is potentially an even darker interpretation in this short poem of four lines. What the poem does not exactly spell out is that to avoid coming to the conclusion, to avoid C, one may undermine one or both of the two propositions. If one wants to walk, if one wants to have grounds upon which to walk tomorrow, one can undermine A or B or both. One can choose to cease respecting the dead, one can actively forget where they died, or one can do both. Because the imperative to walk is so great after the disaster, and because respect for the dead is so difficult to shake, as history has shown, the decision to forget seems to be the most popular avenue. The dead often go unrecalled.

In the context of southern Louisiana, not only is one faced with the loss of ground spurred by the ethical imperative to avoid walking on the dead, if indeed they are recalled, but one is also faced with the literal loss of ground through environmental destruction spurred by a variety of anthropogenic and nonanthropogenic forces: levee construction and soil subsidence, dredging and canalization, chemical poisoning and salt water intrusion, rising sea levels, whiplashing by major storms. All these forces have the ultimate effect of dissolving the ground upon which one can walk and, by extension, performing that most meditative of philosophical and physical activities. The title of Ford's poem, "Earth," is general and planetary, moreover, as if to say that the future's promise in New Orleans does not apply simply there. It is the fate of the whole world.

The kind of ecological dread that surfaces in Ford, Martin, and many others in New Orleans, can be traced back at least to the city's very founding in 1718. The historian Lawrence Powell in *The Accidental City* (2012) notes that during its very first spring of existence, the spring of 1719, the city was inundated by the regular flooding of the Mississippi River. Summing up the city's troubled relationship with its own future even at that time, Powell writes, "It was a tacit admission that the only sure thing between the initial clearing of New Orleans in 1718 and the final order designating it as the new capital more than three years later was that it had no apparent future" (51). This "tacit admission" persists even today, after three centuries, and yet those concerns now operate within a different temporal frame. In the early eighteenth century, the pressing questions were about finding ways to get through the seasonal wave of flooding at hand. Environmental risk, therefore, operated according to a very abbreviated conception of time. Chronophobia was monthly, annual, or at most stretching forward only a few years into the future. In the early twenty-first century, however, after the hurricanes of 2005, New Orleanians think very differently about time and place. Scientists and politicians now refer to the "hundred-year storm" that will come to impact the region with the equal intensity of a Katrina or Rita. The risk involved in the hundred-year storm is stretched out over the course of a century, and that risk is mathematically specified. The phrase uses the time frame of a century to understand risk, but it is also potentially misleading, referring as it does to a storm that will come not in one hundred years but to a storm that has a one percent chance of occurring every year. In this way, the phrase may be read as diluting, deintensifying, or elongating the risk—and with it the dread—over the course of a century, but the phrase also refers to every present moment. It is thus fixed firmly within the time-ticking structure of apocalyptic thought. The hundred-year storm will come because it is already here.

Apocalypse comes from the ancient Greek word *apokaluptein,* a combination of *apo-* or "un-" and *kaluptein* or "cover." The word's etymology helps to explain the uneasiness that arises in moments of its figuration. As an uncovering, it is as if the apocalypse lurks below what we perceive as reality and patiently waits for its time to surface. The disaster of the apocalypse is thus not temporally fixed in the future. Like the hundred-year storm, it spreads itself unseen throughout the past and the present and the future. It is here already; it has been here already, but it has not yet been known. If one is tempted to write off the apocalypse as some unfortunate and hysterical offshoot of religious thinking, some paranoid expression of doom and gloom, one should be quick to note that it extends widely into more subdued and secular manifestations. Many people and groups, including environmentalists, have been drawn to apocalyptic thinking for many reasons. Lawrence Buell, in fact, in *The Environmental Imagination* (1995), calls apocalyptic thinking "the single most powerful master metaphor that the contemporary environmental imagination has at its disposal" (285). As environmental texts, Martin's novel and Ford's poem are not religiously derived or supernatural; instead, they are strictly naturalistic in their conceptualization. No literal god or devil will be coming in the environmental disaster. Ford mentions "the dead," but those entities have no real force in the world; they cannot dictate which grounds are walkable and which are not. It is only their memory housed within the minds of the living that has the power to haunt and compel the ethical question about where to walk with a clear conscience There is no fire and brimstone in their visions of the future, but there is water, and lots of it.

One of the central questions that scholars and theorists of apocalypse are forced to ask is why people would want to live under such conditions. Why would people want to live under threat from a cataclysmic future whose seeds are already firmly planted in the present? Why does apocalyptic thinking exhibit such "extraordinary resilience," as Frank Kermode puts it in *The Sense of an Ending* (1966), and thus can be "disconfirmed without being discredited" over and over again (8)? Why do people "hunger for ends and for crises" (55)? In a new epilogue written for the 2000 republication of his classic work, Kermode looks back on the multiple apocalyptic threats that had arisen since the book's original publication in 1966. "The reason why any date, almost any excuse," he states, "is good enough to trigger some apocalyptic anxiety is that apocalypse . . . represents a mood finally inseparable from the condition of life, the contemplation of its necessary ending, the ineradicable desire to make some sense of it" (186–87). The individual person, for Kermode, needs "fictions of beginnings and fictions of ends, fictions which unite beginning and end and endow the interval between them with meaning" (190). Apocalyptic thinking is a collective expression of the individual desire for narrative unity and meaning. That psychosocial desire, however, like all desires, is not straightforward. It both satisfies and terrifies.

In *Poetic Closure* (1968), Barbara Herrnstein Smith offers an important caveat to Kermode's theory. We do not long for endings in general, Smith claims. Instead, we long for the ones that are more satisfying and less terrifying, and, in order to achieve those, we aspire to endings "that are designed" (1). Apocalypse, in this way, does not signal simply a violently induced ending or some vague cessation of the world as we know it, but a conclusion, a "closure" in Smith's terminology, to the individual and collective story. Smith writes:

> We tend to speak of conclusions when a sequence of events has a relatively high degree of structure, when, in other words, we can perceive these events as related to one another by some principle of organization or design that implies the existence of a definite termination point. Under these circumstances, the occurrence of the terminal event is a confirmation of expectations that have been established by the structure of the sequence, and is usually distinctly gratifying. (2)

The apocalyptic hunger, to expand on Kermode and Smith, is a symptom of the more general desire to achieve this gratification, to see the conditions of the past and present as ushering in a knowable and expected future.

Moira Crone's *The Not Yet* (2012), an unusual novel in the literary history of New Orleans that takes up some of these theoretical concerns, is set in the future, mostly in the year 2121, and may be classified as a "critical dystopia." This fictional genre, a particular expression of apocalyptic thinking, "is a negative cousin of the Utopia proper," as Fredric Jameson explains in *Archaeologies of the Future* (2005), "for it is in the light of some positive conception of human social possibilities that its effects are generated and from Utopian ideals its enabling stance derives" (198). In Crone's critical dystopia, not only is the physical world falling apart as the soil subsides and the Gulf of Mexico rises, but the social world is collapsing too in the face of severe economic disparity and social stratification. This environmental and social decline comes in the aftermath of a stunning scientific breakthrough that allows a specific group of people, the Heirs, to live well past their natural life span for hundreds of years, if not forever. In this way, the disaster of the twenty-first century is generated when some good objective goes bad, when the desire to outwit death leads to a vigorous and destructive self-preservation at the expense of others. As a critical dystopia, in other words, Crone takes the utopic impulse to figure out a better world in which to live and turns it on its head. The drive to improve the human lifeworld in fact engineers just the opposite.

The novel tells the story of twenty-year-old Malcolm as he makes his way to be "treated"—that is, surgically and psychologically transformed into an Heir—in the year 2121. In Crone's world of strict social classification, he is a "Nyet," shorthand for "not yet treated." Malcolm's benefactor is Lazarus, who has lived for two centuries and is holder of his Heir trust fund. His doctor is Lydia Greenmore, who is in charge of the treatment, part of which is pedagogical. Under sedation, Malcolm is educated on history and science from the time of the initial research into the prolongation of life in the 1960s, "the Reveal" in 2005, and the next century of social reclassification, total warfare, and finally the relative peace brought about by the new world order. Behind the scenes is the ever-present WELLFI, the conglomerate in control of medicine, media, and politics.

The backdrop for Malcolm's adventure is the dissolving physical environment surrounding the city of New Orleans. The geographical location is the same as today's, but many things have changed in the future, and these changes are reflected in new topographical names. The Mississippi River is now the Old River after the major watershed jumped course to follow the Atchafalaya in a quicker route to the Gulf. Lake Pontchartrain is now the Sea of Pontchartrain. The city of New Orleans is now called the New Orleans Islands and is further subdivided into Audubon Island, the heavily guarded Museum City (presumably the former Garden District), and the Sunken Quarter. Most of the Heirs have left the city for higher ground on the north shore of the Sea of Pontchartrain, lands protected by the United Authority and renamed Re-New Orleans. "It was crisp and pastel and full of turrets and verandas and pergolas—exquisite, clean, shining, and fashionable," Crone writes (45). Within this protected sphere, "Heirs waved their arms in greeting to each other, calling out, all smiles. They carried packages from the brosia merchants, the genenfabric stores" (45). This place, as Crone describes it, is a kind of suburban hell with a beautiful facade, where kin and kind are shielded from the others, and where retail therapy works.

The scene south of the Sea of Pontchartrain in New Orleans where the non-Heirs live is quite different. Their houses stand half submerged in water where once dry land had been. After "fending off the sea" for years, the non-Heirs could persevere no longer and "had succumbed" to rising tides and sinking earth; and "Yet the occupants had not fled" (29). Abandoned in a kind of "limbo," the non-Heir New Orleanians live a life of precariousness where "no one persecuted them exactly, but no one helped them either" (29). Their non-Heir status causes this precarious limbo, but their ambiguous relationship with the larger nation, the United Authority, is a related part of the problem. They had been "let go" by the nation but at the same time were denied true autonomy (29). "This was a place on the edges," Crone characterizes New Orleans in the mind of the nation, "where what was past could be discarded, forgotten, ignored, occasionally visited for the thrill of the exotic. A place with the fortune, or curse, of not mattering" (203).

Outside the city, and except for the Heir neighborhoods on the north shore of the Sea of Pontchartrain and other prosperous enclosures across North America, the continent is falling apart. "The raw landscape was horrible," Crone writes, full of the "empty ruins, the garbage towns, that weren't needed anymore" (95). The Heirs, however, are shielded from witnessing this ruined world. They move through the continent underground in high-speed tunnels with beautiful and convincing landscapes simulated on the walls. In Crone's future, the New Orleanian zone is not the only one that is abandoned by the nation. Other locales susceptible to natural disaster—the entire Pacific coast of the former United States, for example, as it crumbles westward into the ocean—are subject to political, economic, and psychosocial disaffiliation. The Heirs' wealth and privileged position in a stratified society allow them to ruin and abandon, damage and disaffiliate, but their financial and social status also allows them to live in ignorance of their own actions. Because they can afford the price of the ticket to move from one paradise to the next in a beautifully orchestrated underground, their eyes are not obliged to see that which they destroy.

Like the environments in which they live, the Heirs' bodies have been profoundly transformed. After their medical procedures, the Heirs have eyes that do not blink, lungs that hardly breathe, bodies that retain only uncanny traces of their former selves. Crone describes a bodily movement of Lazarus in this way: "He tried to snap his fingers, but he couldn't, his overskin was too slick for that" (16). Like insects, they "scurry" (45). Their digestive tracts are so fragile that they must eat "brosia," an abbreviation presumably for "ambrosia," the mythological food of the gods. They also lose their original voice after treatment. Crone describes Lazarus's voice: "that voice they all had—full of sizzle, like a rattle" (15). She describes the Heirs as talking with "awful reptile voices" (26).

Unlike other monstrous species that have populated the literary history of New Orleans in the past, the Heirs' bodies of the future register a kind of decadence rather than straightforward horror. In their "elegant emaciation," they do not carry with them the marks of the truly horrible (189). They are, after all, simply aged human bodies slowly aging more. Beneath their elaborately decorated prosthetics, they are becoming barer and barer, being preserved in their decay. Their bodies, as opposed to the vampiric bodies in the gothic world of Anne Rice, are not undead, supernatural, or otherwise ghostly. They do, however, share some traits with those creatures. Like those abandoned to walk the earth indefinitely, Crone's Heirs produce uneasiness in themselves, in the other characters, and arguably in Crone herself and in her readers, because for them the end will never come. Stranded within their "timeless time," they cannot achieve satisfaction; they cannot look forward to an easing of tension that comes only with a general foreknowledge of the end (263). Without this sense of an end, as Kermode warns us, their lives operating as they do perpetually *in medias res* will be without meaning. With the final moment of life suspended indefinitely, as Smith warns us, their lives will not achieve closure.

Such an ontological status of the Heirs reveals the vulnerability at the heart of their being. They may not be living and aging at the normal human pace, but because they cannot stop the passage of time, they are aging nonetheless. They may be injured and killed; they may fall into depression, dementia, substance abuse, and addiction, as well as other forms of instability and madness. They are also at the mercy of the doctors and scientists who sustain them and who all the while do not know for sure where their experiment will end up. While most of the Heirs are comforted by their unflinching faith in the ability of science and medical technology to solve the known problems of today and the unknown ones of tomorrow, other Heirs are not so lucky. Malcolm's benefactor Lazarus, in fact, is unable to cope with his existential dilemma. He is particularly troubled by the monotony of his temporal suspension, and he commits suicide. In his suicide note, the character tries to explain his decision to end his own life, saying, "Now, I think it is the greatest gift of all to have a sense of time" (240).

Where does Crone's world come from? How is she able to envision New Orleans in the twenty-second century and develop the plot of *The Not Yet*? "All plots have something in common with prophecy," Kermode reminds us, "for they must appear to educe from the prime matter of the situation the forms of a future" (83). To make sense of Crone's prophetic plot, then, her readers must make sense of the present in which she prophesies. For Crone, it is the human fear of aging and dying that generates this new world of the twenty-second century. The desire to escape death creates the total state of the world; everything follows from there. Death is so feared—it is, in fact, so despised— that the Heirs do not even utter its name. Instead, they speak sentences like this one that oscillates between euphemistic and childish: "The unlucky do the so-long goodbye" (16). The result is a world of haves and have-nots, those with access to the medical science and technology that will allow them to approach immortality and those without such access. The result is a strict hierarchy of "strats": the Heirs, the Nyets ("not yet treated"), and the Nats (shorthand for "low naturals," or those individuals barred from surgical intervention and thus forced to live a life without artificial prolongation). The strats on the middle and lower rungs of society, furthermore, must demonstrate complete subordination to those on the top. For Crone, it is not some fundamental cruelty in the human species, not some destructive base that makes her characters want to control and oppress, conquer and even—in its most extreme form— annihilate those unlike themselves. Instead, it is a self-preservative drive, an antideath drive, gone berserk. That drive is coupled with a blinding irresponsibility, an utter disregard for the devastation that is multiplying in the worlds outside the Heirs' protective shield.

In the literary history of New Orleans, Crone's novel is highly unusual not only for its profound defamiliarization of the ordinary fixtures of the cityscape but also for the genre in which it is written. For New Orleans, a city in a seemingly endless love-hate relationship with its past, many of the city's most accomplished novelists have turned to historical fiction as a mode of literary invention, setting their narratives in the past in order to answer questions about the present. As we move slowly and unsurely into the twenty-first century, however, New Orleans seems to be even more uneasy about its future than with its past, even if that past continues to haunt the minds and bodies of its inhabitants.

What is it about the future that terrifies in the city of New Orleans? Environmental risks seem to accumulate rather than dissipate through time, and every year the Gulf of Mexico grows in circumference, getting closer and closer to the city. The question is only a matter of timing, when the disaster event, held beforehand in latent form, will surface and make itself known. The Mississippi River, once an agent of land-building as its waters overflowed its banks seasonally and carried the rich alluvium that settled in the marshlands, is now held in check by a vast levee system. The ancient process in southern Louisiana by which continent and Gulf struggle against each other, one trying always to overtake the other, has largely come to an end. Even if the river were let loose to continue the story, the river is not the same river that it was a century ago. The Mississippi River still drains half a continent, as it has done in the past, but now it brings with it all the refuse of modern agriculture and industry from as far away as Montana and Pennsylvania. Through the river's mouth just below New Orleans now flows the continent's life-agents, its fertilizers, and the paradoxical damage they bring, as well as its more straightforward death-agents, its pesticides, insecticides, and all manner of other pollutants.

To complicate matters even further, the petroleum industry's reach along the coastline has radically altered the land, the wetlands, and the open water surrounding the city. In *American Energy, Imperiled Coast* (2014), Jason P. Theriot measures that reach, the great expanse of the petroleum industry in southern Louisiana. "Approximately 191 major pipeline systems," Theriot writes, "originate from the offshore waters and enter Louisiana's vast coastal zone, an area roughly 220 miles across and reaching as much as seventy-five miles inland from the Gulf, most of it marshlands" (4). The sheer geographical scale of the pipelines makes monitoring difficult if not impossible, especially for companies whose bottom line may be negatively impacted by any environmental problem and investigation. One pipeline, owned and operated by Taylor Energy Company, has been leaking continuously since Hurricane Ivan in 2004, and yet that leak has gone underestimated and undermonitored, influenced by the financial incentive simply to ignore it. Many other pipelines promise to do the same as they age, as the ground beneath them shifts, as more wetlands go under and future hurricanes shake their foundations, and as they are left unattended by companies who have long ago cashed in or folded, sold out or simply closed shop. Such human assaults on the earth, on other species, and all the while on each other have profound consequences for the imagination.

For Valerie Martin, Katie Ford, and Moira Crone, the structure of the present seems to be so large, so entrenched and unchanging, that the days to come can only lead to one thing. For Crone especially, in telling the history of the future, political rebellion against strict systems of social classification and stratification, as well as environmental fallout, lead only to violence and squashed hope. For her, this certain future is already formed, lying in wait as "the not yet." One cannot help but wonder, however, to what extent Crone's apocalyptic vision will become truly actualized in the present. *The Not Yet* takes place long after Crone's contemporary readers will probably be dead, in the year 2121. A person born in 2012, the year the novel was published, would have to live to be 109 years old, in fact, to see the chronotope Crone describes. The year 2121 in New Orleans is a time and place that is imaginable without being ultimately verifiable. One hundred years into the future is more thinkable than two, and as Crone's contemporaries live through the twenty-first century, they will be approaching the temporal marker, but they will probably never get to it exactly. It sits just out of reach temporally, just outside the realm of knowability.

Predicting the future has always been a risky business. In hurricane forecasting, for example, as in life, the so-called "cone of error" or "cone of uncertainty" gets wider and wider as the predictive mark gets further and further into the future. In this way, the future's simple promise—for tomorrow, for next year, for one hundred years from now—may not be so simple after all. But despite this lack of simplicity, this cognitive haziness, the current state of the region and the projections for the future are not encouraging, even as there are major efforts presently in the works to mitigate that future. These unprecedented efforts include Louisiana's 50-year, $50 billion coastal master plan and a controversial $48 million grant from the federal government to move a tribal band of Biloxi-Chitimacha-Choctaws from their eroding island to stable land further north. In the face of these best laid plans, however, the haunting prospect still seems to be *anagnorisis sans peripeteia*—recognition without change—as the philias and phobias of topos and chronos keep marching along to that number.

WORKS CITED

Buell, Lawrence. *The Environmental Imagination: Thoreau, Nature Writing, and the Formation of American Culture.* Harvard UP, 1995.

Crone, Moira. *The Not Yet.* U of New Orleans P, 2012.

Ford, Katie. *Colosseum.* Graywolf, 2008.

Jameson, Fredric. *Archaeologies of the Future: The Desire Called Utopia and Other Science Fictions.* Verso, 2005.

Kermode, Frank. *The Sense of an Ending: Studies in the Theory of Fiction.* 1966. Oxford UP, 2000.

Martin, Valerie. *A Recent Martyr.* Vintage, 1987.

Smith, Barbara Herrnstein. *Poetic Closure: A Study of How Poems End.* U of Chicago P, 1968.

Theriot, Jason P. *American Energy, Imperiled Coast: Oil and Gas Development in Louisiana's Wetlands.* Louisiana SUP, 2014.

Afterwor(l)d

The Future in the Present

JAY WATSON

If this luminous, readable, and often entertaining collection is any indication, the future of southern studies is bright, and environmental studies will be a driving force in realizing that promise. I almost said that the future looks *secure*, but I don't really mean that. Rather, it looks *in*secure in exactly the right ways: dynamic, contested, in ferment. I think of the new ideas and models introduced in these pages, conceptual tools that will shape and complicate my own ongoing work: Delia Byrnes's framework of energy regionalism, Daniel Spoth's slightly queasy category of visceral environmentalism, Joshua Myers's concept of eco-miscegenation, John Moran's models of climatological racism and homonationalism. There's also the resourceful, incisive use to which the contributors put a range of ideas and methodological approaches from inside and outside environmental studies proper, expanding the intellectual purview of ecocriticism: Lisa Hinrichsen's work with affect theory (from Sara Ahmed's "stickiness" to Lauren Berlant's "cruel optimism"); Ila Tyagi's complementary emphasis on perception and visual studies; Joseph Thompson's use of the Deleuzian rhizome and his attentiveness to the geographies and ecologies of the military-industrial complex; Sam Horrocks's focus on the georgic genre and agrarian energy flows; Christopher Lloyd's (and Myers's) gleanings from memory studies; Evangelia Kindinger's from diaspora studies; Jimmy Dean Smith's turn to geology for the concept of the techno-fossil; Sarah McFarland's conjunction of environmental and narrative ethics; Moran's adroit employment of the postcolonial studies critique of tropicalization; Robert Azzarello's work with critical dystopia and the social geographers' categories of topophilia and topophobia. Numerous essayists take up the issue of apocalypse—is there an interdisciplinary field of southern "end studies" in the making here?!—and several address the necessity and the challenge of situating region within and among the shifting scales of ecocritical inquiry. And don't even bother to bring up the Anthropocene! It's everywhere in these pages—much as it's everywhere on (and increasingly in) Eaarth. Finally, there's the striking interdisciplinary, intermedial diversity of the cultural material under investigation here: litera-ture and film, of course, but also public policy rhetoric, documentary photog-raphy and cinema, foodways (and food writing), music, television, internet sites, stand-up comedy. I'd extend Spoth's description of the "fundamental messiness" of southern environmental history to the volume itself: if Timothy Morton invites us to reenvision "the" environment as a mesh (*The Ecological Thought* 8), the collection invites contemplation as a mess. But what a fertile mess it is: a seething intellectual compost that generates all sorts of exciting possibilities for future study.[1]

So it's as an ally and not as a naysayer that I'd urge us to think as well about the directions for future work indicated by what *isn't* in these pages. No col-lection on such a rich, fraught subject can do everything with it, so we can ap-proach some of the more underdeveloped aspects of *Ecocriticism and the Future of Southern Studies* as invitations to take up the good work here and extend it, diversify it, complicate it. It's in that spirit that I'd note that, for all its method-ological and medial range, the collection, like so much environmental human-ities scholarship in the United States, is awfully Euro-American in its focus. Black southerners, for instance, appear more often as characters in white-authored representations—Caroline Hentz's slaves, John Muir's freedmen, Faulkner's sharecroppers, the soul food maestros of John Egerton and Mar-cie Cohen Ferris's food writing, the black New Orleanians of *Treme,* the Af-rican American residents of the Isle de Charles Doucet in Lucy Alibar and Behn Zeitlin's *Beasts of the Southern Wild*—than as authors themselves: only Charles Chesnutt, Bernice McFadden, and Gil Scott-Heron figure prominently as Afro-southern cultural producers. Much the same could be said for the re-gion's Asian American or Latinx storytellers, filmmakers, poets, and other art-ists. Nor, surprisingly, are writers—or really even characters—of the Native South allowed an environmental or ecosophical voice here: calling Linda Ho-gan, LeAnne Howe, Louis Owens, Joy Harjo . . . ! On some level, the characters of *Beasts* surrogate or perhaps explicitly allegorize the plight of the Biloxi-Chitimacha-Choctaw Indians of Louisiana's Isle de Jean Charles, the first fed-erally designated climate change refugees in the United States, but you have to look pretty hard for anything like an Indigenous aspect to Wink and Hush-puppy's Doucet or their lowland neighbors. *Treme* achieves something similarly preliminary and equivocal with its subplot about the Mardi Gras Indians of New Orleans. These make for awkward fellow travelers with Native South writ-ers and intellectuals, and as such poor substitutes for them—an "Indianist" presence rather than a more robustly Indigenous one. Without succumbing to the environmental fantasy-caricature of "ecological Indians," we can do better than this unintentional vanishing-work. For southern ecocriticism to have the right kind of future, it will need to allow more artists—and scholars—of color a seat at the disciplinary welcome table. The intellectual resources and traditions of resilience they stand to contribute to the conversation are more necessary now than ever, as the Anthropocene and the Sixth Extinction usher in more and more widespread, and interspecies, versions of Removal. On this increasingly precarious planet, after all, we're all indigenous.

And while we're being neighborly, what about our hemispheric and Global South neighbors and kin? The transnational tools and archives developed by Jon Smith and Deborah Cohn, George Handley, Valerie Loichot, Kathryn McKee and Annette Trefzer, Elizabeth Russ, Martyn Bone, and other leading lights of the "new" southern studies are not as evident in these pages as one might expect or wish. The lines of flight and force that connect the US South with the Caribbean basin are implicit in the way Louisiana and New Orleans figure so prominently in this collection, from Byrnes's essay in chapter two to Azzarello's at the volume's conclusion. The extreme weather events, diasporic flows, and geographies of uneven development and extractive industry that dominate this collection's Louisiana material could easily be drawn from the environmental histories of the Antilles or other sites along the Caribbean rim. The South's ecological ties to other hemispheric regions south of South are already apparent in Muir's *Thousand-Mile Walk to the Gulf*, where the author weaves observations of floral life common to Florida and Cuba into a latent model of transnational bioregionalism that both grounds and enriches the biocentric cosmology discussed by Scott Obernesser in chapter four; a generation earlier, Audubon had built his own version of Greater Caribbean bioregionalism around similar observations about bird species common to the Gulf South and the islands below. More recently, Leslie Silko's *Almanac of the Dead* and Cormac McCarthy's border novels, especially *The Crossing*, reach similar conclusions about the biomes of the US-Mexican Southwest, where all manner of life forms, including *Homo sapiens* (and not so *sapiens*), follow bioregional itineraries that prove to be no respecters of international borders—surely an insight relevant to the current US border "crisis." And these are just Anglophone examples! Southern environmental studies will only grow stronger, timelier, and worldlier as it learns to embrace a more expansive set of transnational, transoceanic, global, and planetary coordinates for the regional *oikos*.

Put another way: southern ecocriticism could use a dose of Ariel's ecology—and Caliban's.[2]

There are yet other precincts worthy of more thorough ecocritical exploration than they can receive here. In the domain of time, for instance, the volume's principal historical foci are the 1850s and 1860s (Hentz, Muir), the 1930s through the 1970s (Faulkner, Harriet Arnow, David Lilienthal, James Dickey, McCarthy, Scott-Heron, *Thunder Bay* and *Hellfighters,* etc.), and the two decades of the twenty-first century (Bernice McFadden, Ann Pancake, Moira Crone, *Petrochemical America, Beasts, Treme,* Tom Franklin and Beth Ann Fennelly, and so on). That timeline leaves significant gaps, or rather, opportunities for continuing work: the colonial and early national eras (Cabeza de Vaca, Richard Ligon, William Bartram; Jefferson, Audubon, Equiano; Aphra Behn, Eliza Pinckney, Mary Prince), for example, or the "long" era of New South modernization from the 1870s to the 1920s, a period here represented only by Chesnutt's conjure tales, leaving Lafcadio Hearn and Kate Chopin, Booker T. Washington and Mary Murfree, Jean Toomer and Ellen Glasgow, along with dozens of other environmentally attuned voices, to await a fuller place in future conversations. What is more, with the exception of the New Orleans material, southern cities don't come in for much theoretical or analytical attention in these essays. Rural, small-town, and in general under- or depopulated geographies still prevail, a bias with deep roots in US environmental studies. It's understandable that, as circum-Caribbean entrepôt and Global North poster child for the Anthropocene, the Crescent City would command considerable airtime in this volume. But what might southern ecocriticism have to say to, and about, the literatures of Atlanta, Houston, Miami, Memphis, Birmingham, Johnson City, even, perhaps, Washington, DC? (Not to mention Nassau, Havana, San Juan, or El Paso-Juarez.) If not yet here then elsewhere, the region's urban, suburban, and semiurban ecologies seem destined to receive their due. Indeed, contemporary issues like environmental justice and racism have the potential to uncover connections between urban and rural zones in the region and build relationships between their inhabitants. Think of Robert Bullard's groundbreaking *Dumping in Dixie,* for instance, whose featured case studies include Houston, Texas, Alsen, Louisiana, and Sumter County, Alabama. To point out the many ways in which the work in this collection needs to be supplemented is to thrill with anticipation for the field.

In the space I have remaining, I want to exercise the afterwordist's prerogative to proceed a bit unsystematically, even impressionistically, by lingering on a couple of issues this book has gotten me thinking harder about. One concerns the role of energy in southern presents, futures, and representations of the region. The other, not altogether unrelated, takes up the specter of the Anthropocene and its challenges to ecological citizenship, and ponders a few historical and environmental legacies that might equip southerners to play a leadership role in thinking and meeting those challenges.

GRIEVING OIL

For me, the essays in section one represent a particularly rich and timely intervention in the long history of representing the US South as an internal other in the national imagination: colonized, subordinate, primitive, developmentally arrested, or even regressive. Fifteen years ago Smith and Cohn promoted the region from marginal to "liminal" due to its position as economic and cultural intermediary between the United States and other New World Souths (13). But a focus on energy suggests an additional upgrade for the region, from liminal to *central*. Christopher Jones has detailed the interlocking historical, technological, and political reasons why Pennsylvania got a significant head start on the rest of the United States in developing energy resources like coal, oil, and electricity, as well as the related enterprises that the state's energy leadership made possible (*Routes of Power*). As the twentieth century unfolded, however, that mantle clearly shifted southward toward Kentucky and West Virginia coal, Gulf Coast oil and petrochemicals, and TVA electricity. Byrnes's concept of energy regionalism, thought-provoking as it is, may still understate the degree to which the South now serves as core and motor of US energy *nationalism*. Even the crude tapped from the oil shale deposits of North Dakota, site of the latest US extraction boom, must still flow south to Texas and Louisiana for refining and distribution. As the essays by Byrnes, Hinrichsen, and Tyagi make clear, southern energy nationalism has been shadowed by its own versions of the so-called resource curse: pollution, state and corporate indifference to local populations, and capital flight from depleted extraction zones (an externalization of *benefits*—jobs, profits, venture capital—to complement the energy industry's routine externalizations of costs and risks). Still, the region's role as national and indeed global energy center invites us to reconsider, or at least reframe, ideas about southern exceptionalism that have ruled the nation's print, popular, and intellectual cultures for generations.

For all their heuristic potential, however, new ecocritical concepts and models like energy regionalism and environmental affect will need to be handled with care, lest they wind up inadvertently reinforcing old, bad habits of thinking about the South *and* the environment. As a case in point I want to take up the work of a scholar and environmentalist I admire a great deal, Stephanie Lemenager, whose brilliant, passionate study of "petroleum culture in the American century" has powerfully stimulated my own thinking, teaching, and writing in environmental studies. Lemenager's accounts of the close geological, ecological, and conceptual ties between oil and water, and of labor as a crucial environmental epistemology, a means of ecological knowing underexplored by scholars, are proving especially generative not just for the energy humanities but for the environmental humanities more broadly. When we reflect on the role of geography in the organization of *Living Oil,* however, something more problematic comes to light. The book's first chapter locates the origins of American petroenvironmentalism in southern California, in the community and media response to the Santa Barbara Channel oil spill of 1969. Here the West serves as epicenter for representational strategies and forms of activism that have gone on to become fixtures of the US environmental movement in the half-century since the spill: a hotbed of forward-thinking, politically minded environmental stewardship, engagement, and protest. Chapter two anatomizes a petroleum-fueled "aesthetic" of freedom, individuality, mobility, speed, power, and ebullient affect that underwrote and literally energized American identity and US nationalism at midcentury, then maps the blandishments and ironies of this aesthetic along an East-West axis traced by the epic automobile journeys of *On the Road* and *Lolita.* Here Lemenager shows us the value of affect as a tool of environmental analysis and critique, a window onto lifeworlds and forms of awareness shaped by specific environmental regimes, a theme also sounded in these pages by Hinrichsen, Byrnes, Spoth, Kindinger, and Jonathan Villalobos.

But when Lemenager turns to a very different form of environmental affect in her next chapter, a new regional geography takes center stage in the discussion. In chapter three, Lemenager introduces the important concept of "petromelancholia," by which she means *not* an inconsolable grief for the environments and lifeways lost to the onslaught of petromodernity, so much as a very contemporary, Anthropocene grief for the traumatic loss of the pleasures and conveniences of petromodernity itself: the sense of progressive temporality, the utopian accents and aspirations, the promise of personal empowerment that cheap, abundant oil made possible (102–5). Petromelancholics, in other words, are mired in mourning for the petroleum aesthetic itself, for a modernity taken from them before they could fully, properly enjoy it, not for the massive collateral damage it both imposed and mystified. And in *Living Oil*, ground zero for petromelancholia is the US South. This debilitating emotion—along with the critical potential it carries—is not allowed to creep into the suburban landscapes and road trips of chapter two, or it goes unrecognized there, walled off conceptually and geographically from the petroleum aesthetic and its giddy bad faith. One is left to wonder, for instance, how a closer look at Flannery O'Connor's "A Good Man is Hard to Find," with its aborted south-bound road trip to Florida; at the perverse love affairs with the automobile recounted in "The Life You Save May Be Your Own" and *Wise Blood* ("Nobody with a good car needs to be justified!"); or at other examples of mid-century southern writing (even Faulkner's *The Reivers!*) might have complicated chapter two's picture of the petroleum aesthetic, and skewed its regional orientation, in all sorts of productive ways. Instead, the darker side of petromodernity is reserved for coastal southerners reeling from Katrina and Rita, from the Deepwater Horizon blowout, from the slower, chronic violences of pollution and wetland loss, and from the economic and ecological question marks associated with Tough Oil. The effect is mitigated only slightly by chapter four, on the museal curation of petrohistories and -cultures, where a pair of east Texas museums joins Alberta's Oil Sands Discovery Centre and the George C. Page Museum at the La Brea tar pits in Los Angeles in Lemenager's witty survey of the cultural politics of a continental petroleum archive. Lemenager, then, no doubt unwittingly, has built *Living Oil* in a way that maps energy abjection onto the nation's region, implicitly fashioning the South as a sacrifice zone for bad environmental (and national) affect. This is a move, albeit one made with the best of intentions, that Leigh Anne Duck and Jennifer Rae Greeson have exposed and made familiar to southern studies scholars: it's "our South" all over again, as the region gathers and quarantines the grief and loss generated by an entire country's addiction to fossil fuels, and southerners lag, as ever, behind the curve of a national environmental movement that would have them condemn the modernity whose loss they mourn. Even in the hands of an eminent critic like Lemenager, then, energy regionalism can be a double-edged sword. I offer this critique as a cautionary tale for all of us who turn south in our environmental thinking and ecocritique; it's only too easy to fall into these moves, to offer up new myths of southern exceptionalism on an environmental rather than historical or political front, driving new intellectual wedges between region and nation, region and planet, just when the imperatives of the Anthropocene call for more integrated, systems-level perspectives. And I say all this with my eye firmly on the mirror, since in the section that follows I plan to flirt with a "weak" form of such exceptionalism myself.[3]

THE MOREL AT THE END OF THE WORLD

Jimmy Dean Smith takes up Cormac McCarthy's harrowing novel of eco-apocalypse, *The Road,* in these pages to develop a critique of Appalachian highways like US 25E, the paved descendant of Daniel Boone's Wilderness Road, as signs and vectors of the human will to dominate and rationalize nature, and thus as incubators and accelerators of anthropogenic change from local to planetary scales. I have something less grandiose in mind for this section, and to see it we will need to leave the blacktop for a moment and follow the novel's protagonists into the woods—or rather, into the fire-scarred remains of "a rich southern wood that once held mayapple and pipsissewa. Ginseng. The raw dead limbs of the rhododendron twisted and knotted and black" (39–40). There "in the mulch and ash," the man finds "a small colony" of morels, "shrunken and dried and wrinkled" (40). "They're a kind of mushroom," he explains to his son.

> Can you eat them?
> Yes. Take a bite.
> Are they good?
> Take a bite.
> The boy smelled the mushroom and bit into it and stood chewing. He looked at his father.
> These are pretty good, he said.

That evening father and son dine on the morels, sautéed in "the fat pork from a can of beans" (41), and the boy pronounces their campsite "a good place." In a near-lifeless world where the pair hovers constantly on the brink of starvation, this is the ultimate benediction. It's also an ethical touchstone: throughout the novel the normative label "good" applies above all to food, the circumstances of its consumption, and the possibility of its sharing. We're a long way from novel's end here, but these morels will be the only example of "fresh" food—neither canned, cured, nor otherwise preserved by artificial means—that the man and boy manage to glean from the dying biosphere. A good place, indeed.

For the ecocritic, the morels are also "pretty good" to think with, and the environmental anthropologist Anna Lowenhaupt Tsing can help us see why. In her stunningly *sui generis* ethnography, *The Mushroom at the End of the World*, Tsing introduces us to the matsutake mushroom, a fungal cousin to McCarthy's Appalachian morels and a window onto "the possibility of life" in landscapes ruined by capitalist forms of alienation, extraction, and accumulation that hijack human and nonhuman life processes. In the context of what she calls "salvage capitalism" (62–63) and its opportunistic global supply chains, matsutake ecology proves especially significant for two reasons, both pertinent to the environmental thought-experiment McCarthy conducts in *The Road*.

First, like many morel species, matsutake thrive in disturbed environments, including or perhaps especially human-disturbed landscapes. Noting that "disturbance emerged as a key concept in ecology" at the same midcentury, Cold War moment when "scholars in the humanities and social sciences were beginning to worry about instability and change" (160), Tsing suggests that disturbance fields such as the matsutake woods "are ideal spaces for humanist and naturalist noticing." Humanists, she points out, aren't really "used to thinking with disturbance" and tend to associate the concept with "damage." But "disturbance can renew ecologies as well as destroy them. . . . Disturbance opens the terrain for transformative encounters" and "new landscape assemblages." As such, it marks a beginning[4] as much as an end of things, an ongoingness: "always in the middle of things[,] the term does not refer us to a harmonious state before disturbance. Disturbances follow other disturbances. . . . [D]isturbance is ordinary." In the patchy spaces it creates, "each shaped by diverse conjunctures" (161), "patterns emerge, organizing assemblages: unintentional design" (162). Newness enters the world, and the world carries on. The morels represent such newness. They are evidence that even here, even now, at the end of the world, the forest is still thinking.

That forests *think*—that they are fields of intense, incessant semiotic activity within and among species, dense "ecologies of selves" (most of them nonhuman) that foster enchantment, engender futurity, and course through the thoughts and dreams of ecosystem people who depend on them for sustenance but must also contend with them for survival—is the provocative claim of Tsing's fellow "multispecies ethnographer" Eduardo Kohn, and he doesn't mean it figuratively.[5] Kohn's argument, at the juncture of Peircean semiotics, cultural anthropology, and ecosystem ecology, is far too intricate to reproduce here, but because life for him is fundamentally a biosemiotic phenomenon, all living things are in effect "living thoughts" (99–100), thinking beings, and as such, they possess selfhood (73–75). In deeming the forest "enchanted" (72), and thereby contextualizing the animistic belief systems of many peoples who interact with it closely and routinely as a mode of cosmological realism, Kohn means to emphasize that "the world beyond the human is not a meaningless one made meaningful by humans." This world actively makes its own meanings: "means-ends relations, strivings, purposes, telos, intentions, functions and significance." This is what the morels are doing. This is what, and how, they mean, and how they attribute meaning to the forest around them and confer meaning on it: the appearance of the fruiting bodies above the soil is the fungus's way of projecting itself into a possible future on the basis of a representation of the world it has formed from the physical and chemical information available to it. This is emergent thought, and one source of futurity in a world otherwise hard-pressed to deliver such resources for thinking and survival. The symbolic behavior for which humans once loved to congratulate themselves may not deliver a comparable yield. Indeed, the man in *The Road* reaches just this conclusion as he stands in "the charred ruins of a library"—a burned-over forest of symbols—and "thumb[s] through the heavy bloated pages" of books long exposed to the elements (187). Worse than useless, these forays in meaning making, he realizes, are "lies" now, inasmuch as their value and function were always "predicated on a world to come" more than actually generative of one. An unflinching verdict, but also one that acquiesces in the deanimation of the world in its ongoingness.

It's characteristic of the man to think like this. Perhaps reflecting his melancholic sensibility—about which more in a minute—the narrative reserves its one true moment of ecological animism, its sole vision of enchantment, for the final paragraph of the book, and even then pitches it in the key of nostalgia:

> Once there were brook trout in the streams in the mountains. You could see them standing in the amber current where the white edges of their fins wimpled softly in the flow. They smelled of moss in your hand. Polished and muscular and tortional. On their backs were vermiculate patterns that were maps of the world in its becoming. (286–87)

The scene "hum[s] with mystery" (287). These are thinking streams in thinking forests amidst thinking mountains. (McCarthy's wording helps us recognize Aldo Leopold's intellectual legacy[6] in Kohn's forest ecology.) The trout are living thoughts. Like Jacob von Uexkull's famous ticks, they have a "world," an environment charged with meaning (Kohn 84–85; Van Dooren 67–68), and they represent that world in mapping it with their bodies and movements. Strivings. Purposes. Intentions. Significance. The narrator—perhaps the posthumous voice of the man?—can admit such enchantment only by assigning it to an elsewhere or elsewhen, an era before the Event (at a temporal distance) or a counterfactual realm of memory or fantasy (at an ontological remove). Meanwhile, in the here and now of the narrative, the man systematically depopulates the world of possibilities, futures, enchantments, other living thoughts, as we see in the following two scenes:

> Will the dam be there for a long time?
> I think so. It's made out of concrete. It will probably be there for hundreds of years. Thousands, even.
> Do you think there could be fish in the lake?
> No. There's nothing in the lake. (20)

> What are you doing? he hissed. What are you doing?
> There's a little boy, Papa. There's a little boy.
> There's no little boy. What are you doing?
> Yes there is. I saw him.
> . . . Come on, the man said. We've got to go.
> I want to see him, Papa.
> There's no one to see. Do you want to die? Is that what you want?
> I dont care, the boy said, sobbing. I dont care. (84–85)

Small wonder, then, if, on hearing the distant bark of a dog, the boy's first concern is that his father may kill it (82). Within every deanim*ist* lurks the specter of a deanim*ator.*

It's in this light that we should return to the encounter with the morels, or more precisely, the non- or semi-encounter with them. In their sheer precarity, and in the much-reduced landscape that surrounds them, they might appear to offer an instructive contrast with those radiant brook trout from a world elsewhere. Yet I wonder whether the similarities might be more instructive in the end. To be sure, the lowly fungus is considerably less charismatic as a species than those opalescent trout. "Shrunken, dried, and wrinkled" (40), its hum is doubtless pitched along a lower register, softer, harder to hear. And the diminished complexity of the wounded forest in which it resides insures that the thoughts it thinks will be quieter as well, simpler, less mazy and intricate in their patterning. Thoughts they remain, however, and as such resources, opportunities for human thinking, being, surviving—dare we say flourishing? It may not be enough, then, simply to eat the morels and soldier on into another futureless day, one more chapter in the story of the end. The point may instead lie in noticing them, *really* noticing them—harvesting them for thinking. It's this harvest the man seems unequipped or just unwilling to perform. Ironically, he's a consummate noticer of things he and his son can eat, burn, wear, and salvage, and of risks they should avoid. But the intellectual and ontological use-value of this particular resource escapes him. The novel challenges the reader to do better, to be more like the boy: what after all does declaring a denuded woodland to be "a good place" signify if not a recognition of enchantment, however modest, however embattled? The boy and the morels are on the same wavelength.

And like the morels, the boy is another source of newness in this world. If not necessarily a new species, he is nonetheless a strange new posthuman life form, born after, and thus entirely within the new dispensation of, the Event that has destroyed the human civilization and all but extinguished the animal and plant life of the planet. His cognitive and affective life have been shaped within environmental conditions almost allegorical in their austerity. Like the morels, he has emerged and is emerging from the ash and duff of a radically disturbed earthscape. As such, he may serve as a living reminder that *Homo sapiens* is another species that, like matsutake and other forest fungi, thrives in disturbed environments—indeed thrives *by* disturbing them.

As it happens, the US South has been a generative space for the development of disturbance-based ecosystem ecology. From the so-called fire-ant wars between the US Department of Agriculture and one of the region's most iconic invasive species emerged research tracing the natural history of the insects to South American alluvial environments subjected to frequent flooding: the legendary resilience of the indestructible pests was forged in their adaptation to hydrological disturbance regimes (see Buhs). The region's barrier islands have been sites of important research in coastal ecology; their beach, dune, and marsh environments have all coevolved with periodic tidal disturbance that can nonetheless be quite irregular in its intensity. The pine plantations of southwest Georgia and northwest Florida were at the center of Herbert Stoddard's pioneering research in fire ecology (Way 81–115), which demonstrated the crucial role of periodic burning in maintaining the health of many forest and grassland ecosystems—a legacy that continues in the work of southern ecologists like Reid Noss, Janisse Ray, and my University of Mississippi colleague Steve Brewer. Indeed, we might think of the child-hero of *The Road* as the product of a radically scaled-up form of fire ecology, a life form, like the morels, for whom the holocaust has brought not the end of the world but the beginning of one.

Sadly, I think, these lessons, too, are lost on the man. Adept and resourceful as he is at meeting the immediate practical challenges of postapocalyptic survival—fixing things; improvising tools, toys, and weapons; treating wounds; foraging for food and fuel—he still strikes me as one of those humanists whom Tsing says are not very good at thinking with disturbance. Indeed, that obdurate humanism, and its implicit costs, are on display in the very scene we've been examining. After their meal—the morels now *inside* them as well as in the woods *around* them—the man wraps his son in blankets against the cold and tells him bedtime stories, "Old stories of courage and justice as he remembered them until the boy was asleep" (41). The age of the tales, and the humanistic verities at their heart, mark them as relics from the age before the Event, from a world that no longer exists. Such tales don't seek to think disturbance so much as to *unthink* it—to ward it off, conjure it away, by restoring, if only in imagination, a lost world still undisturbed by catastrophe. Products of a melancholy pastoralism, or what I have characterized elsewhere as a kind of environmental Lost Causeism (Watson 158–59), they reveal the extent to which the man isn't mourning that lost world so much as *encrypting* it, in Nicolas Abraham and Maria Torok's strong psychoanalytic sense: taking it into the psyche and entombing it there, morbidly guarding against its permanent loss. In a world so radically diminished that "the last instance of a thing takes the class with it" (McCarthy 28) and the great books of the past lie blackened and bloated "in pools of water" (187), the mind is the only archive left. Passing on the stories, the man likely hopes to build a new archive in the boy's memory, a backup repository for the characteristic thought patterns and value structures of a dead episteme. But he's also performing just the sort of intergenerational transmission of melancholy affect that installs "phantoms" in the young, miring them in vicarious traumas that leave them unequipped to navigate their present lives and circumstances.[7] When the stakes of existence are as high as we find them in *The Road,* the man's melancholy pastoral and morbid humanism amount to a dangerous form of tampering, threatening to tame[8] the genuine alterity of being and sensibility that just might represent the child's best resources for staying with the trouble of a postequilibriated, posthuman, and nearly postbiological environment. Better for this boy might be the lessons of the morels.[9]

A second lesson lies in the morel bed that again is lost on the man but seems to be quickening in his son. As noted above, the visible, edible stalks and caps that rise from the forest floor are actually the fruiting bodies of the fungus, which lies in extensive tissues or mats beneath the soil. Mycologists once considered most morel species to be saprotrophs, organisms that obtain their nourishment from dead things or decaying organic material, a classification that nicely accounts for their rapid and prolific appearance in burned-over landscapes like the ones so ubiquitous in *The Road*. Recent research, however, paints a more complicated picture of morel ecology.[10] Many species are intimately entangled with plants, as symbionts in interspecies groupings called mycorrhiza, in which fungal filaments form assemblages with the root hairs and fibers of plants. From the plant roots the fungus mat receives vital sugars; the fungus in turn secretes chemicals that perform extracellular digestion for fungus and plant alike, breaking down soil material into nutrients each organism can metabolize. Many morel species have coevolved in this way with specific tree species: oaks, elms, pines (see "Morchella"), and occasionally, it appears, mayapples (see Scifres). Here the unit of life is the relationship, not the discrete organism or its selfish genes, leading some scientists to speculate whether it may be the unit of evolution more broadly: as one team of researchers cited by Tsing writes, "Nature may be selecting 'relationships' rather than individuals or genomes" (qtd. in Tsing 142).

The man, on the other hand, is all about individuals. Having taken the boy as "his warrant" (5), he considers himself "appointed by God" (77) to protect the child. This is his "job," his one remaining purpose. "I will kill anyone who touches you," he tells the boy, and on at least one occasion we watch as he carries out his warrant to the letter (66). Admittedly, the Event has left father and son with precious few other species to assemble with; they model their ecologies primarily on a social level, in their interactions with other people. To the man, all others are a threat, to be kept at bay by any means necessary. He practices a radically individualist ethos, as evidenced both by a granular and all-encompassing version of Emersonian self-reliance and by a Manichean rhetoric that divides the world into "good guys" and "bad guys," suggesting that, even in a political landscape where "there's not any more states" (43), or any more nations for that matter, the ideology of American exceptionalism has managed to outlive America itself (see Cant 266–80). For the man, the road cuts two ways: promising as a forage zone, yet ultradangerous as a potential scene of encounter. Insistent on doggedly going it alone, the man seeks to minimize encounter.

The boy, however, seeks it out—with a man struck by lightning, with the old man Ely, with the boy he briefly glimpses, with the barking dog he hears, with a thief who has stolen their grocery cart full of salvage, and, in the end, with the family-like assemblage he joins after his paranoid father has departed the scene for good. Having never known school or even day care, he is nonetheless ready to play well with others. The terms of these wished-for encounters are in every case predicated on care: helping the other, feeding the other, and receiving emotional sustenance in return. For the man, sharing their woefully marginal resources would be tantamount to suicide; for the boy, not sharing them is an explicit act of homicide (260). He advocates a human, intraspecies equivalent of what Tsing calls *symbiopoesis,* in stark contrast to the man's stubborn pursuit of human *autopoesis* (142). *Making kin,* Donna Haraway would say (161–62). For Bruno Latour it's a matter of being *neighborly,* forming assemblages with other agents, human or nonhuman, animate or inanimate (98–101). Morton prefers the term *coexistence,* making it the centerpiece of his dark ecology (*Dark Ecology* 80–81, 123–35). Ursula K. Heise and Thom Van Dooren might opt for *multispecies community* (Heise 243; Van Dooren 48), though Van Dooren also writes of *entangled becoming* (72). For all of these ecotheorists, this openness to encounter is key to doing ecology, thinking the ecological thought, at the end of the world—or rather, in the disturbed, entangled world that remains in the wake of the Anthropocene and the capitalocene.[11] Tsing tells us why: "Interspecies relations . . . depend on the contingencies of encounter" (142). These are the very contingencies the man tries to control or repress. The man doesn't make it. The boy just might. The novel itself, then, may be "selecting" at the unit of the relationship. Perhaps this is the moral of the morel at the end of the world.

Though it may be strange to arrive at this point by way of a novel that voids its territory of any regional content or significance—in which "South" refers not to an American region but only to a point on the compass—I nonetheless want to suggest that, if the demands of the Anthropocene place a premium on recognizing, embracing, and pursuing coexistence and what Heise calls multispecies justice, then southerners, including southern writers and thinkers, may have an important contribution to make in that endeavor. Southerners, after all, have been wrestling with, struggling toward, one particular mode of just coexistence for centuries, have indeed served as the face of the nation in doing so. Once again, it's a social ecology at issue here rather than an interspecies one, but the challenges of racial coexistence have underlain the region's histories and identities from its colonial beginnings. Southerners, then—black, white, brown, Indigenous—have long been on the front lines in the fraught work of making kin and being neighborly in the Americas. They haven't always gotten it right—when it comes to coevolving, I would claim no inherent virtue for southerners, only long, hard, unavoidable experience with the problem. But as the history and human centers of gravity of the Freedom Struggle illustrate, for instance, it's a problem that has elicited enormous creativity, intelligence, imagination, and energy from southerners, not just resistance. Here, then, is my bid for a "weak" southern environmental exceptionalism: as the task before us widens to encompass additional and potentially even more challenging forms of coexistence, including interspecies ones, southern thinkers, including the region's organic intellectuals, may be poised to play a leadership role, since in some important respects they've had a head start in the struggle—much as they're getting an unasked-for head start on climate change.

CO-X-ISTENCE

The reverse may also be true: dramas of ecological or interspecies coexistence may help us reconsider, reframe, or reengage with histories of racial and other forms of human coexistence on southern ground. I think, for instance, of Jeff VanderMeer's endlessly thought-provoking *Area X* trilogy (2014), a speculative fable of the terror and enchantment of interspecies—or possibly even interstellar—intimacies unfolding along Florida's Forgotten Coast. There a massive terraforming event of mysterious provenance—human? nonhuman? extraterrestrial?—has created an uncanny forbidden zone subsequently dubbed Area X, warping time, space, and ecology in radical but poorly understood ways. In order to understand them better, the Southern Reach, a government agency tasked with managing and studying this newly (or once again?) alien territory, sends in a team of researchers to gather data on Area X, data that will include whatever transformative effects the team may experience there as human guinea pigs. This expedition is the subject of volume one of the trilogy, *Annihilation*. At this early point in the series, the human encounter with Area X is governed by fear; to the state and its representatives, the weird domain signifies most immediately as an existential threat to personal, species, and even planetary life. Hence the apocalyptic title of the first book.

That emphasis shifts in volume two, *Authority,* where the principal action takes place outside rather than inside Area X and the mission of the Southern Reach lies less in understanding the phenomenon than in containing it, as its ecological and ontological "reach" proves to be gradually but inexorably expanding. With the breakdown of that containment effort, as the headquarters of the Reach, the seat of state and human authority, is itself engulfed by Area X, we proceed to volume three, *Acceptance,* which, as its title implies, traces a philosophical and ecological reorientation toward the force that governs and animates Area X, a force now understood not as mortal enemy but as inescapable fact and part of ongoing life on Earth. The revolution occurs both at a macro level, as the terraforming algorithm of Area X colonizes ever more territory, and at the micro level of the human person. For the individual characters who encounter the unknown life form that inhabits Area X, exposure to its replicating mechanism—germ? pollen? spore? virus?—initially brings on a host of disease-like symptoms (fever, fatigue, hallucination), but before long more violent transformations ensue. The affected humans ultimately transpeciate, becoming plants or animals in the ambient ecosystem, while the aliens replicate their host organisms, masquerading as human in order to infiltrate (or is it merely to "explore"?) the unfamiliar terrestrial habitat beyond Area X, a habitat, not incidentally, that seems to be as toxic to them as Area X is to its human explorers. For the exposed humans, however, there is another symptom of their "contamination," a mysterious "brightness": a more-than-human awareness that encompasses a heightened sensorium, unusual intellectual and intuitive acuity nearing clairvoyance, and elements of elation, vitality, and wonder. Seen one way, alien encounter augurs death, the destruction of the human organism. Seen another, "brighter" way, however, it brings about an interim of coexistence that enhances and enchants life. This is creative destruction in ecological action, the stuff of which worlds are born and kin are made. The trilogy, and especially *Acceptance,* bears out Roy Scranton's claim that learning how to live in turbulent worlds like the Anthropocene—a planetary-scale terraforming experiment that is making of Earth an Area X, a massive unknown variable—entails learning to die there as well.

From yet another angle, VanderMeer's fable of southern ground as scene of a maturing human stance toward forms of coexistence whose outcome cannot be known in advance offers a retrospective gloss on histories of racial encounter and kin-making in the region. From colonial times at least through the antebellum period, the Anglo settler culture was haunted by visions of racial coexistence as a downward plunge into "annihilation": slave insurrections, Indian wars, even, in the case of Bacon's Rebellion in seventeenth-century Virginia, multiracial uprisings threatening violent class revolt. In the nineteenth century, the specter of coexistence elicited efforts by state and federal "authority" to limit interracial encounter and keep subaltern populations from mixing and making kin with the settler population: Indian Removal, Jim Crow segregation, and other border control projects not so unlike the containment fantasies of the Southern Reach—or the contemporary alt-right schemes for the US-Mexico border at the nation's southern reach. In the aftermath of civil rights and social justice activism by black, brown, and Native southerners, however, and of the intensified flows of people, goods, and capital through the region unleashed by neoliberal regimes of accumulation, financialization, and salvage, southern coexistence is looking less and less like an apocalyptic nightmare and more and more like a daily reality compelling "acceptance." In this light, the arc of VanderMeer's trilogy is the arc of southern history, US history: what is the US South after all but a sort of Area X in its own right, when that chiasmatic symbol is allowed the valence of the placeholder for the erased African name, of the resiliently assertive Indian "x-mark," of the ethnic, cultural, and national crossings embedded in the Mexican, Texican, or even Calexican *mestizajes* of *la frontera,* and of the possibilities and newness that arise from the contingencies and unknowns of intercultural encounter.[12] That "X" can mark the spot of national as well as natural modes of co-X-istence in the new and very old place that is the US South. Once more, the nation's region.

In closing, it may be fitting that these remarks have leaned so hard on a pair of speculative fictions. For as Azzarello's discussion of Moira Crone and McFarland's account of *Beasts of the Southern Wild* also register in their own ways, the US South has emerged in recent decades as a fertile field for such fictions: sci-fi, cli-fi, Afrofuturism, tales of the undead, and other forms of "weird" narrative. Long the leading province of historical fiction in the nation's literary culture, the South seems to be turning over a new leaf, adding a new forte to its literary skill set. Think not only McCarthy and VanderMeer, Crone and Zeitlin, but *True Blood* and *The Walking Dead, Aquemini* and *Sankofa, American War* and *Lemonade.* With all due respect to precursors from Poe to Anne Rice to Octavia Butler, we may have something of a southern SF renaissance on our hands. When you think about it, Crone's title, *The Not Yet*, could easily double as an alternate title for all of these new counterfactual fictions. *The Road*'s bleak landscape of global ecological collapse? Thankfully, not yet—quite. The hard-won lesson in coexistence learned in *Acceptance?* Not yet either—by a long shot. But not yet also means there's still time.

And yet. The arrival of the Anthropocene means the not yet is already here.[13] What is more, giving the lie to that huge archive of cultural work depicting the region as falling (whether benightedly or authentically) behind the curve of history and modernity, the South is out ahead this time. The climate-driven ecocatastrophes of Amitav Ghosh's "Great Derangement" are reaching the US by way of southern shores. Ask anyone around Scott-Heron's Barnwell, South Carolina whether they'd agree that nuclear contamination is a planetary-scale hazard, or whether they'd be surprised to learn that it's already leaving permanent geological traces in the sediment and ice cores sampled by paleogeologists. Increasingly, the region is a window onto the future, not just the past. This is likely why neither McCarthy nor VanderMeer wastes much textual time or energy on pinning down the causes of cataclysmic change in their novels— intelligently engineered? cosmically random? The point would rather seem to be how to go forward, how to live, adapt, and die well amidst massive, unstoppable disruption. In this way the Anthropocene has brought us once more to a crossing of the ways, and from the peculiarly environmental consciousness arising out of that conjuncture is coming good work of a special order, the work of our latest southern Renascence: a literature conscious of the future in the present.

NOTES

1. On the heuristic *and* ecological value of messiness, see Kohn 68, 158, 160, and Van Dooren 147.

2. On Ariel's ecology, see Allewaert.

3. On "weak" theory and critique, see the essays collected in the recent special issue of *Modernism/Modernity* guest-edited by Paul K. Saint-Amour, "Weak Theory, Weak Modernism," *Modernism/Modernity* 25.3 (September 2018).

4. Heise observes that the ability to conceptualize beginnings is sorely lacking—and badly needed—in contemporary environmental discourse: "Environmentalists currently face the challenge of reenvisioning conservation," for instance, "in terms that enable the imagination not so much of the end of species as of their future" (50; cf. 54). All the more so amidst the "ashen scabland[s]" of *The Road* (McCarthy 16). Which is precisely why the morels

Afterwor(l)d: The Future in the Present

and their stubborn pursuit of a future, in a field of severe disturbance, are so important as a resource for the imagination.

5. For a succinct account of multispecies ethnography and its implications for environmental thought and justice, see Heise 195–200. On the ecology of selves, see Kohn 78–81.

6. See the section of Leopold's *Sand County Almanac* titled "Thinking Like a Mountain" (129–33).

7. On the psychological phantom, see Abraham and Torok 185–206.

8. At the risk of straining the analogy by thinking from an interspecies phenomenon to an intraspecies one, I am reminded here of Thom Van Dooren's powerful reflections on "the ethics of imprinting" in contemporary conservation efforts to ward off extinction for endangered bird species like the Whooping Crane (101–8). Such programs, which entangle birds with humans in both productive and problematic ways, succeed in preserving the species as a genetic or genomic phenomenon but often at the expense of what Van Dooren calls their "flight ways," "complex ways of life that have been co-produced and delicately interwoven through patterns of sequential and synchronous multispecies relationship" (58). Acknowledging the functional value of imprinting in the restoration of endangered bird populations, and in some cases in the release of individuals or cohorts back into the wild, Van Dooren also points to the "fundamentally coercive" element involved in imprinting fledgling birds outside their own species in the effort to "save" them, the ethically troubling work of "knowingly manipulating the delicate developmental stages of the other to produce a lifelong attachment: a *captive* form of life" (103). Without condemning such "regimes of violent care" whole-cloth (93), Van Dooren nonetheless insists that we approach them in a spirit of "ethical inquiry" that admittedly "pushes the limits of what we can sensibly talk about" (113). I think the ethical quandary here is not in the end so unlike the social relationship between the man and the boy of *The Road,* whose BCE (Before the Catastrophic Event) and ACE *umwelten* are so fundamentally different as to approach the paradigm of species-difference. In imprinting his own flight ways on the boy, the man may well be preempting the development of alternate ways of living, being, and experiencing potentially better suited to the demands of what is in effect the new planet he occupies.

9. For more affirmative reflections on the critical potential of environmental melancholy as a means of extending recognition to and acknowledging love for creatures, systems, or whole landscapes whose value goes un- or underrecognized in the wider culture, see Heise 34–35 and Van Dooren 140–43. In this way, and by serving as "a powerful emotional catalyst in environmental thought and writing" (Heise 35), melancholy "can be considered an integral part of the environmentalist worldview." True enough, perhaps, but it's difficult for me to see this sort of upside in the man's crushing ecomelancholia in *The Road.*

10. See, for instance, Buscot and Kotke 425, 429–30; Dahlstrom et al. 279, 282–83; Kaiser and Ernst 1; and Pils et al. 31, 34, 38–39.

11. On the capitalocene, see Haraway.

12. On the history and politics of the native "x-mark," see Lyons. On the intercultural encounters and mixings along and across *la frontera,* see Anzaldúa.

13. Heise calls this trope "the presentification of the future" (219) and identifies it as one

of the most characteristic ways in which contemporary SF conceptualizes its own present. Little wonder, then, that she declares the idea of the Anthropocene, which again and again elicits such characterizations and scenarios, to be itself a "trope" (217) or generic "offshoot" (218) of speculative fiction. See 215–20 more generally.

WORKS CITED

Abraham, Nicolas, and Maria Torok. *The Shell and the Kernel: Renewals of Psychoanalysis.* Ed. and trans. Nicholas T. Rand. Chicago: U of Chicago P, 1994.

Allewaert, Monique. *Ariel's Ecology: Plantations, Personhood, and Colonialism in the American Tropics.* Minneapolis: U of Minnesota P, 2013.

Anzaldúa, Gloria. *Borderlands / La Frontera: The New Mestiza.* 4th ed. San Francisco: Aunt Lute Books, 2012.

Buscot, F., and I. Kotke. "The Association of *Morchella rontunda* (Pers.) Boudier with Roots of *Picea abies* (L.) Karst." *New Phytologist* 116 (1990): 425–30.

Cant, Robert. *Cormac McCarthy and the Myth of American Exceptionalism.* New York: Routledge, 2008.

Dahlstrom, J. L., J. E. Smith, and N. S. Weber. "Mycorrhiza-like interaction by *Morchella* with species of the Pinaceae in pure culture synthesis." *Mycorrhiza* 9 (2000): 279–85.

Duck, Leigh Anne. *The Nation's Region: Southern Modernism, Segregation, and U.S. Nationalism.* Athens: U of Georgia P, 2006.

Ghosh, Amitav. *The Great Derangement: Climate Change and the Unthinkable.* Chicago: U of Chicago P, 2016.

Greeson, Jennifer Rae. *Our South: Geographic Fantasy and the Rise of National Literature.* Cambridge, MA: Harvard UP, 2010.

Haraway, Donna. "Anthropocene, Capitalocene, Plantationocene, Chthulucene: Making Kin." *Environmental Humanities* 6 (2015): 159–65.

Heise, Ursula K. *Imagining Extinction: The Cultural Meanings of Endangered Species.* Chicago: U of Chicago P, 2016.

Jones, Christopher F. *Routes of Power: Energy and Modern America.* Cambridge, MA: Harvard UP, 2014.

Kaiser, Cheryl, and Matt Ernst. "Truffles and Other Edible Mycorrhizal Mushrooms." CCD-CP-83. Lexington: Center for Crop Diversification, U of Kentucky College of Agriculture, Food and Environment, 2016. *http://www.uky.edu/ccd/sites/www.uky.edu.ccd/files/truffles.pdf.*

Kohn, Eduardo. *How Forests Think: Toward an Anthropology beyond the Human.* Berkeley: U of California P, 2013.

Latour, Bruno. *Facing Gaia: Eight Lectures on the New Climatic Regime.* 2015. Trans. Catherine Porter. Medford, MA: Polity, 2017.

Lemanager, Stephanie. *Living Oil: Petroleum Culture in the American Century.* New York: Oxford UP, 2014.

Leopold, Aldo. *A Sand County Almanac.* 1949. New York: Oxford UP, 1968.

Lyons, Scott. *x-marks: Native Signatures of Assent.* Minneapolis: U of Minnesota P, 2010.

McCarthy, Cormac. *The Road.* 2006. New York: Vintage International, 2007.

"Morchella." Wikipedia. https://en.wikipedia.org/wiki/Morchella. Accessed February 5, 2019.

Morton, Timothy. *Dark Ecology: For a Logic of Future Coexistence.* New York: Columbia UP, 2016.

———. *The Ecological Thought.* Cambridge, MA: Harvard UP, 2010.

Pils, David, et al. *Ecology and management of morels harvested from the forests of western North America.* Gen. Tech. Rep. PNW-GTR-710. Portland, OR: U.S. Department of Agriculture, Forest Service, Pacific Northwest Research Station, 2007.

Scifres, Bill. "Mushroom Hunting—When and Where." March 25, 2002. *All Outdoors.* http://www.bayoubill.com/archives/2002/032502column.html. Accessed February 5, 2019.

Scranton, Roy. *Learning How to Die in the Anthropocene: Reflections on the End of a Civilization.* San Francisco: City Lights, 2015.

Smith, Jon, and Deborah Cohn. "Introduction: Uncanny Hybridities." *Look Away! The U.S. South in New World Studies.* Ed. Smith and Cohn. Durham, NC: Duke UP, 2004. 1–19.

Tsing, Anna Lowenhaupt. *The Mushroom at the End of the World: On the Possibility of Life in Capitalist Ruins.* Princeton, NJ: Princeton UP, 2017.

VanderMeer, Jeff. *Area X: The Southern Reach Trilogy.* New York: Farrar, Straus and Giroux, 2014.

Van Dooren, Thom. *Flight Ways: Life and Loss at the Edge of Extinction.* New York: Columbia UP, 2014.

Watson, Jay. "The Other Matter of the South." *PMLA* 131.1 (2016): 157–61.

Way, Albert G. *Conserving Southern Longleaf: Herbert Stoddard and the Rise of Ecological Land Management.* Athens: U of Georgia P, 2011.

CONTRIBUTORS

ROBERT AZZARELLO is associate professor of English at Southern University at New Orleans. He is the author of *Queer Environmentality: Ecology, Evolution, and Sexuality in American Literature* (2012) and *Three Hundred Years of Decadence: New Orleans Literature and the Transatlantic World* (2019).

DELIA BYRNES is a PhD candidate in the Department of English at the University of Texas at Austin, where she studies post–Civil War American literature, with a focus on the US South in contemporary fiction, film, and television. Her dissertation examines cultures of energy in the Gulf Coast and the ways in which energy regimes shape American literary imaginations. Her work on oil and the southern imaginary has previously appeared in *The Global South*.

LISA HINRICHSEN is associate professor of English at the University of Arkansas and President of the Society for the Study of Southern Literature. She is the author of *Possessing the Past: Trauma, Imagination, and Memory in Post-Plantation Southern Literature* (2015) and coeditor, along with Gina Caison and Stephanie Rountree, of *Small-Screen Souths: Region, Identity, and the Cultural Politics of Television* (2017).

SAM HORROCKS is a PhD candidate in the Department of English at West Virginia University, where he teaches rhetoric, composition, and American and Appalachian literature. His writing seeks to establish an agrarian vision and practice appropriate to the twenty-first century's global ecological context. He raises vegetables, maple syrup, and poultry at Maryland Line Farm in Hazelton, West Virginia.

EVANGELIA KINDINGER is associate professor of American Studies at Humboldt University of Berlin, Germany. She is the author of *Homebound: Diaspora Spaces and Selves in Greek American Return Narratives* (2015), and coeditor of *After the Storm: The Cultural Politics of Hurricane Katrina* (2016) and *The Intersections of Whiteness* (2018). Her research interests include southern studies, gender studies, critical whiteness studies, class(ism) in American popular culture, and nineteenth-century American culture.

CHRISTOPHER LLOYD is lecturer in English literature at the University of Hertfordshire, UK. He is the author of *Corporeal Legacies in the US South: Memory and Embodiment in Contemporary Culture* (2018) and *Rooting Memory, Rooting Place: Regionalism in the Twenty-First-Century American South* (2015). He has also edited three special issues and written numerous articles and book chapters on contemporary US culture. His work sits at the nexus of southern studies, memory studies, and African American studies. Lloyd is also Reviews Editor for the *European Journal of American Culture* and the founder of the *Southern Studies in the UK Network*.

SARAH E. MCFARLAND is professor of English at Northwestern State University, in Natchitoches, LA, where she lives in the piney woods with her multispecies family. Her current research explores the convergence of critical animal studies and postapocalyptic speculations to theorize diverse subjectivities in climate change fiction. McFarland has published a number of journal articles and book chapters and is the editor of *Animals and Agency: An Interdisciplinary Exploration,* with Ryan Hediger.

JOHN MORAN is an MFA student in fiction at Brown University, where he teaches creative writing. He holds a PhD in cultural anthropology from Stanford University, where he completed a dissertation on the cultural politics of environmentalism in the Florida Panhandle. The oral histories with local naturalists he collected for that project are deposited at the University of Florida's Samuel Proctor Oral History Program. His fiction, poetry, and criticism have appeared in *Little Star, Subtropics,* and *Southern Cultures.*

JOSHUA MYERS is a PhD candidate in English at Louisiana State University. He researches environments and ecologies in US literature of the nineteenth and early twentieth centuries, specializing in ecocritical approaches to fictional representations of rural people and places. Currently, he is writing his dissertation: "Provincial Ecology: Rural Environments as Isolated Imaginary in American Literature." Previously, he taught at Thiel College, where he received the 2015 Award for Distinguished Adjunct Faculty.

SCOTT OBERNESSER is a PhD candidate at the University of Mississippi. His dissertation, titled "Road Trippin': Petrocultures and Material Affect in American Literature from *On The Road* to *The Road,*" argues that the road is a site of cultural, material, and ecological convergence central to the shape(ing) of human interiority and contemporary environmentalism throughout the late twentieth century. His forthcoming article, "What It Means to Be On the Road: Mobility and Petrocultures at the Midcentury" is forthcoming in *Interdisciplinary Studies in Literature and Environment (ISLE)*. He is the recipient of the Ventress Summer Fellowship through the University of Mississippi Graduate School and began a postdoctoral fellowship with The Obama Institute of Transnational Studies at Johannes Guttenberg University in Mainz, Germany, in the fall of 2018.

LUCAS J. SHEAFFER completed his PhD at Temple University in 2018 and is currently completing a project titled *Damming the American Imagination,* which examines the intersection of the literary imagination and the Tennessee Valley Authority's massive damming and redevelopment projects between 1930 and 1960. In addition to his scholarship, Lucas teaches widely in environmental literature, twentieth-century American fiction, and composition in both the United States and New Zealand. Currently, he works as the Director of First Year Courses and Lecturer of Interdisciplinary Studies at a liberal arts college in Pennsylvania.

JIMMY DEAN SMITH lives on a partially recovered stripmine site outside Barbourville, Kentucky, with his wife, Sharee St. Louis, and their cats and dogs. He is professor of English at Union College and was the Director of its Honors Program from its inception to its recent demise. He has recently published articles on Ron Rash, Flannery O'Connor, precarity in the small liberal arts college, and the unsilencing Affrilachian poetics of Frank X Walker.

DANIEL SPOTH is associate professor of literature at Eckerd College in St. Petersburg, Florida. He received his BA from Reed College and his MA and PhD from Vanderbilt University. His work has appeared in *ELH, Mississippi Quarterly, Journal of Ecocriticism, Americana,* and *The Eudora Welty Review.* Spoth is particularly interested in how historically misused environments are reimagined in modern and postmodern contexts, and he is currently at work on a manuscript on that subject. When not teaching, writing, or traveling, Daniel enjoys exploring the unique oddities of the Floridian landscape with his wife, toddler, and cats (though the cats generally stay at home).

JOSEPH M. THOMPSON is assistant professor of history at Mississippi State University. He recently completed a PhD in the University of Virginia's Corcoran Department of History. His dissertation, "Sounding Southern: Music, Militarism, and the Making of the Sunbelt," traces the economic and symbolic connections between popular music and the US military during the Cold War. This project places particular focus on the country music industry's role in military recruitment since World War II to show how this relationship between genre and militarism helped create the sonic and political color lines of the late twentieth century. He was a predoctoral fellow at the Smithsonian's National Museum of American History and a Mellon/ACLS Dissertation Completion Fellow. His work has appeared in the journals *American Quarterly* and *Southern Cultures,* as well as the edited collection *Reconsidering Southern Labor History: Race, Class, and Power.*

ILA TYAGI is a writing lecturer at Yale–NUS College in Singapore. She completed her PhD in American studies and film and media studies at Yale University in 2018. Her research fields include the environmental humanities, science and technology, and modern and contemporary Anglo-American literature and visual media. She received a Bachelor's degree in English Literature from Brown University in 2009, and a Master's degree in American studies at Columbia University in 2013. Tyagi worked as a public relations executive between college and graduate school, handling accounts in the renewable energy sector. Her writing has appeared in *Oxford Bibliographies, Senses of Cinema,* and the *World Film Locations* book series.

ZACKARY VERNON is assistant professor of English at Appalachian State University. In both his teaching and writing, he focuses on American literature, film, and environmental studies. Vernon's research has appeared in a range of scholarly books and journals, and he is the coeditor of *Summoning the Dead: Essays on Ron Rash.* Vernon is also currently finishing a manuscript entitled *Haunted by Waters: The Hydropolitics of American Literature, 1960–1980.*

JONATHAN VILLALOBOS earned his PhD in English from the University of Nevada–Reno and is presently assistant professor of English at Ranger College in Ranger, Texas, where he teaches composition, American literature, and British literature. His research considers the intersections of environment and horror in southern literature, with a particular focus on the cultural affect of ecohorror. He is presently in the planning stages of a manuscript on ecohorror in post-1900 southern literature and has a chapter in the forthcoming collection *Appalachian Ecocriticism* (West Virginia UP) on nature striking back in Ann Pancake's *Strange as This Weather Has Been*. He has presented ecocritical analyses of works by Flannery O'Connor, Zora Neale Hurston, Toni Morrison, and Daniel Woodrell, among other southern authors.

JAY WATSON is the Howry Professor of Faulkner Studies at the University of Mississippi. In addition to numerous scholarly articles and book chapters, he is the author of *Forensic Fictions: The Lawyer Figure in Faulkner* (1993), *Conversations with Larry Brown* (2007), *Faulkner and Whiteness* (2011), and *Reading for the Body: The Recalcitrant Materiality of Southern Fiction, 1893–1985* (2012). Watson is also currently Director of the annual Faulkner & Yoknapatawpha Conference, and he is a coeditor of several conference volumes, such as *Faulkner's Geographies, Fifty Years After Faulkner,* and *Faulkner and the Black Literatures of the Americas*.

INDEX

Abadie, Ann J., 3
Abbey, Edward, 217–18
Abraham, Nicolas, 262
Abram, David, 196
Absalom, Absalom! (Faulkner), 114, 118–21
activism, environmental. *See*
 environmentalism
Adair, Paul Neal "Red," 58
Adams, Jessica, 44
Adamson, Joni, 3
affect, 8, 23–34, 131, 133, 215
African Americans, 10–11, 17, 170, 251–52;
 displacement of, 9, 41, 44, 49, 96–107,
 164, 176–77; Hurricane Katrina and, 14,
 176–77; memorialization of, 204, 206–8;
 plantation tourism and, 46–47; slavery
 and, 78–81 (*see also* slavery); soul food
 and, 133–34; U.S. defense spending and,
 96–107
agency, 189–90, 193, 240
agrarian ecologies, 12, 114, 117–22, 125. *See
 also* farmers; plantation ecologies
agrarianism, 11–12, 39, 42, 125n1; Jeffersonian, 147, 155, 157n9; race and, 11, 113–25.
 See also Nashville Agrarians
Ahmed, Sara, 28, 30, 250
Alabama, 151
aliens, 265–68
Allenhurst, Florida, 103
Allewaert, Monique, 232
Allied-General Nuclear Services (AGNS),
 105
American exceptionalism, 153, 263–64
American Petroleum Institute (API), 53–54,
 61
Amin, Samir, 27
Anderson, Eric Gary, 3, 165

animality, 16, 235n8
Anthias, Floya, 26
Anthropocene, 1, 17n2, 91–92, 94, 136, 163,
 168–69, 172, 178–79, 250, 255–56, 268
anthropocentrism, 72–73, 145–47, 149, 151,
 155–56, 179, 188
anthropogenic change, 84, 240
apocalypse, 91–92, 193, 241–48, 250. *See also*
 postapocalypse
Appalachia: coal mining, 8–9, 23–34, 221–
 22; demeaning depictions of, 215, 221;
 disease and, 158n12; floods in, 161, 220;
 roads in, 10, 84–94
Appalachian Regional Commission (ARC),
 94
Appalachians Against Pipelines, 5
Area X trilogy (VanderMeer), 265–68
Armbruster, Karla, 3
Arnow, Harriette Simpson, 10, 85–89, 92,
 94, 253
Ashland-Belle Helene Plantation, Geismar,
 47
As I Lay Dying (Faulkner), 161
Atkins-Sayre, Wendy, 131
atmosphere: environmental conditions of,
 1, 194; sense of place and, 26, 28, 33–34
Atomic Energy Commission (AEC), 104
Audubon, John James, 253
authenticity: New Orleans and, 174; southern foodways and, 130–31, 135
autochthonous identities, 32
automobile emission standards, 216
Ayers, Edward, 23
Azzarello, Robert, 16, 250, 252, 267

backcountry roads, 87–89
backwardness, 74, 77, 81n1